Project Risk Quantification

Volume 2

Project Risk Quantification

Quantification

Volume 2

A Practitioner's Guide to Realistic Cost and Schedule Risk Management

by John K. Hollmann

Probabilistic Publishing

Associate Editor: Nancy Winchester
Cover Illustration: Haesel Charlesworth Holbrook

Probabilistic Publishing   www.decisions-books.com
                                  e-mail: dave@decisions-books.com

1702 Hodge Lake Ln
Sugar Land, TX 77478
281-277-4006

Written, designed, and printed in the United States of America.

Library of Congress Control Number: 2024952571

ISBN: 1-941075-15-0   Kindle version: 1-941075-16-9
ISBN 13: 978-1-941075-15-9   Kindle version: 978-1-941075-16-6

To my wife Cindy with whom risk and reward are everyday realities.

Volume 1 Reviews

"Working at a private equity firm that invests in mining projects, Mr. Hollmann's *Project Risk Quantification* text is a must read and will be my go-to-guide for many years to come. Private equity investment is all about identifying risks and how to capture these risks quantitatively. John's book takes a smart two-part approach that lends itself perfectly to understand and implement risk quantification at any stage in the project life cycle. It is clearly and concisely written and fills a gap that currently exists in the field of risk management." –Edward van Doorn, Project Controls Manager, Resource Capital Funds.

"John Hollmann's *Project Risk Quantification* text makes an important contribution to the practice of project appraisals and to project risk management. Realistic quantitative methods–*absolutely*–are needed for calculations and meaningful communication. I found special interest in the parametric cost estimation details and the novel discussion of and methods for projects tipping into chaos." –John Schuyler, Principal Consultant and Instructor, Decision Precision and PetroSkills; author of *Risk and Decision Analysis in Projects*.

"For those in the trenches of project cost engineering in general, and risk analysis in particular, it is difficult to find practices that are practical and reliable; i.e., that will work on every project. John Hollmann's book not only lays out an integrated set of methods in detail, but documents their basis in empirical reality. The stories are interesting too. For credibility, organizations need strong risk quantification competency in-house and this book provides a great guide for building that competency –Prashant Srivastava, Manager, Cost Engineering Systems, Enbridge Pipelines, Inc."

"John Hollmann is well known for his necessarily blunt honesty about project performance and risk, and as a result he is a rare and valued resource to clients and colleagues alike. He tells it as it is, and offers advice in a pragmatic fashion, often accompanied by vigorous debate. Characteristically, this book does the same, imparting decades of hands-on capex risk management and quantification experience in a readily-accessible, engaging, and conversational tone. It provides a practical guide to projects as dynamic systems, and risks that impact both project decision-making and performance. Run, do not walk, to your nearest bookseller." –Alexia Nalewaik, Vice President of Major Projects and Program Management, WT Partnership.

"John's book demonstrates to users how realistic estimates and forecasts can be created using historical data and proven techniques. A thought provoking guide that delivers a practical starter tool for those who are new to risk quantification and provides experienced parametric estimators with a laser sight for large and small projects." –Laurie Bowman, Principal, Synchrony.

"Currently, no book in the marketplace addresses the question of integrated project risk analysis and quantification in a realistic way. As Mr. Hollmann makes clear, the prevalent methods fail to predict the cost and schedule overruns that frequent process and other industry projects. His book finally addresses the age-old challenge of how to realistically forecast cost and schedule accuracy while also keeping it practical. The book is comprehensive and addresses all the issues in detail along with interesting examples and anecdotes. Everyone will enjoy reading and using this book!" –Kul B. Uppal, Consultant, AACE Technical Director, and former Estimating/Risk lead at oil & gas majors.

"At a time when capital-intensive industries are very prudent with their investments and tempted to demand certainty from project teams, this book comes in handy to equip risk professionals and management with the framework and toolset required to understand, quantify and communicate project risks. Whether you are risk pro or a senior manager, set aside your pre-conceived notions about what makes capital projects successful; follow John as he debunks industry beliefs about capital projects risks and guides you through tried-and-tested methods you can apply to quantify them. Once your organization produces reliable base estimates, the next challenge is to understand, quantify and communicate the uncertainties inherent to capital projects. Whether you are a risk practitioner or a senior manager, John's approach will help you frame the challenge based on years of research and experience, and offer an extensive toolset that can be readily applied by professionals." –Julien Saillard, Team Lead-External Benchmarking, Royal Dutch Shell

"Nobody knows for sure what will happen tomorrow, but it is critical that we make the best predictions possible for the cost and schedule of our projects and programs. John Hollmann's book on *Project Risk Quantification* provides owner cost engineers and decision-makers with tools and methods that are practical and, as the book demonstrates, realistic in order to improve our return on capital. It offers the first truly integrated approach to project risk quantification over the project life cycle that I have seen. It will be my guide for training." –Andres Pereira, Cost Engineer, Strategic Asset Management, Ecopetrol

"This is a great guidebook and reference on risk quantification for cost and schedule professionals in the process industries but also for those in infrastructure and elsewhere. It is a particularly great resource for owner companies for investment decision making, including national-owned companies. It contains a wealth of practical experience including useful examples. I recommend that everyone in the capital project business get a copy of this book" –Johnson Awoyomi, General Manager Cost Engineering, Nigerian National Petroleum Corp.

"John Hollmann's new book on risk quantification is an engrossing and thought provoking read for anyone dealing with capital investment in the process industries. He starts by providing a very good summation of the common errors and misconceptions that are prevalent in dealing with uncertainty and risk. In this, his use of real life examples adds relevance to the text. He then goes on to propose practical methodologies to account for uncertainty and risk that draw on his many years of experience in the field. His emphasis on the need to seek practical solutions that can be proven to work is refreshing." –Gordon Lawrence, EMEA Manager, Capital Project Consulting Practice, Asset Performance Networks LLC.

"John Hollmann's work has opened up a world of empirical knowledge and a type of common sense that have had a profound impact in my career. This book gives everyone access to a breadth of knowledge and practical advice regarding risk analysis in capital projects which cannot be found in existing literature. I am confident that other professionals will find this book to be an invaluable tool for dealing with all the challenges risk analysis poses for capital projects and portfolios." –Claudia Villegas Timm, Lead Portfolio Management Improvements, Wind Power Projects, Vattenfall.

"This book is a must read for any owner, contractor or business person who needs to understand risk quantification and accuracy of estimates and schedules on capital projects and programs and how to avoid the pitfalls. John Hollmann demystifies risk analysis, challenging common industry practices and pointing the way forward with methods that provide greater confidence and credibility for informed judgement and decision-making on capital investments. It is a straight talking guide backed up by a lifetime of industry experience, anecdotes, research and recommended practices." –Les McMullan, Global Director, Project Controls, EPC Firm

"John Hollmann shares his vast expertise while giving you practical, functional tools and a pragmatic guide to implement risk quantification methods at your own organization. I can confirm that the integrated, empirically-based methods that John shares are simply the fastest, least cost and, most importantly, the most accurate available. If you are frustrated with your organization's inability to accurately quantify risk and tired of unexpected cost overruns and schedule slips, this book is your answer!" –Matthew Schoenhardt, Principal at MS Consulting.

Preface and Acknowledgments

The acknowledgements made in the original Project Risk Quantification, published in 2016 (now referred to as Volume 1), remain pertinent. I would like to extend my gratitude to the numerous readers of that volume for their engagement in lively discussions about the book's themes:

- ◆ Online (mainly on LinkedIn),
- ◆ During meetings and presentations,
- ◆ In risk workshops, and
- ◆ At training sessions.

This includes the Australian "book tour" in 2018 and virtual "book club" meetings held during the Covid lockdown thereafter. It was a pleasure to resume face-to-face meetings post-Covid. Volume 2 has been enriched by the questions and feedback (always constructive) from many readers, a fact for which I am continually humbled, especially when individuals share their well-worn copies of Volume 1 adorned with notes and bookmarks.

I would also like to express my appreciation to my colleagues and associates at Koff & Guerrero Consultants S.A., whose assistance has been instrumental in bringing the cloud-based www.ValidRisk.com software to fruition in 2022. This software applies the core methodologies covered in Volume 1.

To rectify an oversight from Volume 1 regarding AACE International, I extend my thanks to my friends and colleagues Mr. Larry Dysert CCP CEP DRMP Hon. Life of Conquest Consulting Group and former Chair/VP of the Technical Board, and Mr. Christian Heller, AACE International Director, Technical Guidance. They have been invaluable "techie" partners in the development of the AACE Total Cost Management Framework and Recommended Practices (RPs) for almost three decades. Larry and I have collaborated since our time at Kodak in the 1990s and on various consulting projects throughout the 2000s. The celebration of the release of the 100th AACE RP in 2021 was a significant milestone. Several of the latest RPs encapsulate practices initially outlined in Volume 1.

For Volume 2, I extend my thanks to friends and reviewers, alphabetically listed: Chris Carson, Colin Cropley, and Greg Ramsey. Chris, an authority in project controls, provided insights into diverse industry and contractor approaches to risk quantification. Colin, a leader in integrating cost and schedule risk analysis with the parametric method, contributed invaluable expertise. Greg, an expert in contractor risk analysis and quantification, provided insights into the contractor's perspective in collaboration with owners across various industries. However, it's important to note that the book represents my perspective on these subjects, so any disagreements should be attributed to me alone (i.e., their acknowledgment does not imply endorsement).

Lastly, I extend my heartfelt thanks once again to my publisher/editor Dave Charlesworth for his unwavering encouragement and dedication, and to his daughter Haesel Charlesworth for the outstanding cover art. I hope Volume 2 will attract new readers and foster further connections and dialogues in the years ahead.

–John K. Hollmann, June, 2024

About QR Codes

We have added QR Codes where there is additional information about a topic discussed in the book. These can be scanned using a smartphone or tablet. With an iPhone, use the camera and it will bring up a small box with the link that you click to go to the web page once it focuses on the Code.

However, please note that the internet changes continually (people add and delete content), so please be patient if a link doesn't work.

Here's one you can practice on: our Probabilistic Publishing company home page, www.decisionsbooks.com.

Enjoy!

Publisher's Note

We sincerely thank all of you who purchased *Project Risk Quantification*. We especially appreciate those of you who took the time to leave reviews on Amazon!

We also appreciate John's ability to continue to expand and elaborate on the material covered in the book as the state-of-the-art progresses.

Our original thoughts were to publish a second edition of *Project Risk Quantification*. We started working towards that goal and got about half way through the book. However, there was an issue with that approach: John had a *lot* of new material that he wanted to present, and the original book was already quite thick. We didn't want to publish a book that was three or four inches thick! Also, some of the updates we were making, although technically correct, didn't add clarity to what was already well covered. So, after spirited and productive discussion, we decided to leave the first book alone and add a second volume.

As with Volume 1, we're making Volume 2 available on the Kindle platform so that it can be inexpensively purchased anywhere in the world. Even though printing and shipping costs have gone up, we're pricing Volume 2 low enough that if you prefer the printed edition, it is still affordable.

Note that we used ChatGPT to edit some of the text in this book, however, ChatGPT was *not* used to develop or write *any* of the content itself.

–Dave Charlesworth, December, 2024 Probabilistic Publishing

Contents

1

Introduction

The original *Project Risk Quantification* book, referred to as Volume 1 from this point, begins with the following paragraph:

> Project risk analysis and quantification can seem to be an "Alice in Wonderland" world where nothing is reliable: a world where strange things happen and cost and schedule outcomes seem impossible to predict (although many people tell you they can do so). In the project world, significant cost and schedule overruns are the norm. Blowouts are common and rarely predicted, despite applying seemingly sophisticated risk analysis methods.

All of that remains true. Some argue that things are worsening rather than improving! However, Volume 2 will provide evidence that at least some improvements are being made.

Volume 1 also emphasizes the fact that...

> ...risk quantification failures largely result from poor internal capital and project management practices and our failure to recognize our weaknesses or to take ownership of them if recognized. The problem is typically not about poor base estimates or schedules and usually is not even about risk events themselves. Taken together, the project strategy, processes, practices, organization, and stakeholder interaction form a system. If this system is immature, weak, or broken, that is the risk that matters most!"

Once again, this remains true; one might consider it the fundamental truth of risk quantification. With an increasing focus on sustainability and social license in both the public and private sectors, the systemic risks are only escalating.

As for why the situation isn't changing much, I attribute that in large part to two generations (40 years) of dependency on purely subjective Monte Carlo simulation (MCS)-based QRA methods (e.g., "ranging") and the powerful "illusion of control" bias fostered by risk registers. The uncertainties and risks that matter (systemic risks) are mostly absent from these methods. Change is difficult.

What is Covered in Volume 1?

Volume 1 begins with a top-ten list of reasons why risk quantification fails. This list remains highly relevant and has proven very popular with readers. While tempted to add more to the list in the context of Volume 2 (e.g., public infrastructure projects, contractor perspective, etc.), upon review, the original list seems universally applicable.

Instead of repeating that list (or any other Volume 1 content), I kindly ask the reader to revisit or read Volume 1. Volume 2 is not a standalone book; Volume 1 provides the necessary *quantitative risk analysis* (QRA) terminology, data, and methods foundations. For instance, if one is unfamiliar with the term *systemic risk*, what a *parametric risk model* entails, or how *cost growth and schedule slip are measured*, Volume 1 is essential reading.

Volume 1 primarily focuses on capital project cost growth and schedule slip research, basic empirically sound QRA methods, and other project practices within process-related industries such as oil & gas, chemical, mining, and metals. It emphasizes the asset owner's perspective rather than the contractor's.

Volume 1 delves into extensive content on empirical cost and schedule accuracy research. Based on this research, it stresses the need to view projects as *systems* and describes *phase-gate* scope development systems, the fundamental risk management method. It underscores that *systemic risks* are the primary driver of cost and schedule uncertainty and stresses the importance of utilizing historical data to develop or validate *empirically valid* QRA approaches, which requires some understanding of basic statistics, also addressed.

To better comprehend the project system and the context for applying QRA, Volume 1 includes content on capital investment decision-making, estimating and scheduling, project control, and budgeting for risk. Risk quantification does not occur in a vacuum.

Lastly, concerning QRA methods, Volume 1 outlines the core, integrated QRA methods of:

(1) empirically-based parametric modeling of systemic risk,

(2) expected value with Monte Carlo simulation (MCS) for critical project-specific risks, and

(3) probabilistic cost escalation modeling.

It also describes how complex megaprojects are subject to non-linear risk behavior and provides a *tipping-point* model that warns of potential blowouts.

Volume 1 concludes with an extensive glossary. In summary, Volume 1 documents the fundamentals of project risk quantification for engineering and construction projects, with principles applicable across industries for both owners and contractors.

What is New in Volume 2?

Volume 2 introduces new content to demonstrate how fundamental principles apply to selected non-process industries and to contractors. It also introduces specialized QRA methods or extensions and offers worked examples of applying QRA methods in various contexts.

Non-Process Industries

Volume 2 reviews additional research on major projects in sectors crucial to achieving net-zero carbon, including transportation infrastructure (rail, road, and pipeline) and renewable and low-carbon power generation (hydropower, nuclear, wind, and solar). Phase-gate discipline and empirical research still lag in these industries. Given this lag, the volume addresses how well process industry accuracy research and QRA models apply to these sectors (a preview: they apply very well). Concerning phase-gate, this volume addresses the problematic focus on the tender phase in public infrastructure (Class 2) rather than the front-end (Class 4), which is the focus of the for-profit process industry.

While Aerospace, Defense, Information Technology, and other non-engineering and construction projects are not covered, the principles of systemic risk are universal.

QRA Method Extensions

In terms of broader methods, Volume 2 better addresses QRA use in programs and portfolios, as well as addressing situations with multiple live options, specifically for AACE Class 10 and 5 estimates. It also describes how to apply the hybrid parametric and risk-driven critical path method schedule (CPM) with MCS, now an AACE Recommended Practice.

Commercial Software

Volume 2 also discusses cloud-based commercial software (ValidRisk®; see www.validrisk.com) that applies the core methods covered in Volume 1 and the specialized methods now covered in this Volume. This software entered the market in 2022.

Worked Examples

Volume 1 readers requested worked examples of the core QRA methods as applied in typical project contexts (different phases, owner vs. contractor, etc.). Volume 2 helps address this issue.

Other Additions

I continue to conduct QRA analyses, study cost growth and schedule slip data (e.g., calibration studies to support parametric modeling), and support QRA practice improvement, including contributing to AACE Recommended Practices. I also keep a close watch on relevant developments in machine learning/artificial intelligence (ML/AI), which is advancing rapidly. ML/AI emphasizes the importance of data; thus, those applying the empirically-based methods in this book will have an advantage! Volume 2 includes new learnings and key references wherever applicable.

A Phase-Gate Rosetta Stone

Chapters 2 and 3 of this volume delve into non-process industry accuracy research and contractor risk quantification applications. These additional perspectives introduce more complexity to the phase naming conventions of phase-gate processes. As discussed in Volume 1, Chapter 3, owners in the process industries typically use the following phase naming convention (with FEL standing for Front-End Loading):

♦ Class 5 is FEL 1/Assess
♦ Class 4 is FEL 2/Select
♦ Class 3 is FEL 3/Define
♦ Class 2: There is no FEL designation, as FEL 3 is usually the final investment decision (FID) gate in the process industries, and the FEL 3 plan serves as the basis for project cost and schedule control purposes moving forward.

In the process industries, the Cost Estimate Classification (Class) per AACE International Recommended Practices is widely recognized and used internationally. However, this is less common in the non-process world and in contract strategy treatments. In that context, the Class 2 gate is of primary importance as the prevailing FID gate, where construction contract solicitations are issued (with less focus on early phases and risk quantification). In the for-profit process industries, the Class 4/Select gate is the main focus because projects are rarely canceled after this single option scope selection gate, so owners are rightly concerned with understanding the risk at that early stage.

Table 1.1 provides a more complete Rosetta Stone for phase naming conventions for reference going forward. It is important to note that a party's use of a particular phase name does not necessarily correspond exactly to the AACE Class RPs. This is a significant advantage of using the parametric QRA method, as it explicitly and consistently assesses the status of scope definition. The shaded cells indicate the typical FID gate.

AACE	FEL	Process	Mining / Minerals	Non-Process / Commercial
5	1	Conceptual	Scoping	Pre-Design
4	2	Basic Engineering	Pre-Feasibility	Schematic
3	3	Front-End Engineering and Design (FEED)	Feasibility	Design Development / Feasibility
2		No common name: FID / control estimates re-baselined using construction contractor input		Construction Documents or Tender / Bid
1		No name: engineering is near or at 100%; used for changes		

Table 1.1: Typical Phase Name Conventions Compared to AACE Classifications

Who Should Read This Book?

Volumes 1 and 2 target the same audience, as described in Volume 1:

- ◆ Investment and bidding decision-makers, including C-level officers, VPs, and senior business managers, as well as the project's financiers.
- ◆ Program directors, project managers, contract managers, and project engineers who need to understand the needs of senior management while also grasping their own requirements for tactical-level decision-making and project control.
- ◆ Team members involved in or conducting risk analysis and/or risk quantification.

Together, the volumes aim to align:

- ◆ The business manager, framing the project in a portfolio and working with decision analysis experts to determine investment.
- ◆ The project manager, executing the project.
- ◆ The team members analyzing and communicating cost and schedule risk for management consideration.

Volume 2 introduces more content relevant to individuals working on infrastructure projects, both public and private, which tend to be more structural or civil trade-centric and more politically sensitive. Sustainability and social license issues receive greater attention. Volume 2 also includes more content relevant to those working for contractors.

Is Anything About QRA Getting Better?

Projects still experience phase-to-phase cost surprises, severe overruns, and delays due to poor project risk quantification. The top ten issues highlighted in Volume 1 persist. However, improvements *are* underway.

Firstly, there's greater awareness of systemic risks since Volume 1's publication in 2016. AACE International has continued publishing more Recommended Practices on QRA, focusing on building a risk "toolbox" to address various risks and advance organizational QRA maturity.

Moreover, rapid advances in ML/AI have piqued C-level interest in data and data analytics. In 2016, few executives were willing to invest in data and analytics as Volume 1 advocated. Now, everyone seems eager for better data! While ML/AI will eventually replace most current risk quantification methods, it still has much progress to make in learning from everything in the project system and its interaction with the external world. ML/AI has yet to address systemic risk. This volume discusses how that gap might be closed.

The remainder of the book explores expanded and continually improving paths to successful risk quantification. Readers are encouraged to share their observations on LinkedIn.com, where I regularly post and comment on articles. I also continue publishing papers and supporting RP development via AACE International; I look forward to meeting you at their annual conference!

Acronyms

Table 1.2 lists prominent acronyms (and other items) included in the text. See also Table 11.1 for acronyms specific to Chapter 11.

ACRONYM	DESCRIPTION	DEFINED BY
AACE®	Association for the Advancement of Cost Engineering	AACE
AI	artificial intelligence	
CAPEX	capital expenditure	
CII	Construction Industry Institute	CII
Class	estimate classification	AACE
CPM	critical path method	
DA	decision analysis	
DRMP	decision and risk analysis professional	AACE
ECI	early contractor involvement	
ECRI	Engineering and Construction Risk Institute	ECRI
EMV	expected monetary value	
EPC	engineering, procurement, and construction	
EV	expected value	
FEED	front-end engineering and design	
FEL	front-end loading	
FID	final investment decision	
HILP	high impact / low probability	

Acronym	Description	Defined By
IPA	Independent Project Analysis, Inc	IPA
IRR	internal rate of return	
J-QPD	Johnson quantile-parameterized distributions	UT Austin
JORC	Joint Ore Reserve Committee	JORC
KGC	Koff & Guerrero Consultants S.A.	KGC
LCCE/A	life cycle cost estimating/analysis	
LSTK	lump sum turn key	
MBC	management by cashflow	
MCS	Monte Carlo simulation	
ML	machine learning	
MLR	multiple linear regression	
NPV	net present value	
NSRF	net systemic risk factor	
P	parametric	
P+CPM	parametric plus critical path method	
P+EV	parametric plus expected value	
P+IRA	parametric plus integrated risk analysis	
P3	public-private partnership	
PCI	Project Complexity Index	CII
PDF	probability density function	
PDRI	Project Definition Rating Index	CII
PERT	project evaluation and review technique	
PGD	Professional Guidance Documents	AACE
QRA	quantitative risk analysis	
QCRA	quantitative cost risk analysis	
QRAMM	quantitative risk analysis - maturity model	
QSRA	quantitative schedule risk analysis	
RF	risk factor	
RFQ/P	request for quotation/proposal	
RIMPL	Risk Integration Management Pty Ltd	RIMPL
RP	Recommended Practices	AACE
SME	subject matter expert	

Table 1.2: Acronyms Used in the Book

"The more things change, the more they stay the same (plus ça change, plus c'est la même chose)."
– Jean-Baptiste Alphonse Karr

2

Accuracy and Phase-Gate for Various Non-Process Industries

Volume 1, Chapters 3 and 4, focused on accuracy studies in the process industry (e.g., oil and gas, chemicals, mining, and metals) because that industry segment has the most robust data and research. Naturally, those in non-process industries ask, "How well do the models based on the process industry apply to my projects?" This chapter reviews the more limited empirical cost and schedule accuracy studies for non-process industries and answers the question of whether the Volume 1, Chapter 11 (parametric) and Chapter 14 (tipping point) risk quantification methods and models apply to them. The focus here is on major projects in sectors critical to net-zero carbon, including transportation infrastructure (rail, road, pipeline, and power transmission) and renewable and low-carbon power generation (hydropower, nuclear, wind, and solar). Note that much of the content here is sourced from Volume 1, Chapter 15 to provide an integrated review of the various industries.

Cost Accuracy Data for Various Industries

We will start with reviewing a sample of empirical cost estimate accuracy studies. The base reference is a 2012 article I wrote describing a meta-analysis of industry cost estimate accuracy studies.[1] More recent studies were added to this. The accuracy studies reviewed in this chapter:

- ◆ Included projects large enough to be relevant to the success of the business (i.e., greater than several million $US), and
- ◆ Focused on asking, "What is the accuracy of our estimates and why?"

Cost Data Quality

Readers should be aware that the quality of the non-process industry study data sets is generally poor to fair and is rarely excellent. This is not because of a lack of skill and effort on the part of researchers, but because quality historical project data is simply lacking (see Volume 1, Chapter 18 about historical data capture). The process industry has benefited from long-standing cooperative benchmarking and research organizations (e.g., Independent Project Analysis Inc. and the Construction Industry Institute) that obtained their data in a planned and organized way from the industrial and contracting firms that owned the project data. They were also able to collect project practice information necessary for parametric modeling; i.e., practices are systemic risk drivers. One cannot understand the project system without measuring how the system works.

The process industry owners also had details of the cost estimates so that they could study *"cost growth or schedule slip,"* i.e., the percent increase from the "base" cost or duration estimate excluding contingency, reserves, and escalation so that the study outcomes can be used to develop contingency models.[2,3] Academic researchers tend to rely on off-the-shelf data available from government agencies, financiers (e.g., World Bank), and others and the basis and quality of that data is often unclear (in addition to not having much, if any, project system practice information). That limitation

---

1   Hollmann, John, "Estimate Accuracy: Dealing with Reality," Cost Engineering Journal, AACE International, Nov/Dec 2012.

2   Four of the references in this Chapter's tables are of "cost growth." These empirical industry studies were facilitated by the author.

3   Published schedules usually do not include explicitly identified contingency. However, business cases may allow for a (confidential) time buffer before the in-service date and start of revenue, i.e., a published schedule planned completion date used in contract negotiation may not reflect the business's true planned completion date used in commercial dealings.

applies to this chapter, which mostly reports on references using second-hand data sources (with the exception of the four studies facilitated by the author).

Academic sources usually study *"cost overrun,"* i.e., the percent increase from the total funded amount, which includes indeterminate allowances for risk and uncertainty (e.g., contingency, reserves, and escalation). To use cost overrun data for developing contingency models, one must first deduct those risk allowances to approximate the cost growth from the base estimate. The good news regarding making adjustments for data analysis is that the cost contingencies that most agencies and companies include in their budgets are both low and generally consistent. That is because most use rules-of-thumb (e.g., 10, 15, or 20 percent for Class 3, 4, and 5, respectively), or, if based on quantitative risk analysis, use methods that generate those values. Besides, for the cost overrun measure ambiguity, other quality issues in published accuracy studies include:

◆ The only project attributes typically documented are per-haps type of asset, size (physical and cost), and overall durations with ambiguous measures of what the start and end milestone dates were.

◆ Published data rarely document the impacts of critical risk events or explains outliers.

◆ Studies may or may not adjust for escalation, and when they do, most use inflation rates. As discussed in Volume 1, Chapter 14, escalation often differs greatly from infla-tion, sometimes by an order of magnitude in a given year and situation.

◆ What is included in actual cost and durations is often unclear. For example, did the project cost include front-end spending and tail-end commissioning, or were they expensed and not included in CAPEX? When did the owner declare the project "complete" (and was it actually operable at that point)?

◆ Descriptive statistics are reported in ways that are difficult to analyze and compare. For example, some sources re-port mean values and others report medians; some report ranges and others report standard deviations (standard deviation is of little use for non-symmetrical distributions); some include outliers and others don't, and so on.

◆ Inferential statistics (for example, regression of cost or schedule overrun versus attributes) are usually not con-

trolled for dominant risk drivers such as the level of scope
definition and complexity, which make the statistical
models highly suspect.

In short, readers must be cautious in drawing conclusions from and
making use of most published accuracy data and metrics. That applies to the assessments that follow, which are indicative in nature,
not conclusive.

Selected Non-Process Studies for Cost Comparison

Table 2.1 (from Volume 1, Table 15.1) summarizes the selected
cost estimate accuracy study comparison sample results. Each published study provided statistics on the distribution of cost growth or
cost overrun outcomes for its sample of projects. For example, reference [F] calculated the cost growth (increase in cost from the base
estimate without contingency) for each of its 24 projects and then
reported the $p10/50/90$ for the distribution of cost growth values (in
that case, the p-values were from a fitted distribution).

Often, studies provide a mean and a standard deviation. In
that case, $p90/p10$ values can be approximated by transforming
the reported data to an estimate/actual ratio and then assuming a
normal distribution, for which the $p90$ and $p10$ values are the mean
plus and minus 1.28 times the standard deviation, respectively. For
some studies, the $p90/p10$ values were roughly scaled from histogram
or continuous distribution diagrams of varying qualities. Note that
the tilde (~) symbol indicates approximation and the Greek letter
mu (μ) represents the mean.

The $p90/p10$ cost growth or overrun ranges in Table 2.1 clearly
exhibit wide variability. They range from +34% to −21% for US pipelines (and similar figures for wind, solar, and power transmission)
to about +300% to −20% for global hydropower, with similarly high
values for nuclear. The questions of interest here are:

(1) Do the empirical process industry-derived methods and models
from Volume 1, Chapters 11 and 14 predict these non-process
outcomes considering the typical systemic risk drivers for these
types of projects?

(2) If not, what is driving the accuracy differences?

STUDY ATTRIBUTES				ESTIMATE ACCURACY OF SAMPLE		
REFERENCE	PROJECTS	REFERENCE POINT	Adjust-ed?	p10 or Similar	p50 or Mean	p90 or Similar
[A] Figure 1	258 Transport, Global	"Decision" estimate	Time	~–15%	~+15% μ = +27%	~+100%
Flyvbjerg, Bent, Mette Skamris Holm and Søren Buhl, "Underestimating Costs in Public Works Projects; Error or Lie?," APA Journal, 68:3, 279-295, 2002.						
[B] Table 2	167 Transport, Swedish	Varied reference	No	~–32%	μ = +15%	~+62%
Lundberg, Mattias, Anchalee Jenpanitsub and Roger Pyddoke, "Cost Overruns in Swedish Transport Projects," CTS Working Paper 2011:11, Centre for Transport Studies, Stockholm Sweden, 2011.						
[C] Various	250+ Transport, US compilation	From "Planning"	?	~0%	~+20% μ = +40%	~+100%
Harbuck, Robert, "Are Accurate Estimates Achievable During the Planning of Transportation Projects?" AACE International Transactions, 2007.						
[D] Pg. I.3.4	56 Hydropower, World Bank	From "Appraisal"	Time	–15%	μ = +24%	+65%
Merrow, Edward W. and Brett R. Schroeder, "Understanding the Costs and Schedule of Hydroelectric Projects," 1991 AACE International Transactions, 1991.						
[E] Figure 2	245 Hydropower, Global	From "Budgeted"	Time	~–20%	+27% μ = +96%	+300%
Ansar, Flyvbjerg, Budzier and Lunn, "Should we build more large dams? The actual costs of hydropower megaproject development," Elsevier Ltd, 2014.						
[F] Table 2	24 Hydropower, Canadian	Est By Phase (Cls 5,4,3)	Scope & Time	–11%	+14%	+53%
Hollmann, John. et. al., "Variability in Accuracy Ranges: A Case Study In the Canadian Hydropower Industry," AACE International Transactions, 2014.						
[G] Various	61 Hydropower	Ambiguous ("Estimated costs")	Time	?	μ = +71%	?
	180 Nuclear			?	μ = +117%	?
	35 Wind			?	μ = +8%	?
	39 Solar			?	μ = +1%	?
Sovacool, Nugent and Gilbert, "Construction Cost Overruns and Electricity Infrastructure: An Unavoidable Risk?" The Electricity Journal, May 2014.						
[H] Database	188 US Pipeline	FERC filing	No	–21%	0%	+34%
Oil & Gas Journal Online Research Center, US Pipeline Study 2009; Actual vs. Estimate (database for fee), Penwell Corporation, Houston TX, 2009.						
[I] Figure 1	Process Plant Turnarounds	From "Budget"	?	–11%	+9% μ = +16%	+59%
Lawrence, Gordon, "Analysis Yields Turnaround Benchmarks for Allowance, Contingency," Oil & Gas Journal, April 2, 2012.						

Table 2.1: Selected Industry Cost Estimate Accuracy Studies

Interpretation of the Various Industry Cost Accuracy Data

The following assessments of the various studies in Table 2.1 aim to answer the questions above. The assessment considers the known drivers of uncertainty and accuracy ranges, including:

♦ The level of scope definition, and

♦ The level of complexity, technology, and process/service severity.

The assessment then examines publicly funded transportation infrastructure projects specifically to challenge the claim by some that cost overruns for these projects are largely explained by behavioral factors (optimism bias) rather than identifiable systemic risk drivers.

Level of Scope Definition

Most accuracy studies do not control for the level of scope definition at the time of the estimate. Most studies report cost overruns from either some published or announced cost or a final investment decision (FID) amount based on unclear levels of definition. The non-process industries have lagged in applying phase-gate system application and discipline rigor, which is evident in the studies. This is problematic because process industry research shows that the level of scope definition is a dominant risk driver. The Table 2.2 study comparison demonstrates why scope definition uncertainty is important to understand. It compares two global hydropower studies that are not controlled for the level of scope definition to a Canadian hydropower study that was controlled.

REFER-ENCE	PROJECTS	REFERENCE POINT	p10 or similar	p50 or mean (μ)	p90 or similar
[D]	56 Global (uncontrolled)	From "Appraisal"	−15%	μ= +24%	+65%
[E]	245 Global (uncontrolled)	From "Budgeted"	~−20%	+27% μ= +96%	+300%
[F]	24 Canadian (controlled)	Class 3/Define	−11%	+14%	+53%
		Class 4/Select	−6%	+28%	+97%
		Class 5/Assess	+12%	+64%	+186%

Table 2.2 : Comparison of Hydropower Cost Estimate Accuracy Studies

Note that level of definition or phase naming convention used in the tables is AACE Class when a Class could be reasonably interpreted (see Table 1.1 for various phase names used in different industries). However, Class designation usage does *not* mean that the projects met the AACE requirements. Unless noted, the Class name is just indicative.

Clearly, the $p90$ values in Table 2.2 vary significantly. However, on closer inspection, the cost growth in the controlled Canadian Study [F] for Class 4 estimates is close to the cost overrun in Study [D], while the cost growth for Study [F] Class 5 estimates is close to the cost overrun in Study [E]. Furthermore, the differences in the $p50$ values of studies [D] and [F-Class 4], and the mean of Study [D], are not statistically significant. As to the $p90$ differences, the large sample in Study [E] included a small number of extreme outliers, which pulled its mean and $p90$ far away from the median. This sample included a group of projects centered at about 500% overrun and one project that overran by more than 5,000%!

The conclusion that the uncontrolled Study [E] authors drew from its data was that hydropower cost overruns were so dire that, *"Policymakers, particularly in developing countries, are advised to prefer agile energy alternatives that can be built over shorter time horizons to energy megaprojects."* In other words, they suggested that "big is bad." Conversely, the statistically controlled cost growth Study [F] showed that defining hydropower project scope well before sanction (or allowing for empirically valid contingency as recommended by this book's methods) can lead to reasonably reliable outcomes. Additionally, the Study [E] mean and $p90$ values were influenced by extreme outliers, raising questions that we will examine later.

The controlled Study [F], which included all the large projects built in the participating Canadian provinces, was specifically intended to determine if the reported process industry accuracy applied to the hydropower industry. The finding was, *"The Canadian hydro experience is similar to that of other process industry projects, as well as of hydropower projects in other regions funded by the World Bank."* In other words, the parametric model in Volume 1, Chapter 11 is "self-correcting" for differences in technology, complexity, and other factors between process plant and civil-oriented/regulated hydropower projects. The next section explores this conclusion further.

Levels of Complexity and Technology (and Outliers)

Most studies do not measure or control for the level of complexity and technology. They typically just identify the type of project (e.g., road vs. rail) and leave it to the reader to speculate why projects of these asset types might differ in terms of accuracy. As with the level of scope definition, this is problematic because the level of complexity and technology are known strong systemic risk drivers.

Study [G] in Table 2.3 illustrates the importance of complexity and technology. That study analyzed hydropower, nuclear, wind, and solar project types using the same approach for each (and assumed similar funding decision estimate bases). The mean cost growth for these project types exhibits wide variability. The question is, are the differences explained by the process industry parametric model, which quantifies the cost impact of the level of complexity and technology?

REFERENCE	PROJECTS	MEAN (μ)
[G]	61 Hydropower	μ= +71%
	180 Nuclear	μ= +117%
	35 Wind	μ= +8%
	39 Solar	μ= +1%

Table 2.3: Comparison of Cost Estimate Accuracy for Power Projects

To compare Study [G] to the Volume 1, Chapter 11 parametric model, we need to assume model inputs. Initially, we assume that, on average, the projects were sanctioned at Class 4 equivalent scope definition (as indicated in the previous scope definition analysis). Nuclear and wind/solar projects are opposites in terms of their level of complexity, technology, and process severity. In physical and execution terms, nuclear projects are much more complex (although offshore wind floating structures and subsea elements also present considerable challenges). Likewise, nuclear processes are more technologically advanced and have more process severity challenges (e.g., radioactivity) than wind or solar projects. Table 2.4 shows these and other rating assumptions for testing parametric model application (see Volume 1, Chapter 11).

Based on the Table 2.4 inputs (and also assuming that the study projects included nominal 10% contingency in their budgets), Table 2.5 shows the Volume 1, Chapter 11 parametric model outcome compared to Study [G] for nuclear.

At first glance, nuclear projects in Study [G] had higher mean cost growth than predicted by the parametric model. Complexity, technology, and process severity were rated as high. Note that the parametric model excludes the impact of critical specific uncertainties and risk events, including high impact/low probability risk events (HILPs). It is also essential to account for the influence of extreme outliers on mean values. For example, the hydropower Study [E] had a high mean value of +96%, similar to nuclear projects, but its median (*p*50) was only +27% (almost one-third of the mean value)!

If Study [G] is adjusted for analogous outliers (HILPs, blowouts, etc.) that greatly drive up the mean value but not the median (which is likely in a sample of 180 projects), the mean values of Study [G] and the parametric model would likely align more closely. The process industry model seems applicable provided that HILP critical risk events and blowout risks (i.e., tipping points) are quantified uniquely by the analyst using the methods outlined in Volume 1, Chapters 11 and 14. However, this conclusion remains speculative because Study [G] lacked useful range or risk event data. We will revisit the outlier issue later. Also, a nuclear industry parametric tool calibration study conducted by the author, discussed later, confirmed parametric model applicability to that industry.

RISK DRIVER	NUCLEAR RATING	WIND/SOLAR
Scope Definition	Average 4	Average 4
New Technology	15%	5%
Process Severity	9	1
Complexity	9	2
Team Development	Poor	Poor
Project Control	Poor	Poor
Estimate Basis	Good	Good
Equipment	15%	35%
Fixed Price	<10%	20-30%
Bias	Low	Typical

Table 2.4 : Systemic Risk Ratings for Nuclear versus Wind/Solar Power Projects

INDUSTRY	REFERENCE	P50	MEAN	P90
Nuclear	Study [G]	?	+117%	?
	Parametric Model	+32%	+36%	+115%

Table 2.5 : Nuclear Study versus the Parametric Risk Model

Wind and solar power projects were evaluated next (as shown in Table 2.6) with respect to their complexity and technology impact (again, assuming the projects included a nominal 10% contingency in their budgets). Wind and solar were combined due to their similar outcomes and risk driver attributes relative to the parametric model.

INDUSTRY	REFERENCE	P50	MEAN	P90
Wind and Solar	Study [G]	?	+1 to 8%	?
	Parametric Model	+4%	+8%	+47%

Table 2.6: Wind and Solar Study versus the Parametric Risk Model

In this case, the Study [G] and the parametric model mean cost growth are less than 10%. Lower complexity, technology, and process severity impacts are particularly evident in the parametric model's $p90$ value for wind/solar projects, which is approximately one-third of the $p90$ of the parametric result for the nuclear case.

Wind and solar projects face fewer high impact/low probability risk events (HILPs) and blowout outliers. This is corroborated by a more recent 2017 study encompassing 51 onshore and offshore wind farm projects, which built upon the findings of reference Study [G] and provided insights into the range of outcomes. The $p90/p10$ range for onshore wind projects' cost overrun was remarkably tight at about +10%/-5%, while offshore wind projects exhibited a wider range of about +35%/-5%, with the largest offshore cost overrun reaching approximately 45%.[4] Mean values stood at 1% for onshore and 10% for offshore, consistent with the parametric model results in Table 2.6, particularly when accounting for the greater physical and execution complexity of offshore projects relative to onshore. Offshore wind project technology and complexity are on the rise, especially with the increasing prevalence of floating structures at greater water depths (although newer floating types were likely not included in the study).

Regarding the narrow range observed for onshore wind projects, wind and solar projects experienced significant cost increases due to supply chain disruptions and price escalations in 2021/22. In particular, some wind project developers and turbine manufacturers encountered financial difficulties due to their failure to anticipate

---

4   Sovacool, Benjamin, "Cost Performance and Risk in the Construction of Offshore and Onshore Wind Farms", Wind Energy, Volume 20, Issue 5, May 2017.

this risk in their fixed-price contracts (see Volume 2, Chapter 3 on contractor risks).

Table 2.6 also sheds light on the oil and gas pipeline Study [H], which reported a mean cost overrun of 0% and a low $p90$ of +34%. Run-of-the-mill pipeline projects resemble wind and solar projects in terms of their low complexity, technology, and process severity (i.e., the parametric model inputs for most pipelines would align with wind/solar inputs in Table 2.4). Additionally, the major pipeline company referenced in Volume 1, Chapter 8 has reported success in utilizing the risk quantification methods outlined in this book. However, pipeline projects can present complexities, such as megaprojects traversing mountains or environmentally sensitive areas, and may also be subject to HILP and tipping point outliers (e.g., the Trans Mountain pipeline project in Canada completion was delayed by 4 years).

Road and Rail Transport (Optimism Bias?)

This section evaluates road and rail transportation projects. These are usually taxpayer funded and are owned by the government (although public-private arrangements are becoming more common). This exposes the projects to added uncertainty stemming from political factors. One such factor is the announcement of project costs in the absence of adequate scope definition. Transportation project Study [A] in Table 2.1 is examined here; it is widely regarded as one of the most referenced studies on cost estimate accuracy in any industry.[5] It's important to note that the projects analyzed in Study [A] were all completed prior to the year 2000, a period when phase-gate systems in the transportation industry were inconsistently defined or applied. Study [A] attributed transportation project cost overruns to strategic misrepresentation ("lying") or optimism bias. The subsequent assessment challenges this hypothesis by evaluating whether the parametric model described in Volume 1, Chapter 11 accurately predicts observed transportation project cost overruns. Table 2.7 outlines the parametric model inputs assumed to apply to the dataset analyzed in Study [A].

The level of scope definition rating in Table 2.7 was assumed to be Class 5. This corresponds to the politically-driven "early cost announcement" behavior often observed in public transportation,

---

5   Study [B] also included a table of twenty other international accuracy studies in transportation. The unweighted average cost overruns of those twenty is about 30%, with rail and urban transit projects being closer to 50% on average and roads being closer to about 10% on average.

particularly prior to 2000 when phase-gate systems were not consistently applied in the public sector.

RISK DRIVER	TRANSPORT RATING
Scope Definition	Average 5
New Technology	0%
Process Severity	n/a
Complexity	3
Team Development	Poor
Project Control	Poor
Estimate Basis	Good
Equipment	0%
Fixed Price	>40%
Bias	Typical

Table 2.7 : Systemic Risk Ratings for Transportation Projects

For example, transportation Study [C] indicated that they used the "planning" estimate as a reference base, typically representing the pre-design, conceptual, or appraisal estimate (Class 5). It was further assumed that typical project complexity and level of technology were relatively low, dominated by road projects. While high-speed rail and urban transit projects can be complex, they were presumed to be uncommon in this context. Although there may be instances of new technology (e.g., maglev), such occurrences were also assumed to be infrequent. Similarly, while process or service severity could pose challenges (e.g., pushing limits on load capacity and service duty), such factors were assumed not to be applicable here. Additionally, the test assumed that transport projects typically employ fixed-price or unit-price strategies (although procurement practices were not explicitly described in Study [A]).

Table 2.8 presents the outcome of the Volume 1, Chapter 11 model based on the inputs outlined in Table 2.7 (again, assuming the study projects included a 10% contingency in their estimates). This is juxtaposed with the range reported in transportation Study [A].

INDUSTRY	REFERENCE	P50	MEAN	P90
Transportation	Study [A]	~+15%	+27%	~+100%
	Parametric Model	+15%	+21%	+71%

Table 2.8: Transportation Study versus the Parametric Risk Cost Model

In this instance, the $p50$ values of the parametric model seem to reasonably predict the outcomes observed in Study [A]. While the mean value in Study [A] slightly exceeds that of the parametric model, this variance could be attributed to the exclusion of critical specific risks by the model. Additionally, the Study [A] mean deviates from the $p50$, indicating a fat tail distribution. Several projects in the study reported overruns in the +200% to +300% range, indicative of tipping point blowouts. The relatively high $p90$ value in the parametric model is driven by the low level of assumed scope definition. Based on this limited data, it can be reasonably inferred that the Volume 1, Chapter 11 parametric cost model is applicable, provided a tipping point analysis per Volume 1, Chapter 14 is conducted to assess potential blowouts. Strategic representation and optimism bias are unnecessary to explain the outcomes observed in the study.

Conclusion:
The Process Industry Model is Generic for Cost

While the studies and analyses discussed above are not definitive, they suggest that the process industry-based parametric cost growth model outlined in Volume 1, Chapter 11 can be confidently applied to non-process industry projects. However, these studies also indicate that the cost contingencies allowed for by industries of all types are similarly unrealistic (5% to 15% contingency versus the 15% to 40% predicted by realistic parametric and expected value methods). If realistic risk quantification methods had been employed, the mean overrun values would likely be closer to 0% in all cases.

This analysis underscores the importance of using estimating accuracy studies cautiously, particularly if they are not controlled for known risk drivers such as the level of scope definition upon which the estimate was based. This factor alone explains much of the observed poor accuracy in studies utilizing publicly available data. By simply rating the level of scope definition, complexity, and technology (and analyzing HILP and tipping point risks), the cost overruns observed in various non-process industries are largely explained.

Except for outliers, industry data does not support strategic misrepresentation as the primary risk driver, even for public infrastructure projects. However, this may change if politicians grasp the profession's failure to address the level of scope definition and other systemic risks in risk quantification. Politicians could then exploit this knowledge to manipulate public perception by making premature announcements or securing funding before appropriate scope definition is established.

Another caveat is not to overly focus on mean values, which can be sensationalized for media coverage but offer no insight into skewed probability distributions. Standard deviations similarly provide little relevance to skewed (e.g., lognormal) distribution data; they merely offer a sense of variability. Outliers (HILPs and blowouts) disproportionately inflate mean values, a topic we will delve into later in this chapter.

Industry Schedule Data

Schedule slippage has also been studied for various industries. This section examines selected industry studies on schedule overrun and evaluates how well the Volume 1, Chapter 11 parametric model for schedule duration predicts the study results, including all risk types (e.g., systemic, project-specific, and tipping point).

Schedule Data Quality: What Duration is Being Studied?

Similar to cost studies, the quality of data on published schedule slip or overrun studies varies widely. One challenge in interpreting schedule studies is the lack of clarity regarding the duration being studied (i.e., the definitions of start and end date milestones). Outside the process industry, the absence of standard phase-gate processes adds confusion. Many academic studies only examine one duration, calculated from an ambiguous early project announcement start date to an assumed start of operation end date (though operational commencement may be debatable). This duration is sometimes referred to as "cycle time." Other studies may focus on specific phase durations such as "execution" (encompassing detailed engineering and construction) or, occasionally, solely on construction.

The duration under study may depend on the study's purpose. For instance, the Rand research underpinning the Volume 1, Chapter 11 models focused on determining the appropriate schedule contingency for control during the post-sanction "execution" phase. Contingency as a control concept is less relevant to the front-end definition phases where scope is being defined and optimized with limited resources and limited control discipline. It is also less relevant for controlling post-construction commissioning. Studies of *execution* phase schedule contingency determination look at what the planned execution duration was at each gate review (i.e., Class 5, 4, 3/FID). The duration of and delays during the front-end phases and commissioning are less relevant to such studies. Risk analysis for the front-end and commissioning and start-up phases would utilize the expected value method per Volume 1, Chapter 12.

Conversely, studies of "cycle time" duration encompass all delays during the front-end, execution, and commissioning phases. A concern with cycle time studies is that during the front-end phases, the primary objective is to refine scope and mitigate risks that might occur later during execution. Minimizing front-end delays (which carry relatively low costs) is usually not a primary objective. An exception is schedule-driven projects that accelerate the front-end pace; such acceleration constitutes a risk driver. One study found that *"the quality of front-end loading tends to decline as the schedule priority increases."*[6] If a project requires front-end delays to optimize scope and planning, such delays are acceptable. In other words, delay is a feature, not a flaw, of a disciplined front-end process. However, for the execution phase, after the FID launch button is pressed and hundreds or thousands of workers are mobilized and purchase orders placed, the goal is to minimize duration and costly delays using effective control and risk management. Due to common delays in scope decisions and design recycling behavior during the front-end, cycle time duration accuracy tends to be lower (i.e., wider range) than for execution duration.

Selected Non-Process Studies for Schedule Comparison

Table 2.9 presents schedule slip data from selected studies, with the following notes:

- The Class designation is indicative of the level of scope definition. In particular, Study [K] used a UK phase designation of SBC, OBC, and FBC. These are somewhat analogous to Class 5, 4, and 3, respectively.
- Sources [E, F, and G] are studies referenced in Table 2.1 with both cost and schedule data. The remaining studies, designated with letter labels continuing from Table 2.1, have been added for this Volume.
- For several studies, *p*-values were estimated from histogram or continuous distribution chart illustrations.

---

6   Merrow, Edward W., "Contract Strategies for Major Projects", John Wiley & Sons, New Jersey, 2023.

STUDY ATTRIBUTES				SCHEDULE ACCURACY OF SAMPLE		
REFERENCE	PROJECTS	DURATION INCLUED	Class	p10 or Similar	p50 or Mean	p90 or Similar
[E] (re: 18.1)	239 Hydropow-er, Global	Cycle Time	≈4	?	+44%	~+120%
[F] (re: 18.1)	24 Hydropower, Canadian	Execution	5	-29%	+6%	+109%
			4	-22%	+4%	+58%
			3	-13%	+9%	+46%
[G] (re: 18.1)	<61 Hydro-power	Ambiguous	≈4	?	+62%	?
	<180 Nuclear			?	+62%	?
	<35 Wind			?	+9%	?
	<39 Solar			?	+1%	?
	#? Transmission			?	+7%	?
[J] Figure	~2,000 Process related	Cycle Time	5	-10%	+50%	+115%
		Cycle Time	4	-3%	+19%	+50%
		Execution	3	-3%	+17%	+48%
IPA, Inc., "IPA's Conceptual Schedule Duration Tool," www.ipaglobal.com/news/article, May 18, 2021.						
[K] Table 6 and App A	340 Road, Global	Cycle Time	5	-20% all	+23%	+135%
		Cycle Time	4		+25%	+150%
		Execution	3		+20%	+48%
UK Dept for Transport, "Updating the evidence behind the optimism bias uplifts for transport appraisals," 2020.						
[L] Table 5	100 Transport >$5M, NV, US	Execution	3	~-10%	+14%	~+45%
Shrestha, P, "Magnitude of Construction Cost and Schedule Overruns in Public Work Projects," Journal of Construction Engineering, 2013.						
[M] Table 1 & Fig. 1	28 Transit, Major, US	Cycle Time	4	0%	+34%	+60%
Gurgun, A., "Schedule Contingency Analysis for Transit Projects Using a Simulation Approach", Journal of Civil Engineering and Management, 2013 Vol 19(4).						
[N] study backup	29 Power Trans-mission Canada	Execution	5	-35%	+4%	+53%
			4	-28%	+8%	+45%
			3	-26%	+3%	+25%
Hollmann, et.al., "Variability in Accuracy Ranges: A Case Study in the Canadian Power Transmission Industry," AACE Int'l Transactions 2017 (unpublished study data).						

Table 2.9: Selected Industry Schedule Accuracy Studies
(continues next page)

STUDY ATTRIBUTES				SCHEDULE ACCURACY OF SAMPLE		
REFERENCE	PROJECTS	DURATION INCLUDED	Class	p10 or Similar	p50 or Mean	p90 or Similar
[O] study backup	37 Power Generation & Transmission, US	Execution	5	-15%	+10%	+53%
			4	-30%	+2%	+91%
			3	-14%	+4%	+30%
Hollmann, et.al., "Variability in Accuracy Ranges: A Case Study in the US and Canadian Power Industry," AACE International Transactions 2020 (unpublished study data).						
[P] study backup	39 Minerals Industry	Execution	5	-27%	+11%	+128%
			4	-17%	+14%	+79%
			3	-21%	+2%	+43%
Hollmann, unpublished study.						
[Q] Fig 5	39 Transport, Major, NZ	Execution	3	~-10%	+10%	~+45%
Love, P.L., Ika, J Matthews, "Breaking the Sisyphean Loop: reconceptualizing the treatment of risk and uncertainty in transport projects," Production Planning & Control, 2024..						

Table 2.9: Selected Industry Schedule Accuracy Studies
(continued from previous page)

◆ For power project studies [F, N, and O], schedule slip data was not included in the published papers but was available to the author. The $p10$ and $p90$ values are derived from lognormal distributions fitted to the data.

◆ Study [K] provided information on non-road projects. However, the study values were relatively consistent across all project types and phases. Therefore, only the most extensive road dataset results are included here for brevity.

It is worth noting that researchers and the author have observed a greater number of cost accuracy studies than schedule accuracy studies. Furthermore, studies covering both cost and schedule tend to have fewer data points for schedule than for cost. Also, explicit schedule contingency usage remains unsettled, making schedule accuracy data less sought after than cost data. Fewer studies and less data pose challenges for drawing conclusions regarding schedule duration estimate accuracy.

As was done for cost, the following are assessments of the various studies in Table 2.9 to determine if the process industry derived methods and models of Volume 1, Chapters 11 and 14 predict these schedule outcomes considering the typical systemic risk drivers for these types of projects. As with cost, the assessment looks at known uncertainty drivers and accuracy ranges including the level of scope definition and the level of complexity.

Level of Scope Definition

Six of the eleven studies in Table 2.9 [F, J, K, N, O, P] examined schedule slippage at different levels of scope definition. Four of these studies analyzed execution duration at each phase, while the other two [J and K] assessed the cycle time moving forward for the first two phases. Five of the six phased studies show a marked narrowing of the range as the level of definition improves.

The exception is the UK Department for Transport's optimism bias Study [K], where the wide range remains wide regardless of improving scope definition and the shift from measuring cycle time to execution uncertainty. This quasi-constant outcome contradicts any accuracy study the author has encountered. Study [K] attributes this partly to "anchoring," i.e., projects are not effectively improving their plans from phase to phase. This raises questions about the effectiveness of nascent public transportation phase-gate processes if Study [K] is correct. Unfortunately, no other transportation industry studies were found that examined how the level of scope definition influences schedule estimate duration.

So, how well does the Volume 1, Chapter 11 parametric model address the level of scope definition risk for schedule slippage? Table 2.10 shows the mean and p90 predicted execution schedule slip by phase using the Volume 1, Chapter 11 model for a project of modest complexity, with no new technology, and somewhat less than ideal definition at the Class 3 phase. It also shows the unweighted averages for the five phased studies in Table 2.9, excluding the anomalous UK study.

The first observation pertains to the mean percent schedule slip. The study values are about 0.6 times the mean schedule slip predicted by the model for each phase. One simple explanation may be that the projects in the studies included a schedule contingency (explicit or otherwise) of 5 to 10% in their durations (i.e., the model is predicting slip from a base duration excluding contingency). Another explanation is that some projects are trading cost for schedule (i.e., expending resources to recover time). These explanations would be consistent with the low study $p10$ values (significant underruns), which pull down the study means.

CLASS	CHAPTER 11 MODEL			AVERAGE [F, J, N, O, P]		
	P10	MEAN	P90	P10	MEAN	P90
5	-5%	+25%	+63%	-23%	+16%	+92%
4	-3%	+16%	+41%	-20%	+9%	+65%
3	-2%	+11%	+27%	-15%	+7%	+38%

Table 2.10: Chapter 11 Parametric Schedule Model Versus Study Outcomes

The second observation concerns the *p*90 schedule slip. The study values are about 1.4 times the p*90* predicted by the model for each phase. The high *p*90s may reflect high impact/low probability (HILP) specific risks on some projects and/or the effect of complexity, as discussed in the next section. The low *p*10 and mean values contradict the high *p*90 values, suggesting fat tails. In any case, the range or span from *p*10 to *p*90 for the studies is about 1.8 times that of the model.

Level of Complexity

The two studies in Table 2.9 that stand out for having high mean schedule slip values are [E] and [G], which focus on hydropower and nuclear projects. These types of projects often experience tremendous public scrutiny, reviews, and delays due to regulatory changes, permitting requirements, and social license risk related to external stakeholders. This may also apply to some projects in the transport studies [K, M]. The interactions of external stakeholders with a project system, as well as working in sensitive environments, contribute to execution complexity. However, the hydropower [F] and transport [M] projects did not exhibit high average mean schedule slip values, suggesting that these complexity-related risks are likely project specific rather than systemic.

On the other end of the complexity spectrum are wind, solar, and power transmission projects in studies [G] and [N]. The means (and the *p*90 for Study [N]) are low, further indicating that complexity (or lack thereof) drives schedule slip. The datasets for studies [L] and [Q] from a US state and a New Zealand highway department, respectively, may also have been dominated by lower complexity projects.

While caution is necessary when interpreting limited data of varying quality, it is possible that the Volume 1, Chapter 11 parametric model somewhat underweights the schedule impact of social license-driven complexity, which seems to be increasing over time. However, regulatory and permit-driven delays are most often specific to the project and its location, regulatory regime, and stakeholder interactions. These delays would be best quantified as critical project-specific risks or high impact/low probability events using the expected value method described in Volume 1, Chapter 12.

Conclusion: The Process Industry Model is Generic for Schedule with Caveats

The study data quality and variability do not support making firm conclusions. However, the Volume 1, Chapter 11 parametric model appears to apply generically across all industries. Schedule slip data can be inconsistent. For example, within a given industry (e.g., hydropower or transportation), the observed mean schedule slip can be either less than or greater than the model's predictions. Low mean schedule slip may reflect the fact that schedules can often be "forced" to achieve a planned outcome within reason (i.e., trading cost for schedule or declaring a project finished before achieving operational objectives). Cost/schedule trading behavior may also partly explain the relatively weak correlation between cost growth and schedule slip found in many studies.

Aggressive schedule management may be a systemic behavior or bias that could arguably be parametrically modeled (i.e., by adding a model question about whether the project is schedule driven). The existing model does not have that question but does include a schedule bias rating entry. If one rates the base project schedule bias as conservative, this will reduce the mean predicted schedule outcome. If using ValidRisk®, discussed in Chapter 7 of this Volume, the model mean can be calibrated to adjust for an aggressive schedule management bias if low mean schedule slip is the norm for one's company.

On the other hand, some of the observed $p90$ values of the assessment suggest that while nominal schedule risk impact can be contained by aggressive schedule management and cost/schedule trading, at some point major risks, or the compounding thereof, can overwhelm the ability to prevent delays. There are major risks (e.g., regulatory and permit delays; protests) that are typically specific to the project, location, regulatory regime, stakeholder interactions, and so on, that should be quantified as specific critical risks or high impact/low probability (HILP) events using the expected value method described in Volume 1, Chapter 12.

Parametric Model Calibration Studies by the Author

In recent years, the author has assisted many companies in implementing the parametric risk quantification method, as applied in the ValidRisk® software. As part of tool implementation, a calibration study is recommended to ensure the model accurately reflects the client's historical project cost growth and schedule slip experience. The author has facilitated cost calibration studies for process, mining, transportation, power generation and transmission, pipeline, and nuclear project portfolios. While the particulars of these studies are confidential, it can be shared that the Volume 1, Chapter 11 parametric model for cost has generally been a good fit for all these industries out-of-the-box.

When calibration factors have been applied, it is usually due to the client's base estimating bias, which can be either conservative (predictability cultures) or aggressive (competitive cultures). This is not the same as reference class forecasting "debiasing" for gross optimism bias; the estimating bias is typically nominal because most cost growth and schedule slip are addressed by the model's algorithm (i.e., the model self-corrects for poor definition, weak team development, technology, and/or complexity). Once clients become aware of challenges in their estimating and scheduling practices, they can effectively address them, necessitating periodic calibration updates to track improvement.

For schedule duration, the calibration studies have found that the Volume 1, Chapter 11 parametric model has been a good fit for projects of lower complexity. However, there are indications, as exhibited in some of the studies discussed, that the industry schedule range is wider than the Volume 1, Chapter 11 model predicts for complex projects, even after accounting for specific risk events and HILPs. This wider uncertainty (range) can be easily addressed in ValidRisk® software, which allows separate calibration for the mean and for the standard deviation or range (the two parameters of the underlying lognormal-based algorithm).

Outliers: Beyond the Pale (Beyond *p*90)

In the hydropower, nuclear, and public transport studies, the mean and *p*90 cost and schedule overrun values were skewed by outliers. I refer to these outlier projects as "Beyond the Pale"[7] because their outcomes exceed the *p*90 boundary that many use to represent

---

7   The Pale was an area in Ireland once under the authority of English law; "beyond the Pale" meant outside the rule of English law and order.

the nominal "worst case" in economic sensitivity evaluations. If you focus on the median values of published studies (and the mean when not distorted by outliers), the parametric cost and schedule models work reasonably well for all the industries examined.

It is tempting to label the outliers as "unknown-unknowns" or "black swans" and disregard them, or to say, "they are beyond the $p90$, so why should we care?" However, a premise of these books is that we must quantify the risks that matter, and these outliers matter greatly.[8] For a portfolio of projects, a few such outliers can ruin a company's overall return-on-capital, not to mention jeopardize management jobs and reputations. There are two prevailing hypotheses for what causes extreme overruns:

- Strategic misrepresentation (and its cousin, corruption) (Volume 1, Chapter 5), and
- Crossing the Tipping Point (Volume 1, Chapter 15).

An example of the former is the hydropower study [E], where the cost growth distribution of its 245 projects had a very long tail (median = 27%, mean = 96%). The distribution was somewhat trimodal, with a small group of extreme outlier projects with cost overruns ranging from about 450% to 625%. A few projects overran by even more; the maximum being 5,142%! Among that study's authors is Dr. Bent Flyvbjerg, who is a leading proponent of the theory that optimism bias and strategic misrepresentation ("psychological delusion and political deception," as the study terms it)[9] are largely to blame for the cost overruns of public infrastructure projects.

A Wider Shade of Pale / Dual Tipping Point Behavior

I hypothesize that Study [E]'s long tail reflects a combination of misrepresentation and tipping point risks (on top of weak systems), acting in a combined and sometimes quasi-stepped fashion. The wide part of the tail (a second mode) consists of overruns of 100% to 300%. These are common to tipping point behavior on megaprojects; the tipping point model in Volume 1, Chapter 14 predicts this scale of overrun. However, a much smaller group of projects with about 450% to 625% cost overruns (a third mode) appears to have crossed

---

8   In the case-study book *When Mega goes Giga* by Joseph Brewer about the $20 billion Sadura project, Mr. Brewer relates how his team found that so called "black swans" "were certain to happen" on large scale projects.

9   Op. Sit., Flyvbjerg et. al.

a second tipping point, likely driven by the blowout drivers covered in Volume 1, Chapter 14, plus misrepresentation and/or corruption[10] (see Figure 2.1).

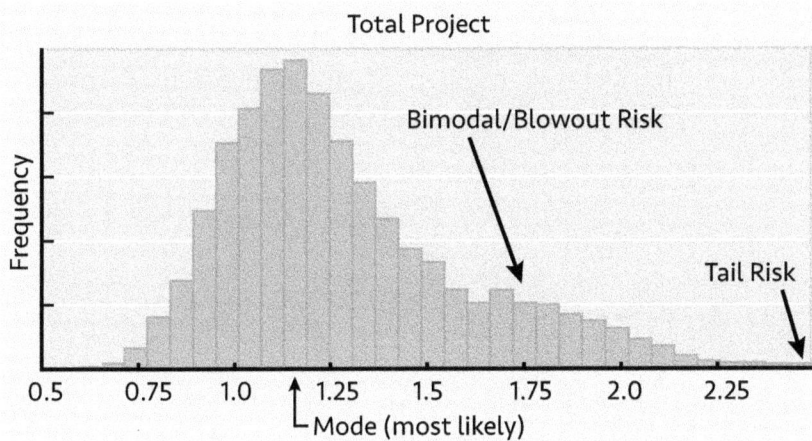

Figure 2.1: The Dual Tipping Point Concept as a Discrete Distribution

In addition, blowouts can be exploited by another risk driver. After punishments are meted out for the initial project failure (e.g., firings, lost elections), the new overseer, free from fault, discovers an opportunity: use the project as a de facto fiscal stimulus (albeit formally unsanctioned and ripe for corruption). In weak economies, some economists promote spending money on infrastructure using debt as beneficial. I suggest that overruns of greater than 300% indicate that the project has transitioned to a de facto fiscal stimulus program. As Rahm Emanuel, US President Obama's former Chief of Staff, said, *"Never let a serious crisis go to waste. And what I mean by that is it's an opportunity to do things you think you could not do before."*[11]

One example is Petrobras's Comperj refinery/petrochemical project in Brazil. A report stated, *"Comperj project is riddled with delays, cost overruns and reckless management, a state audit found, as it listed numerous modifications that raised the cost of the project from $6.1bn to nearly $50bn."* That increase is about 800%, with the

10 There is no doubt that there is misrepresentation in the public sector. At least one politician confessed to it; as shared in Chapter 4, Mr. Willie Brown, former mayor of San Francisco wrote: *"In the world of civic projects, the first budget is really just a down payment."*

11 Seib, Gerald, "In Crisis, Opportunity for Obama," Wall Street Journal, Nov. 21, 2008.

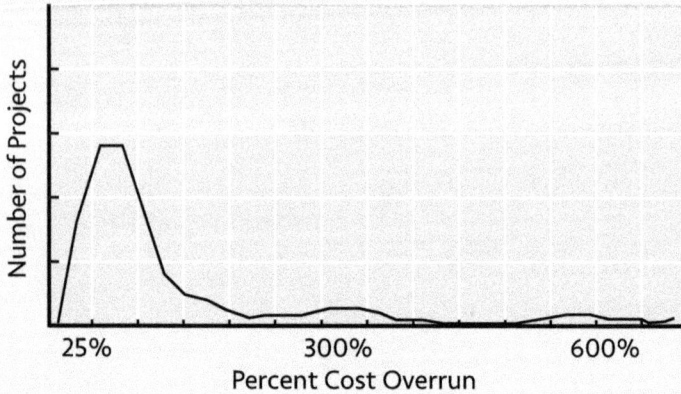

Figure 2.2: The Dual Tipping Point as an Example Continuous Distribution

project starting in 2004 and finishing in 2014. The report continues, "*In the audit, the TCU (Brazilian Federal Accounting Court) did not mention corruption, embezzlement or theft. However, it did find excessive risk-taking and a disregard of standard operating procedures.*" The article adds: "*The audit warned that the project is threatening Petrobras with heavy losses.*"[12] Granted, the project also made repeated "*massive revisions*" to scope, but I would posit that scope changes are a feature, not a risk, when a project becomes something other than a project by any traditional definition.

To illustrate the dual tipping point thesis, Figure 2.1 depicts a simplified discrete distribution of 245 projects, including 214 orderly but mediocre projects with a 25% average overrun, 20 blowouts with a 300% average overrun, 10 exploitative disasters at 600%, and one absurd project-turned-something-else at 5,000%. This distribution as a whole has a median of 25% overrun but a mean of 100%. This is designed to emphasize Study [E]'s way of viewing the overall statistics.

Of course, the actual distribution is continuous, as represented in Figure 2.2. A quote by a subsea contractor summarizes this stepped impact phenomenon: "*When a project begins to have problems it is often followed by more problems.*"[13]

In any case, both charts highlight that outliers are truly exceptions and "beyond the Pale." Misrepresentation, exploitation,

---

12 ICIS News, "Overruns, Recklessness Riddle Petrobras Comperj Project – Audit," Oct. 20, 2014.

13 Siem, K., "Update on the Guara-Luna NE Project Offshore Brazil," Subsea 7 conference call transcript, June 27, 2013.

and corruption are real and must be recognized and managed, but extreme cases should not be used in any representation of the typical state of an industry and arguably should not be included in mean values (unless a study's real purpose is to garner sensational headlines). Showing means with and without exceptional outliers would be most informative and less biased in its own right, but this is rarely done.

Nuclear power projects in the US also display an apparent second tipping point. However, in the nuclear industry, the aggravating risk factor is regulatory change or churn, plus an adversarial culture common when public safety, health, and environmental concerns are high and project durations are long. A recent nuclear power plant project in the US provides an example of complexity, technology, and regulatory risks (plus general poor performance) acting together and compounding. The Vogtle project in Georgia, once viewed as a symbol of possible nuclear rebirth in the US, was completed by the Southern Company in 2023. It was seven years late and $17 billion over budget.[14] As pressure increases to meet net-zero carbon objectives and governments announce aggressive deadlines, this type of risk will likely increase.

This risk impact is not inevitable for nuclear projects. For example, one study pointed out that France did not share the US cost overrun experience partly because, as one report states, *"France's regulatory process was also less adversarial than America's – and, for better or worse, doesn't allow legal intervention by outside groups once construction gets underway."*[15] China, with 21 nuclear plants under construction in 2023, mitigates adversarial challenges as well. An article explained, *"They don't have any secret sauce other than state financing, state supported supply chain, and a state commitment to build the technology."*[16] In the US, the government and industry have formally recognized the need for a regulatory risk mitigation approach and efforts are being made to standardize designs,[17] with a

14   Amy, Jeff, "Georgia nuclear rebirth arrives 7 years late, $17B over cost," AP, May 25, 2023.

15   Plumer, Brad, "Why America abandoned nuclear power," VOX, Feb 29, 2016.

16   Clifford, Catherine, "How China became the king of new nuclear power, and how the U.S. is trying to stage a comeback," CNBC, Aug 30 2023.

17   U.S. NRC, "Backgrounder on New Nuclear Plant Designs," December 2015.

current focus on small modular reactors (SMRs). However, this will likely do little to mitigate interventions by external stakeholders.

Schedule Overrun Outliers

While most studies have focused on cost overruns, schedule overrun studies also include significant outliers. Some examples have already been mentioned, including the Trans Mountain pipeline and Vogtle nuclear power projects, which were completed 4 and 7 years late, respectively. Another example is the hydropower Study [E] in Table 2.9, which included one project that overran its schedule by 750%. The cost overrun distribution for that study was approximated in Figure 2.2. Study [E] also included a schedule overrun distribution with the same general profile as cost overruns, except the multiple schedule modes occur at about half the percentage values of the cost overruns, i.e., at about 150% and 300% for schedule overruns versus 300% and 600% for cost overruns.

Another example of schedule slip outliers and possible tipping point behavior is shown in Figure 2.3, derived from data in Study [O] in Table 2.9. The histogram shows schedule slip (i.e., 1.4 = 40% slip) from the estimated execution duration at Class 3 (FID). (Note: the Table 2.9 values differ somewhat from the histogram as they were from fitted distributions.) As can be seen, 2 of the 20 projects are outliers with greater than 80% schedule slip. Study [Q] also included a similar histogram with 3 of its 39 projects exhibiting greater than 65% schedule slip.

The discussions about cost outliers and their cause also apply to schedule. However, the schedule slip may be of somewhat lesser percentage magnitude than for cost growth.

Modeling Multi-Modal Behavior

These outlier hypotheses represent my opinions and experience. However, there is sufficient evidence to propose a second tipping point adjustment model. This MCS model adjuster would be developed similarly to the method described in Volume 1, Chapter 14, with the difference being that the added risk factors/stressors to rate are the following:

♦ Likelihood of political influence (e.g., as in monumental publicly-funded projects),
♦ Likelihood of regulatory change (e.g., as in nuclear and high carbon projects) and/or public intervention, and
♦ Susceptibility to corruption.

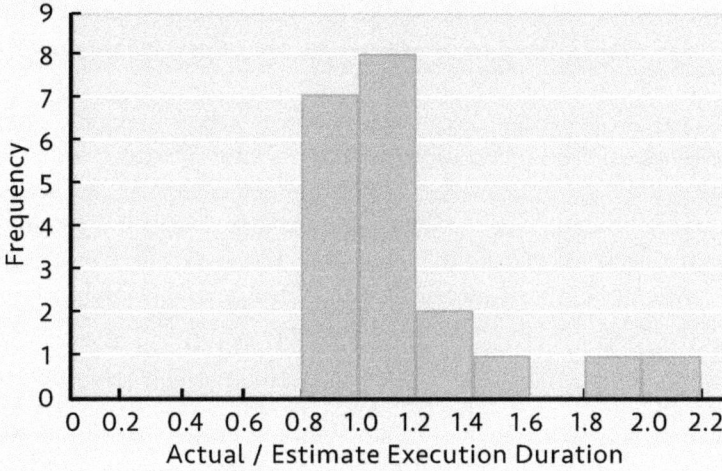

Figure 2.3: Example of Schedule Slip Outliers/Possible Tipping Point

Some have fittingly called these "strategic risks." They can be rated on a 5-level Likert scale, ranging from 1 = very low to 5 = very high. Political influence and public intervention would be difficult to rate objectively; perhaps past project outcomes for that government entity and culture could be used as an indicator if historical data are available. The corruption rating could be measured using something like Transparency International's Corruption Perceptions Index (CPI) as referenced in Volume 1, Chapter 2. In a tipping point model, as the combined rating score increases, it would increase the percentage of MCS iterations subject to this risk's impact multiplier.

Such a model would be both practical and realistic – an objective way to communicate the full risk reality for investors and stakeholders when appropriate. This approach is far better than resorting to vague terms like "unknown-unknowns" and "black swans." We can provide more precise insights than that. While caution is needed in interpreting and using limited studies with varying data quality, the studies indicate that the probability of projects crossing the second tipping point is at least several percent – enough to matter. For communicating potential worst-case business case exposure for complex projects, some rules of thumb are that cost overruns could be about three times and schedule duration two times the $p90$ values generated by the realistic Volume 1, Chapter 11 QRA methods. For example, if the $p90$ is 100% growth or slip, the worst case might be around 300% for cost and 200% for schedule (these multipliers would be doubled if subjective, unrealistic QRA is used).

Summary

This chapter reviewed published cost and schedule accuracy data for selected industries. While not exhaustive, it sufficiently demonstrates that the parametric cost and schedule models of systemic risks covered in Volume 1, Chapter 11 for process industries, and included in ValidRisk® software (see Chapter 7) provide a reasonable basis to quantify risk for engineering and construction projects across all industries. However, the variability in study results suggests that parametric model calibration is advisable for each company. It also underscores the importance of closely monitoring critical specific risks and HILPs.

Additionally, the assessment indicates that a second tipping point MCS adjustment model, developed similarly to the model in Volume 1, Chapter 14, would be beneficial for projects highly susceptible to political influence, regulatory change, and/or corruption. Given the public pressure to achieve net-zero carbon by announced deadlines, understanding these risks is critical.

So far, all data, methods, and model discussions have focused on the owner's perspective. The next chapter will delve into how contractors may employ these methods and models for their purposes, which often differ from those of the owner(s).

Questions

1. When stating that parametric models are "self-correcting," what does this mean?

2. Why could solely reporting mean and standard deviation values in cost and schedule accuracy studies be misleading?

3. What factors might contribute to widely varying findings in cost and schedule accuracy studies within the same industry?

4. Which two overarching systemic risk driver types seem to account for most discrepancies in reported cost growth and schedule slip accuracy studies?

5. What reasons could explain why studies focusing on "cycle time" tend to exhibit wider accuracy ranges compared to those focusing on "execution"?

6. The chapter proposed a dual tipping point concept to explain extreme outliers. What are the three suggested risk drivers behind such overruns?

Volume 2 Perspective

After over 25 years of studying cost and schedule accuracy data and research, I remain frustrated by the generally low quality of published accuracy research, as highlighted in this chapter. This frustration is particularly pronounced in the public infrastructure sector. I am hopeful that recent advancements in machine learning and artificial intelligence, primarily focused on public infrastructure projects, will help improve this situation.

Ultimately, each agency or company must take responsibility for effectively capturing and analyzing its historical data if we are to have any chance of enhancing project risk quantification performance. Encouragingly, the higher-quality data and research emerging from the process industries are proving to be broadly applicable to engineering and construction projects across all sectors.

"It's a very sobering feeling to be up in space and realize that one's safety factor was determined by the lowest bidder on a government contract."

– Alan Shepard, the first American in space

3

Accuracy and QRA Methods for Contractors

This chapter focuses on the prime or general contractor's point of view (POV) regarding data accuracy and project/contract risk quantification.[1] The owner's POV is prevalent in Volume 1. However, contractors have different objectives, processes, experiences, data, and needs from risk quantification than owners.

The chapter also addresses owner/contractor interactions and how their differences impact risk management, data, and quantification, ideally benefiting both parties. Because owners and contractors ultimately work within the same project system, attributes of their working relationship are significant systemic risks.

Generalizing about contractors' needs and approaches to risk quantification in a single chapter is challenging. For instance, Engineering-Procurement-Construction Management (EPCM) con-

---

1   The chapter does not cover the POV of trade subcontractors. In general, they are smaller and their risk management, risk quantification, and data analytics capabilities are more limited given their tight margins. That is not to say they do not carry major risks relative to their scopes or that they are ineffective in their risk practices; it is just that the nature of their situation and practices typically differs from those addressed by this chapter.

tractors in the process sector, dealing with "proposals" at Class 3, may have a broad "project risk" perspective and use QRA methods similar to those used by owners. Conversely, Design-Bid-Build (DBB) contractors in the commercial and public infrastructure sectors, dealing with "tenders/bidding" at Class 2, may have a narrower design or construction-only perspective, emphasizing more intuitive risk analyses. This example highlights why this chapter focuses on risk quantification by contractors in different contracting strategies and why the process (Volume 1) and commercial/infrastructure (Chapter 2 of this Volume) sectors often view risk quantification differently.

Regarding accuracy data and metrics, a key differentiating factor between owners and contractors is that the owner's POV encompasses the entire capital cost and duration of a project's total scope from inception through turnover to operations (a strategic view). Contractors rarely participate in all elements of the project scope and/or life cycle. As such, to the author's knowledge, there are no contractor-sourced studies on the accuracy of total capital cost or cycle time estimates. However, contractors have extensive data on the estimated and actual costs and durations, and hence estimate accuracy of detailed activities and items, and sub-elements of project scope in engineering, procurement, fabrication, and/or construction (a more tactical view). This chapter does not offer accuracy metric statistics or charts at the detailed activity/item level, although this would be a good topic for estimating and scheduling texts. However, it describes the general types of data and accuracy that major contractors might have and can use in their project risk quantification.

Regarding risk quantification methods, the contractor's unique objectives and processes are discussed in the chapter, particularly their focus on bid/no-bid decision making (i.e., go/no-go) and then on markup determination. While project risk quantification should be a core competency for owners, some contractors often support owner cost and/or schedule risk analyses, especially if contract strategies involve early contractor involvement (ECI). Their objectives, practices, roles, and potential issues are discussed. After contract award, contractors should use risk quantification at a tactical level during execution, and those practices are also discussed.

An obvious caution for owners using contractor risk quantification services is that contractor business objectives differ from theirs. The owner's objective for capital projects is usually cost and schedule effectiveness, i.e., delivering the least-cost assets in a timely manner for a given asset capability and quality.[2] These contribute to a competitive return on capital. The contractor's objective is usually to maximize contract revenue and profit margin while delivering the specified contract scope. The chapter discusses the "principal agent problem" in this regard.

One thing owners and contractors share is the use of, or at least reference to, phase-gate project systems. As discussed in Chapter 3 of Volume 1, an owner steps through the project process phase-by-phase, improving scope definition, quantifying risk, and making decisions at each gate. Contractors, on the other hand, are mainly concerned with the owner gate at which a tender solicitation or request for proposal (RFP) is issued. To add clarity to this chapter's discussions, refer to Table 1.1 in Chapter 1 of this volume, which outlines the project phases and the varying names assigned to them. The AACE Class designations are preferred because they are industry-generic.

The chapter discusses contractor phase-gate considerations in risk quantification. For example, the phase of most interest to EPCM contractors may be proposal negotiation at Class 3, but if the scope of work is just construction, the contractor will focus on the tender/bid at Class 2. However, a contractor brought in by an owner at Class 4 to support design development or FEED, if given the opportunity, likely has an interest in keeping the work going through FID, a principal agent concern for owners that will be discussed. The last introductory topic is a high-level overview of contract strategy. Any discussion of contractor risk quantification requires a basic understanding of it.

Contract Strategy

Contract strategy is largely about risk allocation between the owner and contractor. Therefore, you might ask why it is not a lead chapter in Volume 1, or why the parametric risk model does not include a pick-list of contract strategies. Edward Merrow, founder and owner of Independent Project Analysis, Inc. (IPA), addresses

---

2   Some owners, when driven by finance and/or in a punitive culture, sub-
    stitute the word "predictable" for "least" and "timely" in this sentence.
    However, predictability as a primary goal tends to drive overly conserva-
    tive estimates and it usually results in higher absolute project cost and
    duration (i.e., reduced capital effectiveness). Balancing predictability
    and effectiveness is a huge challenge.

this question in his essential book on contract strategy.[3] His book identifies ten principles of contracting. I mention only two here, but all ten are spot-on (read his book).

The first principle is that *"there is no free lunch."* This means somebody will pay for risks. A contract does not make them go away, and the owner often ends up paying one way or another. A contract strategy's effectiveness in managing and allocating risk is situational (or "project-specific" in this book's parlance). A contract strategy that meets objectives in one situation may be a *"mess"* in another; there is no silver bullet. Related to this is the *"principal agent problem,"* wherein owner and contractor goals may not align.

Merrow's second principle is that *"contractors do good projects well and bad projects poorly."* The reason is that *"owner behavior shapes contractor performance."* An owner with a weak project system, team, and practices is unlikely to get good or expected results from a contractor regardless of the contract strategy or which contractor gets the award. Therefore, contract type is a secondary issue regarding the risk profile from an owner's perspective. This helps explain why a given contract strategy's statistical significance to cost and schedule outcomes gets washed out in empirical modeling that considers more dominant systemic risks. That is not to say that contracting is unimportant. Merrow's book is unique in including findings from IPA's empirical research that help owners select a contract strategy best suited for a project's specific situation.

To indicate why contract strategy is difficult to model as a risk driver, consider the following sample of contract strategy permutations (i.e., delivery methods) considering contract scope and compensation structures. The lists are not all-inclusive. The word permutation reflects the fact that the structure and compensation schemes can be mixed in various ways. Plus, there are numerous fee and incentive schemes that can be applied. This complexity is part of the reason Merrow's book subtitle calls contract strategy *"the most difficult element of project management."*

Compensation Structures

1. Reimbursable
   ♦ Cost Plus or Time-and-Material
   ♦ Target Price or Guaranteed Maximum Price (GMP)

---

3   Merrow, Edward W., *Contract Strategies for Major Projects: Mastering the Most Difficult Element of Project Management*, John Wiley & Sons, Hoboken NJ, 2023. Words and phrases *italicized* are from this book.

2. Fixed
- ◆ Lump Sum (LS)
- ◆ Unit Price Construction (fixed, but reimbursable for quantities)

3. Mixed
- ◆ Design/Engineering-reimbursable and Construction-fixed
- ◆ LS Conversion; EPC w/early Engineering-reimbursable and Construction-fixed

Scope structures (with typical compensation structure [#])

Services/Limited Role
- ◆ Project Management Contractor (PMC) [1]
- ◆ Construction Management (CM) (may be CM at risk with GMP) [1]
- ◆ Design-Preliminary or Front-End Engineering and Design (FEED) [1]
- ◆ Design-Detailed or Engineering [1 or 2]

Engineer/Design or Construction
- ◆ Design-Bid-Build (DBB) (separate design and construction contracts) [2]
- ◆ Split Form: Engineer-Procure (usually by FEED) then Construction [1 then 2]

Engineer/Design and Construction or CM
- ◆ Design-Build (DB) [2]
- ◆ Engineer-Procure-Construct (EPC) or EPC-Turnkey (LSTK) [2]
- ◆ Engineer-Procure-Construction Management (EPCM) [1 or 2]

Front-End, Engineer/Design, and Construction or CM
- ◆ Front-End + EPC (FEPC) [1 then 2]
- ◆ Integrated Project Delivery (IPD) [1]
- ◆ Alliancing [1]

Own/Operate
- ◆ Public-Private Partnership (P3) [Concession]

Given that contract strategy is largely about risk allocation, most contracting references provide a chart such as Figure 3.1 to indicate roughly the degree of party risk ownership for some common contract strategies.[4,5] Keep in mind, every contract is different. This is not a chart of the degree of risk but of who is most impacted by the risks that do occur. For example, IPD should reduce risks; however, when risks occur, depending on compensation structure, the owner tends to be the most impacted (remember, "owner behavior shapes contractor performance"). The further to the left the contract type is, the more a contractor needs to emphasize realistic risk quantification.

P3	DB	DBB	IPD	Various
	EPC	Split Form	Alliance	Cost Plus
		FEPC		
		EPCM		
		EPC LS Conv		
Contractor	<--- Risk Carried By --->			Owner

Figure 3.1: Risk Allocation by Contract Parties

This section of the chapter is based on the principle that understanding data and accuracy is fundamental to empirically valid risk quantification (refer to Volume 1, Chapter 4). It assumes that contractors will capture and analyze their project data. Unfortunately, due to tight overhead budgets, analytics is not a strong suit for most contractors, especially smaller ones. For those who do engage in analytics, their risk quantification methods will need range inputs for Monte Carlo simulation (MCS) based models and driver data to support parametric (or future machine learning/artificial intelligence) models. Accuracy metrics require data for both actual and estimated costs and durations.

Contractors generally do not have actual data covering the entire project cost and life cycle duration. While some have project roles that allow data capture close to that of owners, no contract structure gives contractors access to all of the owner's costs. The owner's costs are an increasing percentage of project costs as owner

4   See example in AACE International, Recommended Practice 67R-11,"Contract Risk Allocation – As Applied in Engineering, Procurement, and Construction", latest revision.

5   See example (and good discussion) in: Carson, Chris, "Control of Project Risk for Owners," Arcadis.

work scope increases, such as for addressing regulatory requirements, conducting additional front-end studies, performing community consultations, addressing legal challenges, and so on.

So, what data can contractors capture and use? The following
are some contract structures and scopes with the typical cost and
schedule data these structures may yield to support the contractor's
internal risk quantification methods:

♦ Engineering or Construction Phase Only (e.g., E, C, or
  parts of DBB): Data is limited to phase-specific activity
  durations and item or unit cost and hours for the phase
  deliverables. The detailed data is often at a trade/discipline
  level that usually rolls up to some aspects of the work
  breakdown (e.g., civil, mechanical, electrical).

♦ Broader Contract Scope, but Usually Not Including Front-
  End (e.g., EPCM, PMC): Cost and duration for detailed
  engineering, procurement, and construction, but excluding owner's costs (which may include owner-procured
  equipment and materials). This may include contractor
  support of start-up and data on some construction details
  but limited first-hand subcontract details.

♦ Broad Contract Scope, Usually Including Design Devel-
  opment/FEED (FEPC, EPC Turnkey, DB, IPD, Alliance):
  Cost and duration for design development/FEED, detailed
  engineering, most procurement, and construction, but excluding owner's costs (which may include owner-procured
  equipment and materials and most start-up). This may
  include data on some construction details but limited
  first-hand subcontract details.

Unfortunately, few major contractors do their own construction.
Some prime contractors may self-perform some work, but most construction work is subcontracted to parties whose database management practices are usually less than ideal. If a major contractor has
limited hands-on actual construction cost data, their cost estimates
will not be thoroughly validated, resulting in more uncertainty than
either the contractors or the owners typically assume. Note also
that for megaprojects, work is increasingly bid by contractor joint
ventures, where a venture partner may have limited or no access
to the other partners' data.

What contractors have in the way of accuracy metrics depends
on the work they do and/or track. For example, they have the esti-

mated and actual material quantities, estimated hours, and so on. If they do not have actual construction hours, these can often be approximated. They will also have the estimated and actual durations of activities within their scope. This data is usually confidential and rarely shared or published.[6] The data they do capture and process is usually mean values (e.g., unit hours or costs). Contractors generally do not extensively study their data variability or accuracy. They may have high-level +/- range or standard deviation values but rarely study the causes of the variability using inferential statistical methods.

There are numerous survey-based studies of respondents' opinions regarding the causes of contract cost increases and delays. For example, Arcadis publishes an annual survey on contract disputes; in 2023, they found that most respondents felt that disputes were due to errors and/or omissions in the contract documents.[7]

Contractor accuracy data, if available, is most useful for "ranging" risk analysis where low and high values are entered in a QRA model built on the detailed elements of the cost estimate (quantities, hours, materials, etc.) or schedule activity durations in a CPM model, and MCS is run. Figure 3.2 provides an example of a detailed accuracy metric that contractor data could support if analyzed. In this case, the distribution is of activity duration slip (percentage that actual duration varies from the estimate) for all activities in a database of over a half million schedules to support ML/AI.[8]

A glance indicates that this will be a challenge to use in a three-point ranging with an MCS model. If an empirically valid ranging analysis is desired, should the team use +150% for their high value in three-point entries (given no correlation to cause in the data)? This example suggests why extensive analytics and empiricism are rarely brought to the table for ranging QRA methods.[9]

---

6   As a neophyte estimator 30+ years ago, I learned that every senior estimator, whose careers tend to be mobile, carried binders of data and metrics from their prior employers.

7   Arcadis, "13th Annual Construction Disputes Report, North America - 2023."

8   Hovhannisyan, V et.al,, "Data-Driven Schedule Risk Forecasting for Construction Mega-Projects," AACE International Transactions, 2023. (nPlan data: this figure is approximated from the source's Figure 1.)

9   Three-point probability distributions in ranging QRA models have usually been limited to Triangle and PERT. These do not work well with typically highly skewed data such as is shown in Figure 3.2. This paper

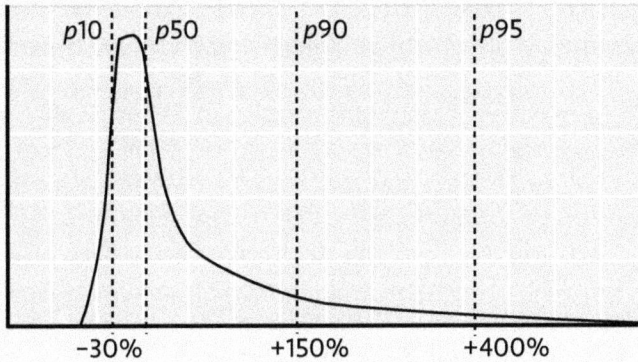

Figure 3.2: Example Activity Duration Accuracy

The contractor's prevalent exposure to details within limited pockets of project scope creates a bias for ranging QRA methods that focus on details. However, as discussed earlier in the book, ranging only quantifies "inherent" uncertainty. The cause or driver of variation, especially systemic risk, is not considered, except perhaps through the subjective opinions of participants in risk workshops or interviews. Furthermore, "ranging" models are of limited use with front-end estimates, which typically have limited detail (e.g., factored or analogy estimates). In short, contractor accuracy data is generally useful for tactical or situational, but not strategic or general project risk quantification.

One thing contractors will always have is data on the planned and actual margins (i.e., profit/loss) of their projects. They will know if a contract was a success or failure from their perspective, and their closeout files will usually include lessons learned in that regard. This data is often used to support bid/no-bid decisions, bid markups, and pricing risk quantification. While contractors may capture feedback from their owner clients, their databases usually do not have much information on whether an overall project was a success or failure from the owner's viewpoint. As such, it's difficult for contractors to understand project risk from an owner's point of view.

---

describes a three-point distribution that can replicate distributions such as Lognormal: Hollmann, J, and J Eric Bickel, "Defining a Lognormal Distribution Using 3-Point Entry: The J-QPD Distribution," AACE International Transactions, 2024.

Contractors and Overruns

I have not found useful published empirical studies on the accuracy or variability of contractor margin estimates (i.e., variability driven by unrecovered cost increases). An example of a margin metric of interest would be (contract revenue)/(contract cost), where revenue includes the original contract value plus all income from recovered changes, claims, and so on.[10] The topic is commercially sensitive, and data is unlikely to be shared; few owners would favor a contractor with a history of cost overruns and delays. Most available data is therefore anecdotal. Contractor overruns are usually only published when the contractor company is publicly held and the overrun is large enough to become financially material. There may also be audit reports published or claims disputes that become fodder for the press. Examples of such reports include:

- The Samsung sidebar story in Volume 1, Chapter 15 [Contractors: Taking One's Lumps]: They lost about 18% of the $5.6 billion EPC lump sum contract value.

- The Bechtel sidebar story in Volume 1, Chapter 5 [Nobody Wins]: This details liquidated damages on a power plant project: *"...claims between the parties (the owner and Bechtel) exceeding $500 million."*

- A report by Siemens: This report discusses *"€310 million in project charges related primarily to two high-voltage direct current (HVDC) transmission projects in Canada."*[11]

- A report by Subsea7: At about 60% completion of a Brazilian offshore project, Subsea7 stated, *"Re-evaluation of the offshore risks based on experience to date, and the extended timeline of the project, has resulted in us increasing the estimate full-life project loss by between $250 and $300 million."*[12]

- In reference to a major Texas LNG project, a legal agreement..."settles months of legal charges and several years of difficult relations among the parties over costs,

---

10 The Engineering and Construction Risk Institute (ECRI), made up of contractor companies, likely shared such metrics (ECRI was dissolved in 2023), but their data and presentations were confidential.

11 Siemens AG, "Mixed Performance, Outlook Confirmed," Munich, May 7, 2014.

12 Siem, K., "Update on the Guara-Luna NE Project Offshore Brazil," Subsea 7 conference call transcript, June 27, 2013.

payments, major layoffs and stalled work at the estimated $11-billion LNG megaproject. The issues eventually led to bankruptcy proceedings by Zachry begun in May for the corporation and 20 units, citing 'significant financial strain' from ongoing cost and schedule disputes. The owner, Golden Pass LNG LLC, later filed an emergency court order to remove the contractor from the site."[13]

When such failures occur due to underestimated bid pricing, usually involving failure to price risks of one or many kinds, it is often called the "winner's curse." Whether due to a few significant blowouts like the above examples or too many modest overruns and slim margins, the end result for construction contractors is often insolvency. The inflation of 2021/2022 and the failure to include sufficient escalation allowances resulted in many contractor bankruptcies. For example, an article reported that *"between July 2022 and April 2023, 1,709 construction companies across [Australia] entered administration."*[14] This number included not just small subcontractors but also large ones such as the Clough Group, which had about A$10 billion of projects underway.

These anecdotes highlight the fact that contractors are exposed to all the risks discussed in this book at some level, and they can benefit from the book's empirically valid risk quantification methods. To help avoid such outcomes, contractor risk quantification methods and practices, and owner considerations of risk quantification done on their behalf, are discussed in the next sections.

Risk Quantification by Contractors for Owners

Most owners use major contractors to prepare their estimates and schedules for the Class 3 phase and later gates. This contractor role may be integral to the contract structure if it includes early contractor involvement (ECI) such as in DB, FEPC, IPD, or Alliances. In these cases, the owner may also have the contractor perform cost and schedule risk quantification for the project, focusing on the determination of owner contingency and reserves. The owner may or may not supplement this with their own risk analysis as a check and/or to address risks that are confidential for use in busi-

---

13 Rubin, Debra, "Zachry Exits Big Texas LNG Project in Deal With Exxon, Qatar Energy," Engineering News-Record, July 23, 2024.

14 Dervisevic, H, "Hundreds of Australian construction firms have collapsed," abc.net.au, 27 Sept 2023.

ness case considerations, with a focus on the worst-case scenarios in profitability sensitivity analyses.

In the situations above, contractors tend to perform project cost and schedule risk quantification using the same methods as the owners. Traditionally, contractors have relied upon subjective ranging methods. AACE Recommended Practice 123R-22 documents a typical approach using a combination of estimate ranging for inherent risks (with subjective ranges) and expected value for project-specific risks with MCS (R+EV).[15] However, as discussed in this book, this method is not recommended for projects with significant systemic risks because it misses most systemic risks and is not empirically valid on average. As such, it is only appropriate for smaller projects of low complexity and no new technology.

For major projects, the hybrid parametric plus expected value (P+EV) with MCS method from Volume 1, Chapter 11 (i.e., AACE RP 113-20),[16] and the tipping point method from Volume 1, Chapter 14 (if applicable) should be used by contractors doing a risk analysis on behalf of the owner. These methods are included in ValidRisk® software.

For major projects with schedules that have concerns about key intermediate milestones, the contractor should also perform a hybrid parametric plus CPM (P+CPM) with MCS risk analysis using either the methods from Chapter 4 of this volume or AACE RP 117R-21.[17] Using both the P+EV and P+CPM methods provides a cross-check and better quality assurance.

Unfortunately, contractors have been late adopters of parametric or other empirically-based QRA methods. Some mistakenly view systemic risks as an "owner thing" and of limited use for their bread-and-butter internal bidding-related or tactical, execution phase risk quantification needs. Additionally, contractors are handicapped in being unable to calibrate a parametric model to best represent project outcomes for a specific owner's project system. However, calibrated

---

15 RP 123R-22, "Integrated Cost and Schedule Risk Analysis and Contingency Determination Using Estimate Ranging and Expected Value with Monte Carlo Simulation," latest revision, AACE International.

16 RP 113R-20, "Integrated Cost and Schedule Risk Analysis and Contingency Determination Using Combined Parametric and Expected Value," latest revision, AACE International.

17 RP 117R-21, "Integrated Cost and Schedule Risk Analysis and Contingency Determination using a Hybrid Parametric and CPM Method," latest revision, AACE International.

or not, an example of an EPC contractor using the methods covered in this book is provided in Volume 1, Chapter 8.

Cautions for Owners as Risk Quantification Customers

Contractors should not perform risk quantification on the owner's behalf at the Class 5 or Class 4 gates. These phases require close cooperation between project risk quantification and business decision analysis and should examine multiple scope options. Early risk quantification, leveraging empirically-based methods, should be an owner core competency. Execution-focused contractors – and unfortunately many owners – tend to be "contingency-focused" (perhaps "obsessed" is a better word), paying little attention to the most important metric for business, which is a realistic $p90$ (worst case). The $p90$ exposes the real nature of a scope option's risk profile and drives business case sensitivity analyses.

At Class 3 and 2, owners need to push back if contractors insist on using their traditional, subjective cost ranging risk quantification methods for a major project. Contractors using the best methods will still be handicapped by not having a parametric model calibrated to the owner's experience.

Another challenge from the owner's point of view is the "principal agent problem," as highlighted in Merrow's text. If a design development/FEED contractor doing the risk analysis has the opportunity to do later execution phase work, the contractor will have an incentive to help nudge the project past the FID gate (granted, owner personnel may also have that bias). Additionally, having a contractor analyst question the owner project manager and team about the efficacy of the owner's project system (including integration with its various contractors) may not be welcome if there are transparency and trust issues. While this may sound self-serving, it is usually preferable on major projects to have a trusted independent consultant, using demonstrated best practices, lead the risk quantification if the owner is not able to do it themselves.

Risk Quantification for Contractor Bidding

This section discusses project risk quantification by a contractor for bidding decision making. The two main purposes or process steps are:

1. Bid/No-Bid (or Go/No-Go) Decision: Preparing a bid or proposal and estimate can be expensive, particularly for lump sum contracts, which may require significant skilled estimating

resources. Upon receiving an invitation or request for proposal (IFP/RFP) or a tender offer, the contractor must decide whether to submit a proposal or bid.[18]

2. Cost and Time Markup Decision: After preparing the base cost estimate and schedule, the uncertainty and risks must be quantified to support the determination of the price(s) and schedule to be bid to maximize the expected value of the contractor's profit.

These steps are somewhat interrelated, as the bid/no-bid decision must consider the potential profit or loss as a criterion. There is a significant body of literature on decision analysis and modeling for bid/no-bid purposes, particularly in the construction management arena given the size and risks of construction contracts. This chapter adds to this literature by showing how the risk quantification methods of Chapters 11 to 14 in Volume 1 can be applied, particularly concerning markup decisions after a bid decision has been made and the base estimate and schedule have been prepared by the contractor.

Regarding the value of contractors using best risk management practices during bidding and negotiation, an article by Turner and Townsend shares an interesting study. It found that *"The comparative analysis undertaken shows that the project that used the risk management process during the tendering and contract negotiation stages ...benefitted from fewer unexpected/unplanned variations and lower contingency expenditure than the project that did not use the risk management approach. Similarly, the delivery time was improved by the use of the risk management approach."*[19] Hopefully, owners are as savvy as the one in this study and will value the risk management capability of the contractor at bid time.

Bid/No-Bid Decisions

While the term bid/no bid (BNB) is used, this section is about the decision to submit a bid (in response to a tender offer) or a

---

18 A bid in response to a tender offer typically follows strict rules: the successful bidder must enter a contract. A proposal in response to an RFP is more flexible, and proponent can revise or withdraw a proposal.

19 Turner & Townsend, "An effective approach to risk management during tendering and contract negotiations stages," www.turnerandtownsend.com/en/perspectives, 08 August 2018.

proposal (in response to an RFP). The tender/bid process follows competitive bidding laws and usually presents more risk because the selected bidder must enter a contract. The RFP/proposal process is generally less risky because it allows for negotiation flexibility, and the proponent can revise or withdraw a proposal.

There is general agreement in the academic literature that BNB practices can be complicated and stressful, given that the contractor's business success depends on them and the time available for making a decision is usually very short. Other parties may be involved if a contractor venture partnership is formed for major projects. Additionally, information about the project, market, likely availability of subcontractors, and so on needs to be collected and analyzed. In general, the decision analysis methods discussed in Volume 1, Chapter 5 apply to BNB decisions. For small projects, intuition or "gut-feel" may play a central role in the BNB decision, but expert judgment is always significant for large project BNB decisions.

For larger projects, a common approach referenced in the literature is to use a weighted checklist or scoring sheet of factors influencing the BNB decision. A top factor is usually potential profit (and the contractor's need for work in slow markets), but other typical factors may include alignment with the contractor's business strategy, the contractor's experience with the owner, project type and location, the project size relative to the contractor's available resources, and so on.

Risk quantification involves identifying the contractor's exposure to various risks if awarded the contract. Contractors typically have limited financial ability to absorb major losses, as described in previous examples. Therefore, risk factors should be among the factors in the BNB decision model or checklist. Volume 1, Chapters 11 through 13, identifies the general risk types to consider: systemic risks, critical project-specific risks, and escalation.

For megaproject contracts, the contractor also needs to be aware of tipping point risks in lump sum projects, as covered in Volume 1, Chapter 14. The tipping point method is typically not used to support markup and pricing decisions; any bid that allowed for the cost impact of crossing the tipping point would not win. If the project tipping point metrics are high, the contractor should generally decide not to bid.

Contract strategy is about risk allocation, so the BNB analysis needs to consider how much risk is transferred to the contractor in a given contract structure. Some risks to the owner may be opportunities for the contractor. For example, if the scope is poorly defined and likely to be changed by the owner, this might be positive for the contractor if changes and claims can be priced to potentially increase revenue and margin, but that is never a sure thing for the contractor.

The BNB decision is ideal for empirical inferential statistical modeling and ML/AI. Contractors often have a database of project and market attributes (factors or parameters) from their BNB checklists and scoring, plus a record of the BNB decision made, markups applied, award success, and the final margin. For example, one reference describes using regression analysis of 139 construction projects (mostly part of DBB owner contract strategies) in the process industry, with estimates greater than $500 million from eight major contractors, to create a parametric model correlating a project complexity index (PCI) derived from 54 factors used in the BNB with the BNB decision result and the cost and time markups applied.[20] This example highlights an excellent opportunity for contractor risk analysts to get involved in the business end of their projects.

In the end, as with investment decision making and assessing NPV/IRR in Volume 1, Chapter 5, decision trees, sensitivity analysis, and scenario analysis can be used in BNB decision making. This requires an analysis of revenue risk as well as costs. Instead of the owner's focus on NPV/IRR, contractors focus on margin or profit.

The risk quantification methods described in Volume 1, Chapters 11 to 12 (i.e., parametric modeling of systemic risk and expected value for critical specific risks) and Chapter 4 of this volume (i.e., CPM analysis) are not likely to be used directly in the BNB decision. However, the parallels between the systemic risk factors of the parametric model in Volume 1, Chapter 11, and the factors in the PCI metric of the referenced BNB example are strong. Also, the tipping point method of Volume 1, Chapter 14, can flag a no-bid decision. Developing analytical capabilities pays off for both owner investment and contractor bid decisions. The next section discusses how the risk quantification methods of Volume 1, Chapters 11 to 14, can be applied effectively in the cost and time markup decision (in addition to methods such as the example above).

---

20 Faraji, A. et.al., "Bid/Mark-Up Decision Support Model in Contractor's Tender Strategy Development Phase Based on Project Complexity Measurement in the Downstream Sector of Petroleum Industry," J. Open Innov. Technol. Mark. Complex. 2022.

Cost and Time Markup Decision

Once a decision to bid has been made, risk quantification should be applied to determine the contractor's cost and schedule risks. This helps determine how to include those costs and time in the bid price(s), schedule, and/or markups. Each contract strategy allocates risks differently, necessitating distinct contractor approaches to cost and schedule risk quantification and how these results are reflected in the bid. The following discusses typical risk quantification practices that may be applied by contractors at the time of bidding for common contract scopes and compensation structures. Note that these practices are not exhaustive, and the typical scenarios described may be optimistic; the extent and quality of internal risk quantification practices among contractors vary widely.

Reimbursable/Cost Plus (not GMP), including EPCM and PMC

These contracts focus primarily on markups and/or fees, with most risks borne by the owner. Due to the limited contractor risk exposure, the methods described in Volume 1, Chapters 11 to 14, or other standard project-level methods, are generally not directly applicable for contractor decisions regarding reimbursable contract markups.

However, the minimal risk exposure for contractors in reimbursable contracts is not an excuse to neglect risk management and quantification. Celebrating overruns at the owner's expense is unacceptable. For instance, I once reviewed a reimbursable EPCM megaproject that was facing a significant budget overrun. The contractor's poor risk management practices were evident. After the client adjusted the budget, I noted a stock analyst conference where the contractor's executive boasted about increasing their backlog by the overrun amount. Ultimately, the contractor's poor practices on other fixed-price projects led to their downfall; they are no longer in business.

Early Contractor Involvement (ECI) Structures such as FEED, DB, FEPC, IPD, or Alliances

The initial contract award in these structures is typically based on the contractor's qualifications and capabilities, not price. As discussed in "Risk Quantification by Contractors for Owners," the contractor may perform cost/schedule risk quantification with the owner (who ideally leads all risk-related activities) to support the Final Investment Decision (FID) using methods from Volume 1,

Chapters 11 to 14. If the work proceeds to construction on a reimbursable basis, the earlier discussion applies. For fixed-price work, see the following sections.

Unit Price

Unit price contracts largely remove scope/quantity risk from the contractor's responsibility, but significant labor, material, and indirect cost risks remain within each fixed unit price in the schedule of values. One method to quantify these risks is line-item ranging, excluding quantity risk, as detailed in the hybrid ranging + expected value (R+EV) method in AACE RP 123R-22. This practice involves two steps: (1) applying low and high ranges to estimate elements (labor, material, and some indirects) to address inherent cost risk and (2) using the expected value method for specific risk events for which the contractor is responsible, followed by Monte Carlo Simulation (MCS). Quantity underruns pose a risk to unit prices as overhead and other allocations may be insufficient, while overruns may result in a windfall. Contractors should also quantify commercial risks from the RFP terms and conditions and, if applicable, from joint venture relationships.

From the risk quantification cost distribution, contingency can be determined, usually guided by the commercial manager's judgment on what it takes to win the bid or close the deal. This contingency (along with general indirect costs, overhead, and profit) is then allocated to the units to derive the unit price. This often involves some degree of "unbalancing," such as allocating more contingency to items installed or paid out early.

However, this risk quantification method is often limited by its subjective nature and tendency to underestimate systemic risks (such as those arising from the contractor's processes, team, and management, as well as general complexity) and escalation (e.g., incorrectly using inflation rates rather than proper escalation). Ideally, the hybrid P+EV method of RP 113R-20 and ValidRisk® software (referenced in Volume 1, Chapters 11 and 12, using the same EV input as for R+EV) should be applied as a check. Probabilistic escalation per RP 68R-11 (referenced in Volume 1, Chapter 13) should also be applied.

Lump Sum: EPC, Build within DBB, or the C in Split Form EPC; also GMP

For these contract types, most of the risk, including material quantities, is allocated to the contractor; only changes to the contract scope are excluded. This is where the winner's curse strikes, mainly because contractors often underestimate both systemic risk and escalation, as well as the tipping point for megaprojects.

For practical purposes, the industry parametric cost and schedule models of systemic risks in Volume 1, Chapter 11, apply to contractors. Note that the cost growth experienced by owners (originally modeled by Rand) excludes the cost impact of risks transferred to contractors (e.g., productivity). Contractors own these productivity risks (although they may try to shift them to subcontractors), but not the scope change risk carried by the owner. The net effect is typically balanced, except in extreme cases where a contractor goes insolvent or is replaced, leaving the owner with additional costs.

Similar to unit price contracts (but also including quantity risk), the most common cost risk quantification method used by contractors is the hybrid ranging + expected value (R+EV) method with Monte Carlo Simulation (MCS) as detailed in AACE RP 123R-22. From the risk quantification cost distribution, contractor cost contingency can be determined, usually guided by the commercial manager's assessment of what it will take to win the bid.

For schedule risk, contractors exposed to delay risks may use the risk-driven Critical Path Method (CPM) with MCS as covered by AACE RP 57R-11.[21] This allows them to determine schedule contingency to factor into the bid schedule appropriately (or assess whether and how they can meet the required durations). By cost loading the CPM model, contractors can assess both cost and schedule risk in an integrated, detailed (albeit complex) way.

The next task is to allocate the cost contingency, along with all estimated costs, to work elements in the bid payment schedule. While the total price is fixed, the payment phases by the owner are usually defined. As with unit prices, this often involves some degree of "unbalancing," such as allocating more contingency (and other costs) to work elements that are paid early.

These methods are typically applied; however, as stated regarding unit price, the R+EV and traditional CPM methods fail due to their purely subjective nature and tendency to underestimate the contractor's systemic risks. With lump sum contracts, the contractor's risk exposure is similar to an owner's in a reimbursable contract. The contractor's "project system" can be very complex, dealing

---

21 RP 57R-11, "Integrated Cost and Schedule Risk Analysis Using Risk Drivers and Monte Carlo Simulation of a CPM Model," latest revision. AACE International.

with many subcontractors and suppliers, as well as joint venture partners on large projects.

The typical methods should not be the end-all. To address systemic risks, the hybrid P+EV method of RP 113R-20 (referenced in Volume 1, Chapters 11 and 12, and in ValidRisk® software) should be applied. For complex schedules, contractors should use the P+CPM method of RP 117R-21 (referenced in Chapter 4 of this Volume).

An underappreciated systemic risk for construction contractors is the need to get all their "systems" (e.g., organization, procedures, software) up and running in the field within a short time frame.[22] Smaller subcontractors often bring unsophisticated systems, and joint ventures can involve personnel with little common experience and patched-together system parts. Even without a joint venture, many field staff and supervisors may be locally hired just for the job. I have seen many megaproject contractor systems that never achieved a stable, productive state in their operations. This risk needs to be factored into the systemic ratings of the parametric model, whether analyzed by owners or contractors.

Escalation risk, which the contractor has limited control over, is best allocated to the owner in lump sum and equivalent contract types. However, if not protected by an escalation clause in the contract, contractors should use the probabilistic escalation quantification method from Volume 1, Chapter 13. The previously cited 2021/22 contractor failures largely resulted from insufficient allowance for escalation risk. If they had properly accounted for it in their bid price, they might not have won the bids, but they would have remained solvent. A key driver of escalation cost is schedule duration; the schedule risk model output should be an input to the probabilistic escalation model. Once quantified, escalation, like contingency, is usually allocated to work elements in the bid payment schedule.

The discussions above are not an exhaustive review of possible contractor risk quantification applications, especially given the wide variation of contract types, compensation structures, and incentive schemes. A key takeaway is the criticality of addressing systemic and escalation risks to avoid the winner's curse. The next section briefly discusses risk quantification after the contract award.

---

22 Owners are often at fault for not allowing reasonable time to develop a detailed baseline plan and schedule, and get systems set up, between the contract award and notice-to-proceed.

Tactical Risk Quantification (and Optimization) by Contractors

After the award of a contract, risk quantification becomes integral to the project and risk management process defined for the contract scope and organization. If the contract work involves detailed engineering and/or construction, risk quantification varies depending on the purpose, which includes the following:

♦ Setup,

♦ Ongoing Risk Management, and

♦ Change/Opportunity Assessment.

Setup

Estimates and schedules by contractors for bidding purposes are usually completed under tight timeframes and often with limited resources. Bid estimates often utilize a mix of semi-detailed and factoring methods. For example, I reviewed a megaproject where the lump sum contractor reused an estimate from a different plant and simply tweaked it, not realizing the scope was much more different than anticipated; it ended poorly for all parties involved.

In the typically brief period between contract award and the notice-to-proceed and mobilization ramp-up, contractors, in collaboration with the owner, will refine their control plans, estimates, and schedules. This should include updating the risk analysis based on the change and risk management processes established during the setup. The risk quantification used for bidding can be updated or, preferably, started fresh as the full team comes together. The risk quantification methods used during bid price determination are likely to be reapplied.

Ongoing Risk Management

During execution, contractors focus on trade and discipline details as well as specific procurements and subcontracts. Risk analyses may involve allocating contingency to control accounts at that level. For cost, this detailed perspective favors using the ranging plus expected value (R+EV) method of risk quantification. Although R+EV is subjective, the contractor team's first-hand experience with on-the-ground situations becomes more valuable as work progresses. This includes team awareness of the in-place project system and its performance, along with any evident glitches. If the project system attributes are causing uncertainty, it may favor the use of the P+EV method during execution. Risk quantification should be revisited at key milestones or when indicated by adverse trends in performance, cost, or schedule.

Change/Opportunity Assessment

During execution, the contractor project manager (PM) will be under tremendous pressure to achieve the planned margin and earn any applicable incentives. If performance lags (especially for lump sum contracts), PMs may push back hard on perceived negativism, demanding solutions instead of problems. Risk managers (or project controls) may face resistance from unenlightened PMs as they monitor potential theats. Problems (i.e., risk consequences) can compound, sometimes only vaguely perceived by the lean-staffed owner, until they become undeniable (e.g., when contingency is depleted and targets or incentives are out of reach). At that point, the PM, along with contractor headquarters, may require a complete re-analysis and re-quantification of risk using a reliable method based on a fresh, realistic forecast. In the worst cases, contracts may need renegotiation.[23]

On a more positive note, the team often brings solutions to the PM, presenting opportunities. Opportunities typically involve changes, necessitating proactive risk quantification to analyze potential risks associated with the change. These changes may also reflect the evolution and elaboration of estimates and schedules as late-phase work plans (e.g., start-up and commissioning) are fully defined. Risk quantification tools can be used to optimize the proposed solution or path forward, particularly concerning the schedule. While drafting Chapter 4 of this Volume on the P+CPM method, a respected scheduling expert colleague emphasized the value of using full CPM-based risk analysis as per RP 117R-21 in mid-execution major change/opportunity assessment. His success stories of improved outcomes provide a compelling argument for this approach.

Data and Machine Learning/Artificial Intelligence (ML/AI)

An advantage contractors have over owners is the volume of data and records available to them (e.g. past schedules) since projects are a contractor's lifeblood. However, contractors have lagged in the

---

23 See the paper by J. Hollmann and R.S. Bali, "Case Study: Use of the Hybrid Parametric and Expected Value QRA Method on the Keeyask Hydropower Megaproject" in the 2024 AACE International Transactions for an example of megaproject risk quantification and re-baselining in mid-execution with a reimbursable contract.

application of empirically-based risk quantification. This is partly because contractors focus mainly on the execution phase, so their databases are mostly detail oriented. They have minimal systemic risk information, such as few estimates at Class 5, indicating a tactical rather than strategic capital investment focus. Additionally, with tight margins, analytics overhead costs may be seen as a luxury.

However, contractors are increasingly adopting empirically-based risk quantification methods, leap-frogging old-school regression analysis directly into ML/AI applications. An early example is the *"British construction company Kier, also known as Kier Group, has started using artificial intelligence provided by the software organisation nPlan to support its bids for new work. The technology is said to analyse programmes to identify where problems and delays are likely to occur and areas where savings could be made."* The goal was to *"increase its bidding chances for new jobs."*[24]

Another study by nPlan used ML, trained on a dataset of hundreds of thousands of projects, to generate activity duration distributions instead of fixed distributions for use in an MCS model.[25] These applications are likely to become the norm, if they aren't already by the time of this publication.

Summary

This chapter provided an overview of the context for contractor application of risk quantification methods. It does not present new methods but outlines when, where, and with what twists a contractor might consider using methods covered in Volume 1, Chapters 11 to 14, and Chapter 4 of this volume. Contractor risk method usage is focused on bid/no bid and markup decisions rather than investment decisions, emphasizing margin rather than NPV or IRR metrics.

Contractor focus on the execution phase and details has led to a reliance on subjective ranging methods, making them late adopters of empiricism in risk quantification. Contractors who use risk quantification as principal agents for owners but rely on ranging for major projects cannot be said to be acting in the owner's best interest, though owner expectations are often low. Low margins and frequent insolvency highlight the need for contractors to use empirically valid methods. All parties benefit from empiricism, and hopefully, contractors will increasingly leverage ML/AI in the coming years.

---

24 Steers, S., "Kier uses nPlan AI technology to support new work bids," Constructiondigital.com, June 30, 2021

25 Hovhannisyan, V, ibid.

Questions

1) What are the primary contract scope and compensation structures?

2) What are the two primary contractor decisions to be made in regards to bidding?

3) What is the main metric focus for contractor bid decisions?

4) For a contractor, what factors might add systemic risks to their decision making?

5) What is meant by the "principal agent problem?"

6) What is meant by the "winner's curse?"

7) Why might contractors be biased towards "ranging" risk quantification methods?

8) Does the book recommend any risk quantification methods that are unique to contractors?

Volume 2 Perspective

Volume 1 addressed the contractor's point of view only as a side note, dedicating just a few pages in the "Various Industries" chapter. However, growing interest from my contractor peers called for a more robust, full-chapter treatment. Merrow's 2023 empirically-grounded book on contract strategies also provided a valuable reference and is a must-read.

A persistent frustration is that most major contractors still fail to see the value of empirically-valid risk quantification methods, despite their unfortunate record of low margins and insolvencies. As this was being written, the contractor's Engineering and Construction Risk Institute (ECRI) was dissolved, leaving uncertainty about where leadership in risk management and quantification will come from.

There is increasing interest in collaborative, early contractor involvement (ECI) contract structures, which benefit both contractors and owners. However, until both parties use empirically-valid methods to quantify risks, these efforts are likely to fall short in delivering improved owner return on capital and contractor margins. Bid and investment decision quality will be handicapped without empirical methods.

Hopefully, the growing interest in ML/AI within the contracting community will result in more empiricism in contractor risk quantification.

*"I have not failed. I've just found **10,000** ways that won't work."*
— Thomas Edison

4

Hybrid Parametric plus CPM-based QRA Method

(Note to Volume 1 Readers: this Chapter supersedes Appendix A of Volume 1)

A key premise of this book is that the hybrid parametric plus expected value (P+EV) risk quantification method, detailed in Volume 1, Chapters 11 and 12, is the most practical and realistic approach for day-to-day risk quantification on projects of any complexity, at any phase of scope development, and in any industry. It should form the foundation of a company's project risk quantification methodology. For companies focused on investment decision making (e.g., IRR), encompassing overall cost and schedule duration (capex and start of revenue), P+EV fully meets the need.

However, there are two project situations at the final investment decision (FID, typically at Class 3 or 2)[1] gate where the more complex critical path schedule method (CPM) risk quantification method is necessary *in addition* to overall P+EV. These situations or objectives at the FID gate are:

---

1   See Table 1.1 in Chapter 1 for various phase names used by different industries at different Classifications.

1. The need for tactical determination of appropriate schedule buffers (contingency) at key intermediate milestones in a project schedule or at interfaces between projects within a program (with megaprojects almost always being a form of a program).

2. The desire to validate the P+EV findings on strategic projects (aligned with item 1, as most strategic projects have intermediate milestone/interface challenges).

The specific CPM-based method recommended is a hybrid of parametric modeling with the risk-driven, critical path schedule method (CPM) with Monte Carlo simulation (MCS); i.e., P+CPM. To support objective two above, P+CPM can also be cost loaded.

Anyone interested in the P+CPM method should begin by reading AACE Recommended Practice 117R-21, "Integrated Cost and Schedule Risk Analysis and Contingency Determination using a Hybrid Parametric and CPM Method." This chapter's approach streamlines some steps from RP 117R-21 for practicality, aligning with the book's goal of being both effective and efficient, with less reliance on external experts. Understanding the AACE RP in full will help clarify how this chapter's approach differs. (Each project must choose the method or variation that works best in their situation.)

Even when simplified, the P+CPM method is more complex and resource intensive than P+EV (as illustrated in the CPM-based example in Chapter 11 of this Volume). Its application still requires analyst expertise in CPM project scheduling and use of appropriate CPM-based risk analysis software.

Schedulers may be disappointed that this chapter does not cover all CPM-based method variations, details, or the numerous ways CPM-based analyses can potentially benefit projects for different purposes. For example, CPM-based analysis can aid in risk identification and treatment (i.e., risk management), schedule option development, and schedule quality assurance. As per the chapter epigram by Edison, I view CPM's main value as an experimental test bed to refine a project's work plan during planning, i.e., *optimization*.

However, optimization is not a primary objective of the risk *quantification* step. The operative assumption for risk quantification at a decision gate is that the risks have been managed, they are what they are, and the schedule presented is final. If the planning and schedule are of poor quality or otherwise sub-optimal, these deficiencies are quantified as systemic risks that add uncertainty, quantified using the parametric method. If that uncertainty is too great, the gate decision should be delayed, and the project scope development should undergo more rigorous planning, schedule development, quality assurance, validation, and risk identification and treatment.

In short, CPM-based risk analysis is best conducted while the schedule is being developed, not at the end of a phase, several weeks before a gate decision (as is most common). However, if business and project management are satisfied with postponing analyses until the decision gate, desire independent, cold-eyes, expert analyses, are not deterred by added complexity, and/or seek all potential benefits of applying comprehensive CPM-based analysis, they should proceed accordingly.

That aside, the chapter begins by describing the primary objective for using the P+CPM method at the decision gate: quantifying intermediate buffers. This is followed by discussions of some fundamental concepts behind the P+CPM method.

Schedule Contingency and Buffers

Chapter 6 of Volume 1 discusses the concept of schedule contingency (i.e., a buffer activity). It notes that using visible buffers in a CPM schedule is not common practice, with one exception noted later. Schedule contingency, if any, is more often considered in business case development (e.g., determining the start of revenue), negotiation of product sale contracts, and similar scenarios. The project team and construction contractor are often held to the "base" duration or target without contingency. In this sense, schedule "contingency" is often treated as a form of *management reserve* of time not explicitly shown in the schedule.

The exception, as addressed in this chapter, occurs when a project or program has intermediate completion milestones or phasing built into the schedule. For example, in sub-arctic regions, pipeline excavation or trenching work must be done in winter (a seasonal execution strategy). If the excavation work is not completed before the end of the winter season, pipeline installation in the trench and project completion may slip an entire season. In such cases, a buffer activity is planned into the schedule before the intermediate winter season end milestone to mitigate the risk of an early melt causing a lost installation season. Similarly, project or program plans may include major scope elements constructed sequentially (finish-start), where a delay in the preceding scope has major cost and schedule implications for the succeeding scope. Here, an intermediate buffer activity between the scopes of work can help mitigate risks to schedule objectives.

Concepts Behind P+CPM

Start with the Risk-Driven CPM with MCS Method

To quantify where and how much buffer to include, the risk quantification method must analyze the uncertainty of the midstream milestone date(s) of concern. AACE RPs 57R-09 and 117R-21 are both risk-driven CPM with MCS methods (using "Risk Factors") and can model intermediate milestone date distributions. However, they differ in their approach to modeling uncertainties (or risk events). RP 117R-21 is a hybrid approach that incorporates empirically-based parametric modeling of systemic uncertainty, including inherent uncertainty.

Conversely, RP 57R-09 treats systemic risk and inherent uncertainties as separate and unique, viewing systemic risk as a type of event. This approach expects the risk analyst and team to distinguish between these risk types and subjectively quantify them appropriately. This reliance on the analyst and team opinion, rather than empirical data, places a significant burden on ensuring a reliable analysis. The following section further discusses the distinctions between inherent and systemic uncertainty before moving on.

Inherent Uncertainty versus Systemic Uncertainty

Inherent uncertainty, as quantified by project teams, reflects their opinions on how much activity durations (or costs in an estimate) may reasonably vary from the base values. This practice is typically called "ranging." The ranges are based on the team's general experience, their specific knowledge of the project, and their understanding of what the ranges are supposed to represent (which may not always align with analysts' expectations). Team opinions are also influenced by the biases present in the situation. Experiences, biases, and understandings can vary significantly, even with the best workshop or interview facilitation efforts.

Subjective ranging is only reliable when the uncertainties involved are limited and team opinions are grounded in real-time working knowledge of the specific project situation, such as an analysis done in mid-execution. At that point, subjective opinions are quasi-empirical, based on real-time observation. Figure 4.1 illustrates how the value of subjective uncertainty inputs to schedule risk analysis increases as a project progresses and decisions become more tactical. The relative value of subjective inputs increases after the final investment decision (FID) and as engineering is completed and construction ramps up (e.g., after Class 2). An example of a tactical situation is the fine-tuning of construction planning as the start-up phase approaches.

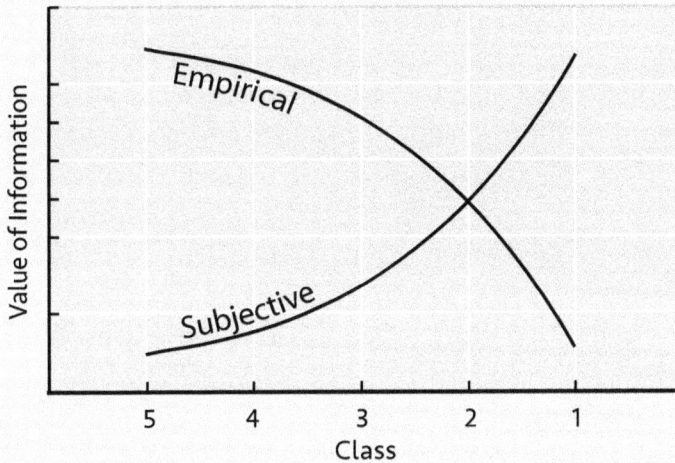

Figure 4.1: Value of Empirical vs. Subjective Uncertainty Inputs by Project Phase

Systemic uncertainty, as quantified in empirically-based parametric modeling, represents the residual uncertainty remaining after accounting for the impact of critical, project-specific risks and uncertainties from historical cost growth and schedule slip data. It encompasses all uncertainties and risks except for those specific critical risks and uncertainties. "All" includes the impacts of day-to-day risk events, nominal weather uncertainty, conditions uncertainty, project system failures, and more – essentially everything except the specific critical risks and uncertainties. This empirical approach assumes that understanding the system behavior is beyond the ability of any team member or analyst to quantify subjectively.

In the RP 57R-09 view, systemic risks may be seen as discrete, identifiable events. For example, a system attribute might generally be strong but has some probability of shifting to a weak state (an event) with some impact. Non-changing systemic attributes, such as complexity, are assumed to be addressed by inherent uncertainty ranging or treated as uncertainties in their own right. Ultimately, this quantification remains subjective and places a significant burden on the risk analyst to manage the process while avoiding their own biases.

Because systemic uncertainty, as quantified in parametric model development, is all inclusive except for specific critical uncertainties, the P+CPM method defined here eliminates inherent risk ranging and minimizes subjectivity and bias, making it more practical for the average scheduler and analyst. This approach sacrifices team input regarding uncertainties, which can make it more challenging to gain acceptance, as people want their opinions heard. Nevertheless, the focus is on more objective risk drivers and methods – systemic uncertainty quantified on an empirical basis, and critical project-specific risks and uncertainties: the risks that matter.

Critical Project-Specific Uncertainties

In the P+EV (Chapter 12 of Volume 1) and P+CPM methods (this chapter), there is one type of uncertainty not included in the parametric modeling results: critical, project-specific uncertainties with a probability of 100%. As discussed in Chapter 12 of Volume 1, these uncertainties fall well beyond typical "ranging" bounds and, in their worst manifestation (the high value of a 3-point range), could cause the project to fail to meet its cost and/or schedule objectives. When creating the parametric model, these extreme impacts were excluded from the analysis, so we need to add them back in. These typically include extreme uncertainties in weather, soil conditions, or skilled labor availability (productivity), among others. Unlike events that have a probability of less than 100% (see Chapter 12 of Volume 1 and Chapter 10 of this Volume regarding the avoidance of "eventification"), these extreme uncertainties are certain but have a wide range of possible impacts. In many cases, empirical data can support their quantification, such as weather records, geotechnical studies, and labor productivity or bidding experiences from nearby projects.

Risk Factors

The following method description refers to "risk factors." A *risk factor* is the percentage by which a duration or cost may vary due to risk or uncertainty. Risk factors are typically entered as a 3-point distribution, e.g., 95%, 100%, and 125%. While I am not endorsing a particular software product, most risk experts using CPM-based methods have been using Safran Risk® (as of this writing) due to its effective handling of risk factors, simple risk mapping, and other features.

Applying Hybrid Parametric Modeling with Risk-Driven CPM with MCS

Differences with RP 117R-21

The P+CPM method described here differs from AACE RP 117R-21 to reduce complexity and minimize the need for external expertise. RP 117R-21 includes ranging of inherent risks and uses a heuristic (i.e., net systemic risk) to deduct inherent uncertainty from systemic uncertainty to avoid double counting. It also quantifies nominal weather uncertainty using weather calendars (i.e., quantifying the range of lost days by period). These steps are not included in this chapter's simplified approach. For more information on those steps, see the worked example in Chapter 11 of this volume.

Steps in the Hybrid P+CPM Method

Figure 4.2 is a process flowchart of the steps of this book's P+CPM method (it is not the same as the RP 117R-21 process; see Chapter 11). This figure can be compared to the P+EV flowchart in Figure 12.1 in Volume 1.[2] The steps are discussed in more detail below. Steps 1 to 4 are the same as for P+EV in Chapter 12 of Volume

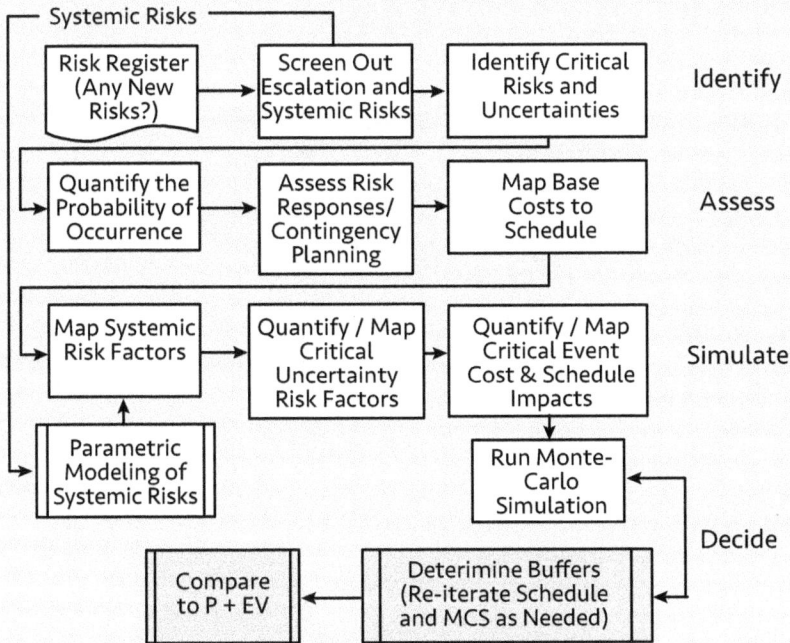

Figure 4.2: P+CPM Method Flowchart

2   See also Figure 10.3 (page 215) of this Volume.

1. Note that considerations for programs, which typically have more intermediate milestones of concern, are covered in Chapter 5.

The steps described do not include conducting systemic and project-specific risk quantification workshops (see Chapters 11 and 12 of Volume 1). Assuming that the foundational P+EV method is always applied first (the premise of this book), the identifying critical risks and uncertainties, event risk probabilities, and bottom-line schedule and cost impacts will have already been completed in the EV workshop(s). For P+CPM, an additional day per project (note that a program involves multiple projects) is required to link specific critical duration risks and uncertainties (typically 5 to 15) to schedule activities or groups thereof (and costs, if included), and to clarify impacts in terms of risk factors. Any information not effectively obtained in the workshop can be gathered off-line in dialogue with the lead project planner/scheduler or other team members as appropriate.

The P+CPM method is most applicable to Class 3 or later analyses. It can be used at the Class 4 phase for special studies, usually focused on alternative selection rather than establishing control plans and budgets. In early phases (e.g., Class 4), "forced-detail" in the CPM method must be used because standard deliverables at these stages don't support the development of a quality CPM schedule. By the Class 3 gate, where most projects are sanctioned (de facto or otherwise), a quality CPM schedule model, incorporating construction input, should be available. However, many schedules are still not of suitable quality when first presented to a risk analyst.

To address quality issues and manage the complexity of schedules (although faster software is making it easier to model large schedules), some analysts create a simplified "study schedule" for risk quantification purposes. This simplification may introduce its own analytic issues, such as merge bias. It is essential to include potential critical paths and intermediate milestones of concern in the study CPM network model.

Here are the steps for the process outlined in Figure 4.2:

1. *Screen the Risk Register*

Readiness: Make sure that any new or modified risks (since the last risk management identification was done) are captured. If additions are extensive, delay the risk quantification workshop until the risk register can be updated to accurately reflect current status.

Characterization: Screen the risks to characterize each with *quantification type*, which can be registered with one of the following designations:

♦ Systemic,
♦ Project-specific, or
♦ Escalation/Exchange.

Often team risk descriptions in registers are ambiguous. If so, the definition must be clarified before proceeding. The rule-of-thumb for quantification type designation is that if the risk description is not specific with respect to who, what, when, where, and how, then it is likely a systemic risk. If a systemic risk is found that was not well considered in the prior systemic risk analysis (e.g., the business thought the team development was excellent, but the team itself raises all sorts of issues), then the systemic analysis may need to be revisited before completing the project-specific risk quantification.

In regard to escalation, if the price-related risk is about a general price trend driven by economic conditions, it is escalation. If instead it is driven by company or project procurement or contracting practices, it is either systemic or project-specific.

Issues: If your risk management process moves issues to its own register, these will need to be reviewed as well. Anything that may result in uncertainty going forward must be quantified (most issues are systemic risks).

2. *Identify Critical Risks*

Having screened out the systemic and escalation risks, sort the register's remaining project-specific risks by their qualitative probability and impact ratings. Usually red risks are critical. The threshold criteria for criticality were discussed previously. Once the critical risks are noted, the workshop agenda can be reviewed to decide on the order in which to assess them (e.g., make sure construction risks are covered while construction leads are present). Also, verify that there is enough time in the agenda to discuss all of the critical risks.

3. *Quantify the Probability of Occurrence*

At this point, each critical risk's probability of occurrence should be refined into a specific percentage value. If the team is having trouble coming to consensus on a value, my suggestion is to lean to the conservative side (i.e., the higher probability) or assess the situation further off-line. A related input needed for MCS is whether the occurrences of any of the risks are correlated. For example, if one risk is a 100-year storm event and another is for a flood damage event (e.g., the cofferdam), these tend to go together (although not perfectly).

Often related risks can be reasonably combined for quantification purposes. For example, if there are multiple risks to the start of construction due to not receiving one or more permits, risks for permit A and permit B might be combined. They both have the same potential impact (it is not cumulative) but the probability of at least one of them occurring can be approximated as the sum of their individual probabilities.

With respect to permits, most projects have a high probability of delay from somewhere in a series of permits. In fact, permit risks are not so much risks but a fact today. It is often more efficient and cost effective to just plan for permitting delay.

4. *Assess Risk Responses*

In this step, a conceptual contingency plan (or set of plans) is developed. The operative question is, "How will we respond if the risk event happens?" The response actions should be aligned with the project cost and schedule strategy (i.e., cost versus schedule driven). Regarding a decision during the analysis, the project's PM should have final say on the answer, but the lead of the phase (e.g., construction) will have significant planning input. In general, the less clear and specific the response, the wider the range of potential impacts will be. This is because the cost and schedule range must cover all possible responses (or lack thereof).

5. *Map Base Costs to Schedule*

This step is necessary only if an integrated cost and schedule analysis is desired to validate the base P+EV method outcomes (i.e., apply P+EV on every project first). The project's quality base schedule model, containing the main inter-dependencies, is overlaid with the project base estimate, split into time-dependent and time-independent costs. Time-dependent costs are loaded into hammock activities[3] and linked to the start and finish of the related activity groups, ensuring that, as those groups of activities vary in duration, the time-dependent costs change proportionally.

---

3   A *hammock activity* is a summary activity with its start and finish linked to the start and finish of a group of lower level activities..

6. *Map Systemic Risk Factors*

The parametric method (refer to Volume 1, Chapter 11) will have already been applied, producing percentage cost growth and schedule slip distributions. For example, the *p*05, *p*50, and *p*95 values from the parametric model might be -20%, 0%, and +55%, respectively. These can be converted to 3-point risk factor distributions (1+ decimal percentage value), resulting in a low of 80% (1-0.20), a most likely of 100% (1-0), and a high of 155% (1+0.55). Given that the parametric tool generates a lognormal distribution, mean and standard deviation of that curve's data can be used to quantify a lognormal distribution. These risk factor distributions are applied to the CPM model activities and costs (or groups thereof) with 100% correlation between them. These risk factors will not be correlated with specific, critical risk factors entered later.

7. *Quantify/Map Specific, Critical Uncertainty Risk Factors*

Specific, critical uncertainties (100% probability of occurrence) will be identified in the risk quantification workshop. For example, if the critical uncertainty is the amount of rock in the soil, the worst-case scenario may result in very slow, costly excavation, potentially doubling the base duration and raising the direct cost to haul the rock away. Assuming there is some small chance of having less rock than planned, the 3-point risk factor applied to the duration of excavation activities might be 90%, 100%, and 200%. The 100% midpoint value indicates that there will most likely be no impact (the rock quantity is as planned and estimated). The non-time-driven cost of rock volume excavation and hauling would have its own risk factor range assigned. If time-driven cost has been built into the model, this will be affected proportionally.

Extreme weather uncertainty for activities at the beginning or middle of an adverse weather period is modeled similarly. However, in a seasonal execution strategy, activities planned near the end of the good weather season may be pushed into the bad period by preceding risks or uncertainties. Running the model with all risks except weather will indicate the need for a buffer. The buffer can then be added, the logic adjusted, and analysis continued iteratively. This type of optimization is why CPM-based analysis should be performed early, well before a gate review.

8. *Quantify/Map Critical Event Cost and Schedule Impacts*

Specific, critical risk events (probability <100%) will be identified in the risk quantification workshop. These are modeled similarly to uncertainties except the 3-point impact range will not be centered at 100%; risk events usually add time and cost. For example, if the risk is the occurrence of an extreme storm event, the 3-point risk factor applied to the duration of activities affected by the event might be 120%, 150%, and 200%.

9. *Run MCS*

After all the risk factors are entered (or mapped) into the model with appropriate correlations, the MCS can be run. This may be iterative if various risk mitigation strategies (i.e., schedule optimization) are applied as part of the analysis.

10. *Determine Buffers (Re-Iterate Schedule and MCS as Needed)*

If the distribution of the key intermediate milestone date threatens the achievement of schedule objectives, a buffer activity before that milestone may be considered. For example, if seasonal work is planned to be completed by November 15 and this is a hard stop, but the $p50$ value of the key milestone shows completion on November 27 (12 days late), the plan and schedule will need to be reworked to reduce the base duration by 12 days so that planned completion is November 3 (or November 15, including a 12-day buffer). By making the base schedule more aggressive, the systemic schedule bias rating will be slightly more aggressive; i.e., the buffer analysis may call for iterative schedule analysis if the buffer is substantial and acceleration of work prior to the buffer changes the risk profile. Iterative analysis takes time and is best done well before locking in date commitments at the gate.

For more details on the hybrid P+CPM method, readers are again directed to the references listed at the start of the chapter, as well as Chapter 12 of Volume 1 for steps where P+CPM has parallels with P+EV. As noted, early, full CPM-based analysis provides significant value in developing high-quality, robust, optimized plans and schedules considering risks, as well as for planning risk treatments (part of risk management).

Applying P+EV for Quantifying an Intermediate Buffer (Special Case)

The P+EV method described in Volume 1, Chapter 12 can be used to quantify buffer durations if there is a single key intermediate milestone where activities before and after the milestone can be viewed as pre- and post-sub-projects. Common examples include projects where construction shuts down for one winter or where the project has two major scope elements with a finish-start relationship. In such situations, the P+EV method can be applied to the pre-milestone scope alone to determine the need for a buffer.[4] However, if there are multiple milestones of concern, the P+CPM method is still recommended.

In this special case, the parametric model would be applied to the pre-milestone scope (e.g., Phase 1). For example, the Phase 1 work may have a more aggressive schedule bias and greater complexity than the later phases. The EV method would then be applied, including only the specific critical risks and uncertainties affecting the Phase 1 work. Costs can be ignored for this intermediate milestone study. ValidRisk® software simplifies assessing special cases such as this. The schedule duration output distribution of the P+EV model would then be used for buffer determination. This can all be done without much-added effort or time over the basic P+EV approach.

Questions

1) For what risk quantification purposes does this chapter recommend the use of the P+CPM method?

2) What P+CPM practice steps used in RP 117R-21 are not used in the practices as described in this chapter? When might it be preferable to use the full RP approach?

3) What are the two types of uncertainties (excluding risk events) quantified in the P+CPM method as described in this chapter?

4) What are "risk factors" and how are they applied in the P+CPM method?

5) In respect to intermediate milestone quantification, what P+EV method variation can be used instead of P+CPM?

Volume 2 Perspective

Volume 1 includes the P+CPM method in Appendix A. This does not address the method's main objective, which is quantifying the uncertainty of intermediate key milestones. Also, AACE Recommended Practice 117R-21 covering the hybrid method was published after Volume 1 and that RP needed to be referenced and discussed as

---

4   As I wrote this chapter, I was supporting a project risk analysis with seasonal phases where an iterative analyze / revise schedule / reanalyze process was called for based on a P+EV analysis.

a point of departure for this Volume's approach focused on practicality. Example 9E of this Volume includes a worked example of the P+CPM method with the addition of the "net specific risk" concept (referred to as P+IRA). This Chapter recognizes that at the Class 3 phase-gate or later, P+CPM should typically be applied on major projects and programs with key milestones of concern.

5
Program and Portfolio QRA Methods

Volume 1 focuses on individual projects, with some, but minimal discussion of program and portfolio cost and schedule QRA. With increasing focus on megaprojects (which are all programs or groups of projects) and the complexity of project interaction, particularly in infrastructure, this chapter goes deeper into those QRA applications. Also, enterprise level capital investment strategies usually involve study and consideration of groups of projects. Managing project groupings adds additional and often unique uncertainties and risks, which calls for tailored or special methods of risk quantification.

Programs and portfolios are the two main types of capital project groupings. The following definitions apply:

◆ A *program* is made up of separate but related projects that together meet one or more focused business objectives. Like projects, programs have a defined beginning and end. The projects in a program can be tied together in an integrated schedule network logic.

◆ A *portfolio* is a broader, less related group of projects and programs collectively addressing one or more general business strategies.

The portfolio is managed at a strategic capital planning level as a more-or-less ongoing process without a clearly defined beginning and end, but typically with strong financial focus on the current or upcoming fiscal year. The projects and programs in a portfolio are typically not tied together using integrated schedule network logic, though the component schedules may all be accessible in an enterprise level scheduling application. However, the business will have schedule objectives that guide strategic planning of the constituent projects and programs.

Ownership of the assets involved and business sponsorship of projects is wider for programs and portfolios than for individual projects. Projects tend to be primarily sponsored by a single owner business unit or entity. Programs and portfolios more often involve multiple business units working together, making for a more complex project organization and system.

Program Risk Quantification

Program-level risk quantification was introduced in Volume 1, Chapter 7 as part of an overall company risk quantification process. Examples include:

- ◆ A greenfield oil refinery/petrochemical program may include multiple process units and utility systems subprojects.

- ◆ In transportation, a multi-modal program may include airport, rail, and road subprojects, which may in fact be subprograms.

- ◆ The rail subprogram may include rail station, track, and tunnel subprojects (or just track in a series of phased projects).

- ◆ Similarly, a mining program may include mine development, processing plant, and infrastructure subprojects (rail, water supply, etc.).

Program constituent projects may be constructed more or less simultaneously or in a phased approach over time. As stated, most megaprojects are programs.

According to Devaux, a key consideration for program risk analysis, distinct from project risk analysis, is that programs often start delivering value (products, services, revenue, etc.) from their

constituent parts before the entire program is complete.[1] Therefore, optimizing the schedule to maximize the overall value to the
business over time (e.g., capturing some value early) becomes an
objective. Schedule risk analysis thus needs to be linked to or done
iteratively with a revenue model. A program may have multiple
critical paths, each leading to the completion of a constituent part
going into operation. Devaux also suggests categorizing constituent
project types as:

♦ *Optional* or *independent* projects: produce value on their
  own.

♦ *Enabler* projects: must occur for other projects to add
  value.

♦ *Kindler*[2] projects: add value to that being generated by
  other projects.

Typically, each constituent project in a program has a project
manager with a scope and budget under their authority, and each
requires its own risk quantification and contingency for managing risks. The projects in a program are tied together in a master
schedule under a program director or equivalent. Often, project
execution plans are interconnected, physical processes and facilities have connections, and regulatory bodies may view some aspects
of the program as a whole. The layering and interconnections add
complexity to the project system, leading to increased systemic risk
and additional integrative risks to programs.

Given the layering, program risk quantification, as discussed
in this chapter, involves making a separate "program level pass"
analysis after the constituent project risk quantifications are done
(though it may be revisited).[3]

---

1   Devaux, Stephen, "The Program-Level Value Breakdown Structure:
    How It Can Revolutionize Program Scheduling," PM World Journal,
    June 2024.

2   The term *Kindler* derives from "kindling" – something added to a fire
    to give it a boost. It compounds the value.

3   There are currently no AACE International Recommended Practices
    for program or portfolio level risk quantification, Also, no comprehen-
    sive papers on the topics were found in their virtual library. There are
    sources on enterprise risk management, and case studies of megaproj-
    ects including some discussion of risk management (e.g., "When Mega
    goes Giga" by Joseph Brewer), but I found no sources that address the
    specifics of program or portfolio risk quantification methods.

Program-level risk quantification focuses on interaction (internal and external), integration, and interface risks, plus added physical and execution complexity. The program-level pass supports the determination of cost contingency and/or management reserves under the authority of the program director, as well as overall schedule contingency and intermediate milestone buffers.

To quantify these program risks and uncertainties, a process is described in this chapter that emphasizes practicality and realism, the book's themes. The risk quantification process is necessarily more complex than a single project risk quantification but no more than needed to meet the basic objectives. The following program-level risk quantification steps will be described:

1. Apply the parametric model using a program-level view of the systemic risks (weakest link approach for ratings).

2. Re-run the project parametric + expected value (P+EV) analyses using the program-level parametric model outputs.

3. Identify critical program-level specific risks and uncertainties in a program-level risk workshop and apply EV analysis; use this to quantify any program-level specific management reserves.

4. Consolidate the cost distribution outputs using Monte Carlo Simulation (MCS) applied to the re-run project P+EV analyses (from step 2) and the program-level critical specific risks and uncertainties (from step 3); use this distribution to determine a program-level general management reserve.

5. Perform a parametric + critical path method (P+CPM) schedule analysis (see Chapter 4 in this Volume) using the program master or study schedule, the program-level parametric model schedule output (from step 1), the existing project critical specific risks and uncertainties (from the projects), and the additional program critical specific risks and uncertainties (from step 3); use this to quantify schedule contingency and buffers.

Prior to this risk quantification process, it is assumed that the business will have worked out an overall schedule to optimize value delivery from the constituent projects (as Devaux described). In other words, there will be base schedule milestones for the start of operations for each part.

Beyond these steps, program-level risk quantification needs to address the following special risk considerations where applicable.

They mostly tie to other book chapters:

♦ Escalation: Long duration and large size add to escalation risk (re: Volume 1, Chapter 13).

♦ Complexity/Tipping Point: Program complexity increases the probability of tipping into disordered/non-linear behavior (re: Volume 1, Chapter 14).

♦ Phasing/Scope Evolution: The scope of projects executed late in a long-duration, phased program is likely to change (include scope change in their contingency/reserves) (re: Chapter 6 in this Volume).

♦ Agility: Risks are more likely to emerge or change nature during long-duration programs; periodic, mid-execution risk quantification will likely be needed.

Program-Level Pass Risk Quantification Process

Volume 1, Chapter 7 described an integrated risk quantification process that a company might follow for its capital projects and programs. The flowchart in Volume 1, Figure 7.1, depicted a "program analysis" step that comes after individual project analyses and before escalation/exchange analysis.[4] Figure 5.1 maps the program analysis step in more detail. On the left of the figure are the base, project-level P+EV methods and outputs, as covered in Volume 1, Chapters 11 and 12. On the right are the additional steps for program-level analysis that build on the constituent project

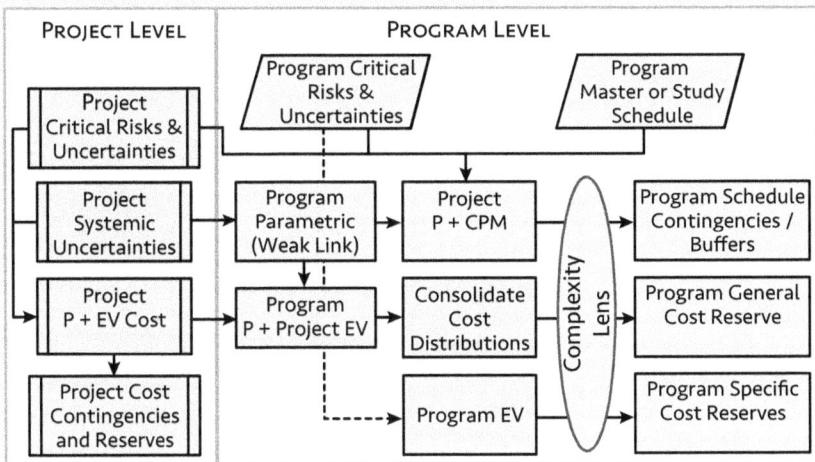

Figure 5.1 Risk Quantification Process at the Program Level

---

4   See also Figure 10.2 (page 206) of this Volume.

analyses. The program analysis focuses on project commonalities, interactions, interfaces, and added complexity.

As in the general process outlined in Volume 1, Figure 7.1, the program analysis in Figure 5.1 distinguishes between systemic and critical project-specific risks and uncertainties. The program analysis applies two hybrid risk quantification methods:

♦ P+EV for costs (Volume 1, Chapters 11 and 12), and

♦ P+CPM (Chapter 4 of this volume) for schedules.

The P+CPM method, if cost-loaded, can assess both cost and schedule risk, but this increases the complexity of the model. A common drawback of depending on cost-loaded CPM is that the necessary cost/schedule integration may not be present for all projects and/ or at the program level, particularly if there is long-term project phasing. The process in Figure 5.1 is flexible even if base estimating and scheduling practices are not of the best quality; the parametric method addresses the systemic uncertainty resulting from planning deficiencies.

Both the P+EV and P+CPM methods are fed by a program-level application of the parametric model (P) using a "weakest link" approach for systemic risk rating, as will be discussed. Both hybrid methods use inputs from a program-level specific, critical risk, and uncertainty workshop. Ultimately, the overall analysis provides program-level measures for a tipping point assessment (i.e., the complexity lens). The outputs of the Figure 5.1 process are program schedule contingency/buffers and cost allowances for program-level general and specific management reserves.

The rest of this chapter provides more detail on the steps of the program-level pass process in Figure 5.1 and discusses the special risk considerations previously listed.

The Program-Level Risk Quantification Process Steps and Methods

Step 1: Program Parametric Model/Weakest Link

At the start of program risk analysis, each project will have assessed its respective systemic risks, noting any project consistencies where applicable. For the program-level pass, the parametric method is applied similarly to a project as described in Volume 1, Chapter 11. However, for the program, the team will rate the systemic risks using a "weakest link" approach. In this approach, the program's scope definition and planning, business ownership, team development, project control, and estimate and schedule basis are rated only as strong as the weakest, most lagged ratings among the significant subprojects. There may be exceptions where a weak project element is largely independent and/or isolated from the other projects. Using the weakest link may seem overly pessimistic, but it is consistent with the nature of systems. In a system, problems in one element (project) tend to impact or infect the others. For example, weak management and poor performance in one project may result in poor morale and motivation that spread through the workforce of other projects, especially in remote projects where workers are housed together in camps.[5]

Consider a greenfield oil refinery program as an example. The process unit project scope definitions may be at Class 3 (P&IDs issued for design), but the utilities are at Class 4 (P&IDs just starting). In that case, the program-level scope definition would be rated Class 4 because scope changes in the lagging projects are likely to result in late changes to those projects that have proceeded.[6]

An example of a possible exception to the weakest link rule is a transit project where the track scope definition is at Class 4, but the station work is at Class 3. It is arguable that the track work, where the definition is driven by right-of-way, interferences, and permits, is largely independent of the station, suggesting the use of a weighted average definition rating of the projects. However, all the projects in a program are working under a common project system umbrella to some extent, so the weakest link still applies to attributes such as business ownership and program control. It is easy to get carried away with making "exceptions" (a form of optimism bias), so a general recommendation is to use the weakest link approach for all ratings (one exception might be for phased projects in a program, which will be discussed).

For program complexity ratings, the physical and execution complexity of a program will generally be greater, or at least no less, than any one of its constituent projects. Using the refinery example, the refinery process complexity may be rated as high while the utilities process complexity is rated medium. The program-level pass

---

5   A welder (injured on the major project that I was assessing and driving my taxi) once told me that he and others were "influenced" to slow the pace of their welding output to that of the slowest welding crew.

6   In my experience, utility and infrastructure scope definition almost always lag definition of the more central process units or core facilities.

may then rate program physical complexity as high, considering the overall total number of process and utility units in the entire plant. The execution complexity (e.g., complex execution and/or contract strategy) will also generally be rated as higher than the rating of the most complex project because a layer of management complexity has been added. As with general systemic practice ratings, if one project experiences problems because of its execution complexity, those problems will tend to affect other projects in the program.

For the program level of technology, where risk manifestations are more in the nature of late design changes and startup issues rather than degraded construction performance, a suggested program-level rating would be to calculate the weighted average of the constituent project technology ratings (weighted by the project costs).

Step 2: Update the Project P+EV Analyses

To support program-level cost distribution determination, re-run the project-level P+EV analyses using the program-level systemic risk rating inputs from Step 1. However, keep the original project-level files intact as they are still the basis of the individual project cost contingencies. This is a quick, straightforward calculation step and does not require new inputs from the team.

Step 3: Identify Program Critical Risks and Uncertainties

In this step, conduct a program-level specific risk identification/ quantification workshop as covered in Volume 1, Chapter 12. This workshop will focus on commonalities, interactions, and interfaces between the projects and with external stakeholders interfacing with the program. Attendees should include business sponsors, PMs, and selected project leads familiar with the interaction/interface risks and uncertainties.

One of the most common interaction/integration risks on programs is a skilled labor shortage. For example, managing 500 workers on one project may seem feasible, but managing 3,000 workers across a program's constituent projects can lead to internal competition for labor resources, causing shortages.

Similar examples may involve supply chains or infrastructure elements over-stretched by program demands or permitting agencies with limited staffs bogged down by submittals from the many varied project elements and stakeholders. There may also be interface risks where disputes arise over responsibility for work where projects physically and/or contractually overlap.

Other common risks include delays in one project pushing another project into an adverse weather season or causing much greater program peak man-loading if the program end date is held constant.

As with a project, screen these program-specific risks to identify those that are critical. Conduct an EV analysis for the critical program risks and uncertainties, including program delays and time-dependent and non-time-dependent costs. In the EV analysis, set the base cost of the program at zero so that the bottom-line cost distribution of the analysis represents added cost to the program.[7] This distribution will be included with the other project cost distributions in the program-level consolidated MCS cost simulation in Step 4. If some risks are high impact, low probability (HILP), consider them for specific management reserve funding at a program level. Usually, all specific HILP risk reserve funds, including those specific to a project, will be under the program director's or higher authority. The overall schedule impact will be addressed in Step 5.

Step 4: Consolidate the Cost Distributions

For each project, as well as for the program-level critical interaction risks and uncertainties identified in Step 3, there will be a cost distribution derived from their respective EV analyses. Using Monte Carlo Simulation (MCS), these can be consolidated into a single program-level cost distribution to determine a general program-level management reserve. For example, the program may fund a general reserve by subtracting the sum of the project contingencies from the $p70$ of the consolidated program cost distribution. Consolidation using MCS is necessary because *only* the mean values of the individual project distributions are additive (e.g., the $p90$ of the consolidated distribution will likely be somewhat less than the sum of the project $p90$s).

The "consolidator" will usually be a spreadsheet[8] wherein the base cost estimates, the defined cost contingencies, and the contingency cost distributions of each project are entered (the base cost of

---

7   Sometimes the program director will be responsible for managing supporting scope elements such as camp and/or other temporary construction. If so, analyze that often loosely connected group as a subproject. As supporting elements, this scope is often affected by the risk impacts of the other program projects (e.g., project productivity impacts may result in late camp additions).

8   Consolidation capability is built into ValidRisk® software.

the program-level analysis of Step 3 will be zero). As shown in Table 5.1, the project cost growth (contingency) distributions are entered as *p*-tables with MCS tool distribution functions (e.g., "riskcumul" in @Risk®) being used to model them. Next, a correlation matrix is set up to define the correlations between the project distributions. Being managed as a program in a common regime, no scope element will be completely independent. Most will be highly dependent (e.g., coefficient of say 0.9), but some may be less so (e.g., coefficients of say 0.5 or 0.7). The project contingency MCS functions are then summed and defined as an MCS output distribution (total contingency risk costs). That output is added to the sum of the deterministic base costs and also defined as an MCS output distribution (total program cost). The program general reserve is determined by subtracting the sum of the project contingencies from the cost at the *p*70 or other confidence level of the total program cost distribution.

	Project 1	Project 2	Program Risks	Total
Base Cost	$1,000	$1,000	$0	$2,000
Contingency	$150	$200	$50	$400
*p*05 cost growth	$ at *p*05	$ at *p*05	$ at *p*05	
... increments of 5				
*p*95 cost growth	$ at *p*95	$ at *p*95	$ at *p*95	
	Riskcumul function including correlation (for each column)			Total of RiskCumul as @Risk output
				Sum Base + Total above as @Risk output

Correlations	Project 1	Project 2	Program
Project 1	1		
Project 2	0.9	1	
Program	0.9	0.9	1

Table 5.1 Example Consolidator Tool Using MCS

Step 5: Perform a Parametric + CPM Schedule Risk Analysis

Using the program master schedule or a specially created program study schedule,[9] conduct a P+CPM schedule risk analysis.

---

9   Study schedules may be needed because schedule development of some project elements is lagging, project interfaces may be poorly defined, general schedule quality may be poor, and/or the number of program activities is simply overwhelming (e.g., schedules with more than 10,000 activities are not uncommon).

This analysis should use:

1. The program-level parametric model schedule output from Step 1.

2. The existing project-specific critical risks and uncertainties.

3. The additional program-level critical risks and uncertainties identified in Step 3.

Chapter 4 of this volume describes the suggested P+CPM method, which has been simplified from the method described in AACE RP 117R-21 by removing the cost-loading and inherent risk quantification steps. Although a cost-loaded P+CPM method can assess both cost and schedule risk, it increases complexity and reduces flexibility.

The output of the P+CPM analysis is a distribution of the overall program schedule completion date. This is typically used in business case model sensitivity analysis (e.g., start of revenue) and/or to manage commercial delivery promises. If projects in the program produce their own products or services (e.g., revenue streams), those project-level completion dates are modeled as well. Other key outputs include the distributions of intermediate and project interface milestone dates, which are used to determine buffers as discussed in Chapter 4 of this volume.

It is important to note that the P+EV method with consolidation can be used for the program schedule duration similar to cost, but only if the projects are sequential (i.e., finish-to-start relationship). However, purely sequential projects in a program are unusual; most program projects are done in parallel to some extent. For example, a program may have four projects where the construction of each takes two years, but the overall program duration may be three years with the program's critical path passing through all its projects depending on the logic.

Special Considerations for a Program

Escalation (Refer to Volume 1, Chapter 13)

The risk quantification flowchart in Volume 1, Figure 7.1[10] shows probabilistic escalation analysis being conducted after the program risk analysis. Typically, escalation will be funded as its own budget account under the authority of the program director. The methods described in Volume 1, Chapter 13 are applied to programs in the same way as for individual projects. The key difference for a program is that the cash flows by account will be the summation

---

10 See also Figure 10.2 (page 206) of this Volume.

of the project cash flows. Additionally, the size of the program will likely necessitate a higher capital market index adjustment factor, as discussed in Volume 1, Chapter 13. This is because megaprojects create their own micro-market, with various projects competing for resources and driving up prices (refer to the Goodyear Rule).

Complexity/Tipping Point (Refer to Volume 1, Chapter 14)

Volume 1, Chapter 14 describes a method for assessing a project's susceptibility to disordered, non-linear behavior, often referred to as chaos or blowout. The assessment acknowledges that complex projects and programs are fragile. It employs a rating concept called the *tipping point factor*. Volume 1, Chapter 14 lists the systemic and specific risk attributes considered in the factor. Research suggests that the following attributes tend to push projects toward non-linearity:

♦ Size: Total cost, number of workers
♦ Decisiveness: Business leadership, ownership, and decisiveness[11]
♦ Team: Team development, staffing, roles, and responsibilities
♦ Aggressiveness: Cost and schedule aggressiveness
♦ Complexity: Process/facility complexity and execution complexity
♦ Critical project-specific risks: stressors

For a program, the tipping point approach mirrors that of a project. However, the ratings of the attributes are typically worse at the program level than for its individual projects. As a general rule of thumb, qualitative program ratings (e.g., green, yellow, red) will be one step higher for the program than the average project-level ratings (e.g., yellows at the project level become red at the program level). The examples below show why this rule of thumb is suggested, understanding that the tipping point method is not an exact science:

♦ Size: If each of the project sizes is large, the program will likely be a megaproject.
♦ Decisiveness: Any indecisiveness at the project level may be compounded at the program level due to the added layer

---

11 Refer to: *Leading Complex Projects: A Data-Driven Approach to Mastering the Human Side of Project Management* by Edward Merrow & Neeraj Nandurdikar, Wiley, 2018.

of management, communication challenges, opportunities for confusion, and inter-project conflicts. Outstanding program leadership is crucial for success.

♦ Team: Competition for resources may result in thinner staffing, less clarity of objectives between projects, and more opportunities for conflict.

♦ Aggressiveness: While project schedules may not be aggressive, the program schedule might be (e.g., projects running in parallel can lead to unrealistic resource loading).

♦ Complexity: More projects mean more physical complexity, especially if project elements are interconnected or interdependent. Execution complexity increases as the number of contractors, suppliers, and stakeholders grows.

♦ Critical project-specific risks (stressors): New interaction, integration, and interface risks are added at the program level.

If a quantitative Monte Carlo Simulation (MCS) tipping point model assessment is desired (as detailed in Volume 1, Chapter 14) to better communicate the threat to cost (e.g., showing bimodal or fat-tail behavior), a unified program-level P+EV analysis is required. This unified analysis should use the program-level parametric model (weakest link) and an EV analysis focused on cost, incorporating all project critical risks, effectively treating the program as a single, very large project.[12]

Phasing (Refer to: Chapter 6, this Volume)

As mentioned, projects in a program may be constructed either simultaneously or sequentially. For example, an integrated petrochemical plant might build oil refining and utility units first, followed by various petrochemical units. Similarly, a linear road, rail, or pipeline transportation program could involve segmented projects, with each segment constructed one after the other.

A program, as discussed in this chapter, is usually sanctioned as a whole, with risk quantification supporting a single investment

---

12 Refer to: J. Hollmann and R.S. Bali, "Case Study: Use of the Hybrid Parametric and Expected Value QRA Method on the Keeyask Hydropower Megaproject" in the 2024 AACE International Transactions for an example of megaproject (program) risk quantification using the tipping point method.

decision. This contrasts with projects that are strategically related but sanctioned and managed individually over time, as markets and needs evolve or as funding becomes available. An example of the latter can be found in the capital spending programs of water and power utilities in a growing metropolis, which must develop long-term plans for an expanding and evolving utility system. Chapter 6 of this volume addresses risk quantification for long-term project planning, assuming that the scope of distant future projects will change and that these projects have not yet entered a formal phase-gate queue (i.e., Class 10 estimates, not Class 5).

For a program sanctioned as a whole, the risk quantification process in Figure 5.1 is applied similarly for both simultaneous (parallel) and phased (sequential) project types. However, for phased programs, a weighted average of scope definition ratings may be used in the program parametric model if the phasing reflects greater independence of the projects. The weakest link approach, where the least defined project (usually the last to be constructed) determines the program's rating, still applies if changes in a later project are likely to result in rework for earlier ones.

A grey area exists for phased programs sanctioned as a whole but spread out over a long period (7-10 years or more), where later projects are expected to experience significant changes in technology, politics, regulations, social license and stakeholder challenges, the economy, and so on. For these later projects, which are Class 10 estimates, alternate scopes and scenario analyses become relevant (see Chapter 6 of this volume). If an owner insists that risk quantification for such a phased program "assumes no major scope changes," this could be a form of strategic misrepresentation to be cautious about and possibly avoid being involved in.

Agility

With increasingly long program durations and prevalent major program cost blowouts, there is a growing interest in incorporating "agility" into the phase-gate system approach. This approach entails mid-execution risk quantification when risk management identifies new or evolving risks and/or increasing uncertainty, or conducting these analyses on a planned basis (more frequently than year-end updates, such as quarterly if the risks are dynamic). Implementing incremental risk treatments as appropriate, rather than waiting for a tipping point blowout that necessitates harsh interventions, is essential (see Volume 1, Chapter 14). Establishing adequate program management reserves will help avoid the disruption and added delay of "cost surprises" and the need for supplemental funding.

Portfolios/Strategic and Sustaining Capital Management

Like programs, a portfolio is a group of projects (which may include programs). However, the projects in a portfolio are typically less related and less interdependent than those in a program. A portfolio typically has no defined beginning or end. Capital management is an ongoing process that approves an annual and long-term capital budget for all the projects in the enterprise's general or specialized portfolios. The projects in a business's or operation's capital budget are often called the *project portfolio*. The mix of projects and the capital budget is usually updated annually in alignment with evolving business strategies. As discussed in Volume 1, Chapter 7, portfolios have integrative risks similar to programs that may not be evident at the project level.

Risk Quantification in Capital Project Portfolios

In general, there are two risk quantification focus areas in capital project portfolio risk analysis:

1. Strategic (Major Projects): The business's concern is selecting an optimal set of strategic capital project investments while considering risks. The key performance indicator being optimized is usually return on investment or another profitability measure (with sales/revenue as the key risk driver). Strategic projects typically constitute the largest share of capital spending (in a growing company, the 80/20 rule tends to apply for strategic versus sustaining capital costs). Strategic projects often have their own entry in headline capital plans. When a strategic project or program overruns, the business is likely to allocate extra funds for that project, quantified using best practices.

2. Sustaining (Small Projects): The business operating unit's concern is selecting an optimal set of sustaining and capitalized maintenance projects within a constrained fiscal year capital budget, potentially considering resource optimization. Key performance indicators are usually focused on maintaining or nominally improving existing asset safety and performance.

Sustaining projects typically make up the largest number of projects (e.g., 20 percent of the capital budget but 80 percent of the number of projects). In a sustaining or small project portfolio, if a project overruns, it will likely be funded (due to escalating commitment bias), but other projects in the portfolio budget will be de-scoped, delayed, or canceled to keep overall portfolio capital cash flow on budget, driven by financial discipline.

Strategic (Major) Project Portfolio Risk Quantification

Strategic project portfolio risk management and quantification are typically handled by the business planning and decision analysis functions within a corporation, using investment decision-making practices as discussed in Volume 1, Chapter 5. The methods used and literature on the subject often resemble those for optimizing investments in a portfolio of stocks and bonds. Specialized software is available for portfolio planning and optimization. Although this book does not focus on deciding the makeup of and managing and quantifying the risk of an overall strategic capital investment portfolio, it addresses the practical needs of a typical project risk analyst. Project analysts will use the risk analysis methods discussed in this book on individual projects and programs within the portfolio. These project and program-level analyses become inputs to strategic business capital portfolio planning and decision analysis.

Sustaining (Small) Project Portfolio Risk Quantification

Sustaining project portfolios are often managed by decentralized (e.g., plant-based) organizations using a "small project system," a streamlined version of the company's phase-gate process. These projects are typically characterized by use of shared teams, where team members work on multiple projects simultaneously. Consequently, less team member time is available, and less rigor is applied to practices such as project control, risk management, and risk quantification for each project. As discussed in Volume 1, Chapter 4, the unspoken[13] cost strategy for small projects is almost always to *"overfund and underrun"* to ensure predictability, optimally returning any excess funds for use on other small projects.

The focus of portfolio management tends to be more on financial cash flow management (predictability) rather than individual project

---

13 "Unspoken" because some key stakeholders (e.g., Finance) would not be happy to hear that capital effectiveness (least cost for a given scope and quality) is not the operative cost strategy.

performance and profitability. No single project receives significant focus, and sophisticated project risk quantification methods are usually not applied to small projects. However, the parametric method discussed in Volume 1, Chapter 11 offers a viable and practical risk quantification method for small projects – it is fast and simple, leaving no excuse for not applying it. As projects become larger, the full P+EV method of Volume 1, Chapter 12 may be employed.

The primary finance and operations risk questions for sustaining portfolios are typically, *"Will we get the planned projects done this year within the budget?"* and/or, *"Will we have money left to get some more work done this year?"* Organizations will also be concerned with managing key resources. Small project portfolio risk analysts may be called upon to perform risk quantification to answer these questions. To do this effectively, they need to understand the financially-driven project management practice known as Management-by-Cashflow (MBC).

Management-by-Cashflow (MBC) on Strategic/Major Projects

Strategic projects are usually funded independently, with necessary funds made available to ensure they meet their strategic objectives. However, companies may sometimes face capital constraints and decide to limit a strategic project's cash flow. Such constraints, common for small projects, can be very costly for strategic projects and programs. Another form of constraint occurs in companies with an over-zealous "capital discipline" strategy enforced by finance, requiring projects to "hit your monthly cash flow target exactly or else."

When financial constraints are imposed (a max limit) or perfection in cash flow is enforced (min/max limits), projects must throttle back activities or use slow payment schemes to stay within max limits. Conversely, they might accelerate work and pay early if there's a minimum spending limit. MBC is a significant risk driver and a common feature in government projects.

MBC is always destructive to project system discipline, particularly project control. Teams in a punitive capital discipline culture become obsessed with cash flow issues rather than effective cost and schedule performance. Ironically, emphasis on certainty in spend rate adds cost and time, increasing uncertainty in total project costs. MBC is a systemic risk that can be addressed using the parametric method. If MBC applies to all projects in a portfolio, its cost and schedule impact should be incorporated into the company's parametric model through periodic calibration. However, project control practices will typically be rated as marginal at best.

A strategic project or program with an imposed spending constraint will need to change its plans, schedules, and estimates. This leads to major mid-stream changes with cost increases and schedule delays, often involving contract claims. Imposition of a constraint is a risk event that can be assessed using the EV risk quantification method. A 2023 study by Independent Project Analysis, Inc. (IPA) reported that projects with a capital spending constraint had 18% longer durations and 13% higher costs than comparable projects without constraints. They also reported that this behavior appears to be increasing.[14]

Unfortunately, this constraint risk occurrence is usually difficult to foresee unless the company or uniquely financed program is in a precarious financial situation. This is likely a high impact, low probability (HILP) risk; however, the possibility of this event underscores the importance of funding projects at a high confidence level of underrunning (e.g., $p70$ or $p80$).

MBC on Sustaining/Small Projects: Probabilistic Cashflow

Sustaining, small project portfolios operate within a fixed annual capital budget constraint, making Management-by-Cashflow (MBC) a way of life. As previously stated, "overestimate and underrun" cost management cultures prevail. Individual small project risk quantification is usually unsophisticated, optimally using the quick and practical parametric method of Volume 1, Chapter 11. As mentioned previously, at the portfolio level an analyst may be called upon to answer key uncertainty questions: *"Will we get the planned projects done this year within the budget?"* and/or *"Will we have money left to get more work done this year?"*

The common risk quantification method to answer these questions is to apply a probabilistic cashflow model that addresses the project cost and schedule uncertainties of the portfolio projects. The purpose of probabilistic cashflow modeling is to help portfolio management decide if more or fewer projects should or can be included in the fiscal year plans. The models allow portfolio management to test alternatives and develop contingency plans for having "shovel-ready" projects to initiate efficiently mid-year if surplus capital becomes available. One objective is to avoid the inefficient and

14 The Domino Effect of Cash-Flow Restrictions on Projects," www.ipa-global.com/news/article, December 1, 2023.

often wasteful "use-it-or-lose-it" mad dash to spend surplus funds in the last month or two of the fiscal year, a common problem with government budgets.

Figure 5.2 highlights the concerns of small project portfolio cashflow risk quantification. The portfolio includes numerous projects with uncertain costs, start times, and durations. Ideally, each project's risks are quantified individually by each team, and those results are incorporated into the collective probabilistic cashflow analysis. The collective analysis may also study the identified risks of the constituent projects (if risks are captured in a common way) to identify commonalities that might be addressed at a business level.

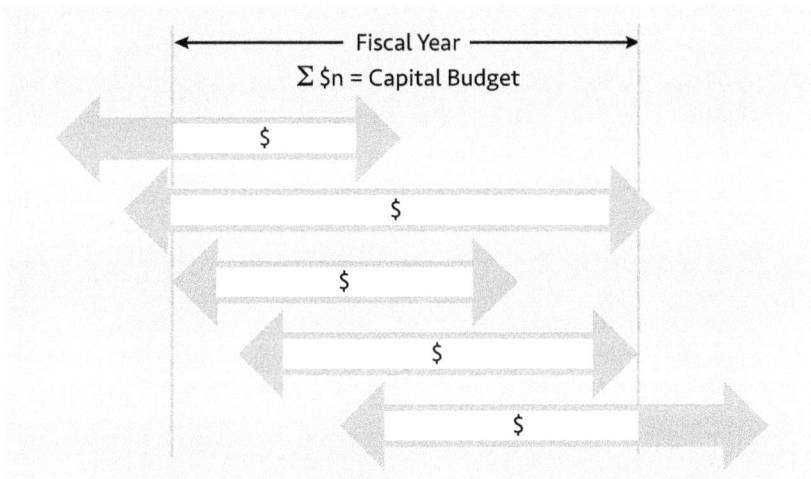

Figure 5.2: Small Project Portfolio Cashflow Risk Elements

Probabilistic cashflow is also used in probabilistic escalation models (see Volume 1, Chapter 13). However, for a portfolio, the focus is on cashflow by project rather than by cost account, as with escalation. There are two general model types:

1. Modeled using cost-loaded critical path method (CPM) schedule risk analysis software, and

2. Spreadsheet-based tools.

Both use Monte Carlo simulation (MCS).

Scheduling Software Analysis

CPM-based analysis can be applied at various levels of sophistication and complexity. If a small project system uses enterprise CPM software where each small project's schedule and cost (and maybe key resource requirements) are already loaded by their teams and forecasts updated monthly, the portfolio's cashflow can be assessed cumulatively. Traditional CPM-based risk analysis with MCS can be applied to each project, so the portfolio will reflect the overall result (although there will be no overall critical path).

In portfolios, there is the added risk that project start dates are uncertain, and some projects may be postponed or canceled. If cost and duration risk factors have been applied by the project team (and possibly at a portfolio level), the final output of interest will be the distribution of current fiscal year total capital spending.

However, managing small project portfolios with hundreds or thousands of projects using CPM software at an enterprise level is challenging, especially if attempting to link related projects using network logic. The modeling task can be expedited if the projects are repetitive by creating templates that can be imported or copied. This requires CPM scheduling and risk modeling competency among many teams and at the portfolio management level.

If the scheduling software incorporates an MCS tool such as Safran Risk® (SR), duration and cost risk factors can be assigned to groups of activities and costs for all similar projects. If practical, risk factors can be characterized for individual projects by SMEs according to the unique known characteristics of the individual projects or according to different classes of such projects (e.g., simple/medium/complex or small/medium/large, or according to the degree of difficulty due to location).

After running the portfolio model in the CPM software (e.g., SR), probabilistic cash flows can be produced for various p values, such as $p50$, $p70$, and $p90$. Due to the duration and cost risk factors, the cash flow curves will spread upwards with cost uncertainty and to the right with duration uncertainty.

A non-enterprise CPM alternative is to create a purpose-specific portfolio study "project" wherein each portfolio project is entered like an activity (or a simplified set of activities such as design, procure, construct) with forecast cost (and perhaps key resource) loading. Some projects will be independent, while others may have logic ties to other projects. Again, there will be no critical path to the portfolio since there is no integrated network. They will have a common date-of-forecast start milestone. Each project can have a time-to-project start activity without resources to address uncertainty about when (or if) a project will start. The uncertainty of the project durations can be entered as risk factors, as can the uncertainty of the project costs. The final output of interest will again be the distribution of current fiscal year total capital spending. This approach requires more effort from the portfolio-level planning team and strong scheduling skills to collect, check, and input the schedules and other data from the teams.

Spreadsheet-Based Analysis

To avoid the IT requirements, software expenses, and scheduling competency needed for a CPM-based approach, probabilistic cash flow can be effectively modeled in a spreadsheet with Monte Carlo Simulation (MCS). Each project would provide its own cost forecast worksheet by month. In the analysis worksheet, each project can have a cost risk factor, entered as a distribution, and applied to the base forecast cost of each project. These base inputs can be determined by project-level risk quantification. An "offset" function can be used to address the uncertainty of when (or if) the project will actually start, shifting monthly spending earlier or later based on a +/- months distribution.

Modeling the risk to duration is more challenging because small project cashflow patterns are often far from uniform or smooth (e.g., months of little activity followed by bursts of spending). However, duration uncertainty is less essential to model because only the current fiscal year is being assessed. The effect of longer durations often pushes spending into the next year, and this effect can be reasonably modeled using the cost factor, adjusted to account for longer and shorter durations that result in more negative and more positive cost range potential in the current year. Studying historical cost uncertainty (e.g., is there an overestimate and underrun culture?), project timing and duration variation experience, and cash flow patterns will support realistic model development.

Chapter 9 of this volume provides an example spreadsheet-based model with MCS for a small project portfolio.

Summary

Given the varied considerations, program and portfolio variations, and available software tools, there is plenty of room for creativity in program and portfolio risk quantification approaches. The processes and methods suggested in this chapter are not the only ways to achieve practicality and realism in quantifying cost and schedule risk and uncertainty, but the chapter provides some example workable methods to compare with other approaches.

Volume 2 Perspective

In Volume 1, program content is scattered between chapters and covered at a high level. This chapter consolidates the content and more fully describes the program risk quantification process (see Figure 5.1) and methods. Interest in program risks is increasing as global "net zero" carbon initiatives drive the need for megaprojects, which are essentially programs.[15]

Additionally, there is more interest in "agility" in managing megaprojects and programs as social demands and technology change at a seemingly faster pace. While being agile may be seen as being more resilient and robust in the face of change, change always adds uncertainty.

Finally, because project-level analysts are often involved in small project portfolio analysis, general methods to model small project capital portfolio fiscal year cashflow uncertainty are included in this chapter. Quantification of strategic (major project) capital portfolio risk to profitability is outside the scope of this book.

Questions

1. Define what programs and portfolios are; how do they differ?

2. How does value generation timing play into program analysis?

3. What are the two typical project timing approaches found in programs?

4. Who typically has authority over project contingencies in a program?

5. What does the "weakest link" approach mean in respect to parametric modeling of systemic risk for a program?

6. What types of specific risks and uncertainties are typically identified in a program-level risk workshop?

7. Why is the hybrid parametric and CPM risk quantification method suggested for programs?

8. How can a single program cost distribution be produced from the various project and program inputs?

---

15 The IMF reports the need for $5 trillion US dollars per year for Net Zero investments by 2030. IMF Blog, "World Needs More Policy Ambition, Private Funds, and Innovation to Meet Climate Goals," November 27, 2023

9. What are the three major outputs of program-level risk quantification?

10. What rule-of-thumb applies to rating tipping point factors for programs?

11. What scope risk situation may arise with very long duration programs?

12. What is the risk called that a finance-driven company may experience?

13. What are the two general types of portfolio capital risk of interest to business?

14. What methods are there for probabilistic portfolio cashflow modeling?

"I try to prepare for everything beyond the extent of preparation."
– Taylor Swift

6

Multi-Option (Class 5) and Long Range (Class 10) Estimate QRA Methods

The Multi-Option and Long-Range QRA Gap

The most widely used AACE Recommended Practices (RPs) are probably its cost estimate classification RPs for various industries. One reason for their popularity is their close alignment with ubiquitous phase-gate project systems. They also align with our traditional perception of contingency and its quantification methods.

However, in one area of capital investment planning, these classification RPs did not go far enough to cover all cost estimates. This is particularly true for long-range capital planning, especially in the public infrastructure sector, and industries that must bond (sureties) the eventual decommissioning and closure of their assets. Long-term estimates are also used in asset life cycle cost estimating (LCCE).

For long-range planning, a project will not enter a formal phase-gate capital management process until far in the future, often 10 to 50 or more years out. For example, a municipal water utility company might update its long-range capital plans annually based on uncertain long-term forecasts of population growth, urban development patterns, and similar factors. They don't know what facility capacities will be required, let alone what technologies will be available or where they will be located so far in the future. For instance, the San Francisco Municipal Transportation Agency published its 20-year (2023 to 2042) capital plan costing $31.3 billion, in which every project and program is itemized, including a brief basis statement such as "estimate based on past similar work."[1]

The problem with long-range estimating is not how to prepare a conceptual base cost estimate for any assumed scope; those estimating methods are well established. The issue is quantifying the cost risk when the potential requirements and scope of the asset and project are very uncertain. The definition of "contingency" (the usual mechanism in phase-gate systems for funding risk) per AACE RP 10S-90 specifically excludes scope change.[2] Traditionally, it is assumed that there is a given scope definition for which the project economics and other objectives are evaluated, and a decision is made to stop, recycle, or proceed with more scope definition.

To address this issue, AACE established an estimate class called Unclassified or Class 10 in RP 111R-20.[3] Recognizing the high uncertainty, the RP states that Unclassified/Class 10 estimates *"are not associated with indicated expected accuracy ranges."* With respect to risk quantification, the RP further acknowledges that the *"estimate is unlikely to be accurate, and the original scope may not be representative of the final solution and associated costs."*

---

1   SFMTA , "2021 20-Year Capital Plan," San Francisco Municipal Transportation Agency, San Francisco, CA, 2021.

2   Scope in that definition refers to change in "business scope," not contract or engineering specification scope. For example, at Class 5 the business scope may consist only of the plant production capacity, product qualities, and time frame. A change in any details assumed for the purposes of estimating is not a business scope change.

3   AACE International, Recommended Practice 111R-20, "Estimating for Long-Range Planning – As Applied for the Public Sector" (latest revision).

In a paper I wrote in 2022, I noted that this scope problem also applies to Class 5 estimates.[4] A single scope alternative is not selected until the Class 4 phase, often called the "Select" phase for that reason. While the scope options or alternatives are clearer for Class 5 than for Class 10, there is still room for very wide cost uncertainty – much wider than included in the AACE RPs (see Figure 4.3 in Volume 1, Chapter 4). Risk quantification at Class 5 fails when project teams estimate the base cost and quantify the risk for only one scope alternative (usually the business's "favorite" option) when there are actually several economically viable alternatives being carried into the later Class 4 or Select Phase for more detailed design.

What is needed for Unclassified/Class 10 and Class 5 estimates is a risk quantification method that effectively models the impact of potential scope change and/or scope alternatives. My 2022 paper included a literature search that failed to find any reliable risk quantification methods designed to address long-range project scope risk (i.e., none that would pass muster as meeting AACE's or this book's risk quantification principles). The primary method I found that does work, but has not been used much for specific project cost risk quantification, is decision tree analysis.

Because the term contingency excludes scope change, the expression "contingency/reserve allowance" is used for the remainder of this chapter. However, it is important to keep in mind that for investment decision making, and the decision analysis tools used for that purpose (e.g., sensitivity analysis), the contingency or contingency/reserve allowance is not the most important risk quantification output. The important values are the CAPEX and duration (i.e., start of revenue) high or worst-case values ($p90$ or $p95$). The worst case best defines the risk profile and largely determines if a capital investment alternative is economically viable.

Use Cases for Long-Range Estimates

There are two typical long-range planning use cases where risk quantification for establishing a contingency/reserve allowance needs to address the cost for likely scope change. These include long-range cost and economic studies and surety (bonding) estimates.

---

4   Hollmann, J, "Risk Analysis and Contingency Estimating for Class 10 Estimates," AACE International Transactions, 2022.

Long-Range Cost and Economic Study Estimates

Study estimates are part of special studies developed to understand the cost and risk of potential future investments and to support structured long-range investment economics and sustainability evaluations. They typically use life cycle cost estimating or analysis (LCCE/A) to support current investment funding, loan, borrowing rate, or other decisions, or for portfolio or systems management. This management considers current and future investments, such as additions, expansions, systems growth, technology evolution, rehabilitation, replacement, restoration, closure, and so on.

There are three typical cost and investment economic study types using long-range estimates of future projects:

- ◆ Single project: A one-off study estimate for a single future project (e.g., a project to build a facility in year X).
- ◆ Multi-project, single alternative asset using LCCE: Multiple projects and estimates to build, maintain, and decommission a facility in years X, Y, and Z. The LCCE feeds a probabilistic NPV calculation.
- ◆ Multi-project, multi-alternative asset options with multiple project LCCEs: Similar to the above but for multi-asset options. LCCEs feed multiple probabilistic NPV calculations for comparisons of the options.

One focus of this chapter is on the risk quantification methods and contingency/reserve allowance determination for the projects within these studies, including potential scope change and strategic risks for each investment.

Surety Estimates

Surety estimates and contingency/reserve allowance quantification determine amounts for insurance reinstatement, bonding, escrow, or other financial liability or assurance instruments to cover the future cost of required investments (for example, asset or facility closure/decommissioning to comply with regulatory requirements). A difference with economic studies is that surety estimates are typically updated repeatedly over the asset life cycle (e.g., every 5 to 10 years).

In surety use, traditional Class 5 estimates and risk quantification methods are used wherein a conceptual scope (allowing for alternatives within that scope) is defined. There is no expectation that a given estimate will cover the cost of project scope change, even though such change is expected in the long range. Instead, scope change is addressed in later surety estimate updates as the asset life cycle progresses. These estimates are not used as the basis to approve or commit to an overall investment amount but to support a narrow surety need, and in general, to assure the current enterprise financial condition is sound until the next surety review. In short, surety estimates are long-range but estimated in the same way as traditional Class 5 estimates.

Probabilistic Decision Analysis Method Context

Before defining risk quantification methods for project contingency/reserve allowance in the aforementioned study use cases, it is useful to further understand the decision analysis context these methods may be part of. Most probabilistic decision analysis (DA) methods fall into the multi-input, multi-alternative use case described above. These DA methods use long-range project estimates (CAPEX) as inputs to NPV, but the uncertainty of each of the various input project cost estimates is not usually a focus of DA methods. Volume 1, Chapter 5 covers investment decision making using decision models and risk quantification focused on NPV. The following common probabilistic DA methods are recapitulated here to avoid flipping back to Volume 1:

- ♦ Sensitivity analysis,
- ♦ Scenario analysis with MCS, and
- ♦ Decision tree analysis with MCS.

Sensitivity Analysis

The definitions of the terms sensitivity and sensitivity analysis in AACE RP 10S-90 are:

- ♦ Sensitivity: The degree to which a change in an element of a model affects the outcome.
- ♦ Sensitivity Analysis: A test of the outcome of an analysis by altering one or more parameters from an initially assumed value(s).

Sensitivity analysis involves altering an input to a model to see the impact on the output. It is a simple concept and most often applied to a current, often detailed, estimate. For cost, an example is varying construction labor rates to see how they impact the total project cost. For an NPV study, an example is varying (e.g., entering lows/highs) the time-to-market, revenue, OPEX, CAPEX, and other NPV inputs, resulting in a tornado diagram ranking these inputs in terms of how much they drive the NPV. Sensitivity analysis is used to show which uncertainties are contributing most to the outcome's (usually NPV) variability. They are also used as a quality assurance step before running MCS to obtain cumulative probability curves.

Expert assessment of the uncertainties *must be done correctly* and documented *before* the sensitivity analysis can be done. Skinner[5] and Charlesworth[6] both devote entire chapters to this topic (chapters ten and six, respectively). Leach warns against simply adding arbitrary amounts (e.g., +/– 10%) to and from the median value.[7]

Avoid using narrow, unrealistic rules-of-thumb or subjective plus/minus ranges in addressing the uncertainty of time-to-market (project duration) and CAPEX (project cost) inputs. Low positions in the tornado diagram result when the ranges are unrealistic. Cost and schedule uncertainties then receive little subsequent attention (revenue tends to get the focus). Investment decision quality suffers.

The subject matter expert assessment protocol at first seems onerous, but once experts get used to going through it, they usually prefer the assessment process. Instead of being tied to a single number estimate that they know is either too high or too low, a credible range of potential outcomes is developed and the rationale for their thinking is documented.

Scenario Analysis with MCS

The definitions of the terms scenario and scenario analysis in AACE RP 10S-90 are:

> Scenario: A description of specific events and conditions and their probable outcomes. Usually limited to likely or probable scenarios versus all possible ones. Frequently, most likely, best case, and worst case scenarios are used to define the most probable outcome and the range of outcomes.

> Scenario Analysis: Methods to assess a range of events, conditions, and outcomes employing specific scenarios. An alternative to simulation methods for assessing ranges.

---

5   Skinner, David, *Introduction to Decision Analysis*, Third Edition, Probabilistic Publishing, 2009.

6   Charlesworth, David, *Decision Analysis for Managers*, Second Edition, Business Expert Press, 2013.

7   Leach, Patrick, *Why Can't You Just Give Me The Number?*, Second Edition, Probabilistic Publishing, 2014, page 33.

Scenario analysis involves applying a model multiple times, with each run using inputs that together reflect artifacts of the selected scenario so that you can see the range of impacts on the output. This is a "big picture" or strategic approach, making scenario analysis more suited to long-range planning than sensitivity analysis. Scenarios can reflect a wide range of future states. Expert input should be obtained to help define the scenarios and *must* be obtained to assess uncertainty ranges.

A common use today is to consider different carbon reduction and climate change scenarios, which may affect many inputs to an NPV or economic cost model, including variations in facility design and construction cost. The concept starts with multiple cost estimates for the respective scenarios, defining appropriate inputs for the scenario, and comparing the respective NPV outputs. This can be done probabilistically at two levels. The most common approach is to use MCS by entering the inputs to each scenario model as probability distributions rather than discrete values, thus obtaining an output distribution for each scenario for comparison rather than discrete outcomes. At this level, scenario analysis is used to develop insights and communicate risk rather than for funding.

At the second level, a simple decision tree can be set up wherein each scenario is assigned a probability for its occurrence (usually with stakeholder and expert input). After running MCS, the output will be a single NPV distribution. Expert uncertainty assessments must be obtained for each uncertainty feeding the MCS, including capital cost and schedule.

Decision Tree with MCS

Decision trees for analyzing NPV for investment decision making are covered in Volume 1, Chapter 5, with Figure 5.2 providing an illustration. The definition of the term decision tree in AACE RP 10S-90 is:

> Decision tree: A graphical representation of the decision process. Sequential decisions are drawn in the form of branches of a tree, stemming from an initial decision point and extending all the way to final outcomes. Each path through branches of the tree represents a separate series of decisions and probabilistic events.

At its simplest, a decision tree may have only the decision node and two chance nodes, each with two discrete outcomes and probabilities of those outcomes occurring. The valuation of the chance node is simply its expected value, i.e., the sum of the products of the discrete probabilities and outcomes. For a cost-based decision, the decision maker would choose the chance node with the lowest expected monetary value. MCS is applied by replacing fixed outcome values with distributions. In Volume 1, Chapter 5, the decision tree is used for deciding between different investment alternatives based on NPV. The use of this concept for project cost risk quantification is discussed in the next section.

The DA/QRA Gap

Before delving into QRA methods for Class 10 and 5 estimates, it is essential to understand the wide variation found in the roles and capabilities of business-oriented Decision Analysis (DA) versus project-level Quantitative Risk Analysis (QRA) and why this distinction matters. Ideally, the business DA function and project QRA functions should be capable and well-aligned, working towards the same objective of risk-informed decision making. This alignment is common in international oil and gas, chemical, pharmaceutical, and other process companies and agencies with a relatively steady stream of strategic capital investments.

However, it is common to find smaller firms or agencies with only intermittent strategic capital investment concerns. In such cases, the business unit's DA function often covers only the basics of NPV modeling, with limited insight into actual project cost and schedule behavior under risk. Meanwhile, the project-level QRA capabilities are typically focused on contingency estimating, often prepared by a contractor with a "just give me the (p50) number" mindset. This is because business and project management are primarily concerned with that specific figure. For these less capable firms, risk assessment is simplified to using "standard" contingencies and range percentages they have somehow come to know, applied to a single favored scope option.

Understanding this is important because project risk analysts, armed with the knowledge and methods from this book and chapter, may face an ethical dilemma. This dilemma arises when, at the Class 5 gate, the business and its DA function seem unconcerned with the uncertainty associated with the fact that there are always viable scope alternatives. Should you simply deliver "the number" for a dictated scope (ignoring this chapter) or question whether there is strategic ignorance or misrepresentation of the risk?

For example, while working on this chapter, I encountered the following situations:

♦ A government entity developing a mega rail project with a duration of over 10 years wanted a QRA of the project cost but instructed that the possibility of evolving scope over that extended time period not be considered.

♦ A business provided a (normally confidential) copy of its draft business case report where the range information on capex and the start of service assumed numbers different from the team's risk analysis. They assumed high of +25% versus QRA results of almost double that. When questioned, the business's response was, "These are the values we use in NPV modeling."

The hope of this chapter is that project analysts, backed by this book as a reference and armed with simple methods and tools, can engage in discussions with the business and their DA function to develop a better approach to risk-informed decision-making.

Risk Quantification Methods for Unclassified/ Class 10 and Class 5 Estimates

Business planning groups do not expect that strategic long-range LCCE/A or other study input estimates will ever be used directly for project funding or other individual commitments. They usually do not perceive a need for rigor in project CAPEX contingency/reserve allowance determination; rule-of-thumb plus/minus or subjective ranges are viewed as sufficient. The prevailing thinking is that nobody will remember or use the project input number later in its own right. In some cases, that will be true.

However, in ongoing portfolio or systems management, these LCCE/A results will be revisited, projects will eventually enter the formal phase-gate queue, and inevitably past project cost values (i.e., "the number," which can drive anchoring bias) will be recalled. The cost engineering objective should be to use fit-for-use, practical risk quantification methods available to produce more reliable results given how far off from reality rules-of-thumb are.

In any case, the estimator/analyst should start analyses by ensuring clarity regarding stakeholder expectations and objectives for the risk quantification and what is to be communicated about risk. Optimally, portfolio management and LCC study processes with appropriate estimate and risk quantification methods, quality requirements, documentation (i.e., basis of estimate), historical data capture, and other elements will be established.

The following summarizes three practical risk quantification methods for determining the risk profile and contingency/reserve allowance values for long-range estimates. They apply to Unclassified/Class 10 estimates, but also to standard phase-gate Class 5 project estimates with viable alternatives within the bounds of the business scope. Note that ValidRisk® software can apply all three (see Chapter 7 in this Volume). These methods are listed in order of increasing levels of long-range uncertainty and risks on the project:

1. Calibrated Parametric Model (Volume 1, Chapter 11): Primarily for more repetitive portfolio projects (e.g., water system growth) where past life cycle data has been captured for use in calibration.

2. Modified Hybrid Parametric plus Expected Value (P+EV: Volume 1, Chapter 11/12): Adds scope variation and strategic risks, along with critical risks; primarily for more unique projects, but with relatively stable foreseen futures.

3. Decision Tree with Scope and/or Scenario Variation Branches (Volume 1, Chapter 5): Primarily for projects with higher complexity and more dynamic external risk situations.

Calibrated Parametric Model

This approach is the same as in Volume 1, Chapter 11 (reference AACE RP 42R-08), which already addresses the need to calibrate a base parametric model to align with a company's experience. The AACE RP provides guidelines for performing calibration, as does Chapter 7 (in regards to ValidRisk software). It is recognized that few companies will have life cycle data to develop a parametric model from scratch using regression analysis. However, it is common and expected practice to calibrate existing models where there is some nominal level of actual/estimate cost data available to do so.

For long-range planning, it is most likely that data will be available for utilities and others who have decades of experience in water, power, transport, or other system planning with relatively *repetitive asset and project types using technology that improves with time, but usually not dramatically so.* The data needed, as discussed in RP 42R-08, is actual/estimate cost data normalized to remove the effect of escalation.

The calibrated parametric model will address the typical systemic risks for Class 5 estimates as well as the long-range scope variation and strategic risk impacts covered by the calibration factors. The calibrated model documentation should clearly note the limitations of using the calibrated parametric model with *descriptions of the types of scope variation observed* in the calibration study. Avoid extrapolating beyond that experience. The model will produce overall project cost and schedule distributions from which a contingency/reserve allowance value can be determined as well as the range for sensitivity analysis. If capital planning indicates that known or likely significant scope change or strategic risks will emerge, the next two methods are preferable.

Modified Hybrid Parametric Plus Expected Value (Modified P+EV)

This method is the same as in Volume 1, Chapters 11 and 12 (refer to AACE RP 113R-20), except that the definition of "critical risks" includes long-range scope variation and strategic risks and their cost impacts. The parametric model, optimally calibrated as discussed previously, will address typical systemic risks for Class 5 estimates and nominal scope change. The EV model will address potential, more significant identified scope changes and strategic risks. Long-range risks would be identified using a workshop approach, involving appropriate business and technical staff in the associated portfolio or long-range planning.

This approach is suitable for long-range projects with more unique, identified scope variations and/or strategic risks than are typical in more repetitive system planning (where the calibrated parametric method alone might suffice). However, these projects should still have *a relatively stable foreseeable future with limited long-range scope change and strategic risk drivers identified*. If there are more than a few discrete long-range risks, the method becomes unwieldy and the quantification less reliable.

Decision Tree with Scope and/or Scenario Variation Branches

This method is a variation of the example in Volume 1, Chapter 5. AACE RP 85R-14 provides the basics of the general decision tree method, although not in a project risk quantification context.[8] Volume 1, Chapter 5 addresses quantifying the uncertainty of NPV

---

8   AACE International, Recommended Practice 85R-14: "Use of Decision Trees in Decision Making," (latest revision).

for investment decision analysis. For contingency/reserve allowance determination, the output is project cost.

There are two use cases:

♦ Unclassified/Class 10 estimates – Scenarios: The branches represent alternate scenarios or strategic risks.

♦ Class 5 estimates – Scope Alternatives: The branches represent viable, identified scope alternatives. The decision tree method should be used for every FEL Class 5 estimate where such alternatives exist.

For practical project risk quantification, the decision tree is usually fairly simple. Figure 6.1 shows an example two-branch tree (although there could be more branches). This example assumes the involvement of a business DA function closely engaged with the project risks analyst. The example is described as follows:

♦ Cost: We're determining a budget-quality CAPEX number to include in the forecast. The tree can either be solved directly, which will yield a cumulative probability tree similar to Figure 5.3, Volume 1, or MCS can be run, which will yield a smooth distribution like Figure 5.4, Volume 1.

♦ Business Environment: Looking forward, the subject matter expert(s) see two differing business environments in the future: Y, and Z. The probability of Y happening is estimated to be 40%; Z is therefore 60%.

♦ Alternatives A and B: Subject matter experts are assessed on the favorability of each alternative given Business Environments Y and Z. Assessment results are shown in the tree: Business Environment Y results in a 90% probability that Alternative A will be favored in the future.

♦ Project risk analysts perform QRA using appropriate methods (including input from subject matter experts) to determine the cost distribution that is simplified here using 3-points ($p10/p50/p90$).[9] If these distributions are affected by Business Environment, they will need to be assessed for each Business Environment and both alternatives.

---

9   This paper describes a 3-point distribution that can replicate distributions with long tails such as Lognormal: Hollmann, J, and J Eric Bickel, "Defining a Lognormal Distribution Using 3-Point Entry: The J-QPD Distribution," AACE International Transactions, 2024.

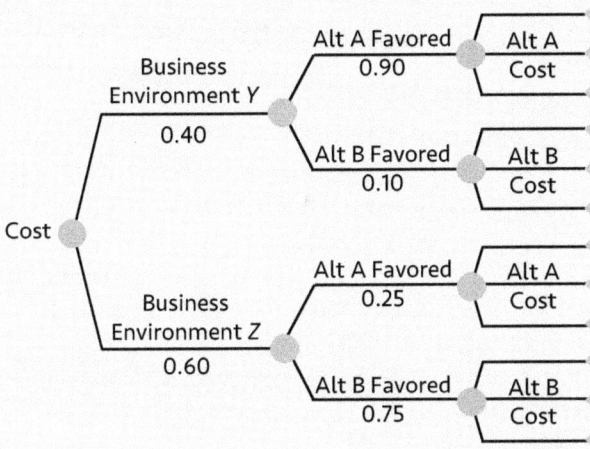

Figure 6.1. Example of a Decision Tree for Project Risk Quantification

After the cumulative probability distribution for cost has been plotted, the decision makers should be engaged to determine what p number they are comfortable using for determining the CAPEX number that will be carried forward in the budget. Optionally, you could use the $p90$ (nominal worst case) to be conservative. However, a realistic QRA may produce a high value that results in a negative NPV. More typically, it would be set using company contingency policy (i.e., the mean or $p50$) but with the range well documented in the business case.

Example Scenario with Limited Business DA Engagement

This example assumes the business DA function is not closely engaged. Scenarios such as the business environment are not considered, and the scope options are only known to the risk analyst. In this case, there are three alternative scopes. The project risk analyst can still reasonably address the overall cost uncertainty presented by those alternatives and hope that the analysis will engage the business's interest.

This example provides a spreadsheet application shown in Figure 6.2 that readers can experiment with. The model is easy to apply in a spreadsheet using an MCS add-on such as Lumivero @Risk®. This simple capability is also built into ValidRisk® (see Chapter 7).

In the example, there are three scope alternatives (numbered 1, 2, and 3) for which the probabilities of occurrence or selection (i.e., the favorability ratings) are entered. In MCS, the scenario/alternative occurrence/selection choice was set up as a "discrete" function such that in each MCS iteration, one of the three choices will be selected in accordance with the respective probabilities.

Next, separate risk quantification analyses are conducted for each project scenario or alternative using the P+EV method. In the example, the P+EV outputs are represented by three triangular distributions. The triangular distributions include an "IF" function that refers to the discrete sampling function, which picks either option 1, 2, or 3 in each MCS iteration. The three option result cells are summed, with the summation being identified as the MCS output for use in determining the contingency/reserve allowance.

	A	B	C	D	E	F	G	H
1	Scenario or Alternative			1	2	3		
2	Occurrence or Selection Chance			%	%	%	(add to 100%)	
3				A	A:=RiskDiscrete((1,2,3),D2:F2)			
4	Scenario or Alternative							
5		L	$ or mos					
6	1	ML	$ or mos	B	B:=IF(D\$3=1,RiskTriang(C5,C6,C7),0)			
7		H	$ or mos					
8								
9		L	$ or mos					
10	2	ML	$ or mos	C	C:=IF(D\$3=2,RiskTriang(C9,C10,C11),0)			
11		H	$ or mos					
12								
13		L	$ or mos					
14	3	ML	$ or mos	D	D:=IF(D\$3=3,RiskTriang(C13,C14,C15),0)			
15		H	$ or mos					
16								
17				E	E:=RiskOutput("total")+D6+D10+D14			

Figure 6.2: Example Decision Tree with MCS Model (using Lumivero's @Risk for Excel)

Chapter 9 (Section 9A) includes a more detailed worked example of using the methodology on a Class 5 estimate.

Decision Tree for Scenarios: Unclassified/Class 10

For Unclassified/Class 10 scenario modeling, the approach begins with a scenario identification process as described in an AACE paper. This process involves three steps:

(1) Identify external factors that could affect project execution.

(2) Focus on internal uncertainties or trends.

(3) Define two to four plausible situational scenarios, avoiding low-probability scenarios.

It also suggests grouping external factors and key uncertainties into a narrative or storyboard to facilitate communication and consensus on the analysis. Although this process is not perfect, it is more robust than analyzing a single base case. A practical approach is to quantify three branches representing low, most likely, and high-cost scenarios.

For instance, in a low/most likely/high scenario identification process, the low project cost scenario might assume no regulation changes and a step change in technology, resulting in the project costing half of the current technology. The high project cost scenario might include regulation changes and a more complex process without technological benefits. The most likely project cost scenario might represent only nominal changes in regulations and technology (status quo). The team would then define conceptual project scopes and prepare Class 5 estimates aligned with these three scenarios. Parametric risk quantification might be applied to each project to determine the cost distribution for each scenario. Finally, the team would quantify the probability of these scenarios occurring.

Decision Tree for Scope Alternatives: Class 5

For Class 5 estimates with viable scope alternatives, the modeling approach begins with the team identifying the scope alternatives and preparing Class 5 estimates for each using typical base estimating practices. Teams often screen alternatives to a manageable set (e.g., fewer than five). If only one option exists (e.g., a repeat process unit train addition project), then a default selection has already been made, and decision tree analysis is not needed.

For example, a hydropower project may have multiple viable alternatives for dam impoundment types and geometry, with the geometry choice depending on geotechnical studies to be conducted in the next scope development phase. Typical Class 5 estimates would be prepared for each alternative, and P+EV risk quantification would be done for each estimate. The team would then assess the probabilities of selecting each alternative, which are expected to depend on the outcomes of the geotechnical study. Both project cost and duration risk can be evaluated this way.

The mode of the output distribution of a decision tree model with MCS will typically be similar to that of a P+EV analysis that considers only the favored alternative. However, if one of the alternatives is more costly than the others, the $p95$ value will be greater than the favored case approach, indicating more tail risk. The extent of this increase depends on the cost and the probability of selecting the high-cost case. Since capital investment decisions often rely on NPV or similar sensitivity analysis, the worst-case CAPEX (e.g., $p95$) is crucial for making risk-aware decisions, as the high value defines the capital risk profile.

Using the practical methods described above can significantly improve the realism of Class 5 estimate risk quantification and the reliability of long-range planning analyses of various types. Ensuring accurate CAPEX (project cost) and time-to-market (project duration) probabilistic inputs is essential.

Questions

1. Describe the distinguishing characteristics of long-range estimates in terms of risk and uncertainty.

2. How do some industries pre-fund future decommissioning and closure projects?

3. What type of analysis addresses the potential impact of situations like long-term changes in climate, political regimes, sustainability concerns, and so on?

4. With respect to the AACE definition of contingency, how might Class 5 estimates differ from later phase estimates?

5. For sensitivity analysis of NPV, what does the statement "the worst-case defines the risk profile" mean with respect to a tornado diagram output?

6. Explain how the decision tree method quantifies the potential cost or duration of scenarios and scope alternatives.

Volume 2 Perspective

This chapter discusses improving the understanding of risks associated with long-range projects. Around the time of Volume

1's publication, utility sector estimators pointed out that AACE's five-phase estimate classification scheme did not meet the needs for long-range capital planning of their utility systems. Other sectors, such as power and transport, echoed these concerns. This led to the creation of AACE RP 111R-20, which introduced a new Unclassified/ Class 10 estimate prepared before the phase-gate system kicks into high gear and where scope change is generally expected.

To support RP 111R-20, new risk quantification methods were needed to address scope change and scope alternative risks. The usual methods were found inappropriate. After many years of questioning why industry Class 5 estimates were so inaccurate (as shown in Volume 1, Figure 4.3), a realization emerged that base estimates were fine, but failure to quantify scope change and alternative scope risks was the major issue. Decision trees could fill this gap in the risk quantification toolkit. The paper written in 2022 and referenced in this chapter delves deeper into this practice, making it a valuable resource for understanding and applying these methods.

"Software is a great combination between artistry and engineering."
— Bill Gates

7

ValidRisk® QRA Software

At the time of Volume 1's publication, no commercial software was available for applying the QRA methods described in the book. Only custom spreadsheet-based tools with associated Monte Carlo simulation (MCS) add-ons existed, limiting potential application and interest of the methods in industry. However, in 2022, ValidRisk® cloud-based software with built-in MCS was released, eliminating the need for users to create their own tools.[1]

This chapter is *not* a sales pitch. Being the only commercial software of its kind, understanding ValidRisk's use and application is crucial for the practical and effective implementation of the methods covered in this book. ValidRisk closely follows the book's methods and steps, to the extent that the book serves as an expanded user guide and training resource (though ValidRisk includes its own tool-specific user guides).

---

1 ValidRisk® is a product that Koff & Guerrero Consultants S.A. (KGC) developed in alliance with the author. The software is described in the ValidRisk.com website. At the time of writing, the software was offered on an annual license fee per nominated user basis.

KGC has achieved ISO 27001:2022 certification for Information Security, Cybersecurity, and Information Privacy. ValidRisk is built on the secure Microsoft Azure cloud platform.

ValidRisk software includes the following book methods:

♦ The parametric method covered in Volume 1, Chapter 11, including:

    o Systemic risk rating matrices for most asset types.

    o Calibration functionality to customize the model for specific assets.

♦ The Expected Value method covered in Volume 1, Chapter 12, including built-in Monte Carlo simulation (no third-party software required).

♦ The tipping point (non-linearity) method covered in Volume 1, Chapter 14.

♦ The program project cost consolidation method covered in Chapter 5 of this Volume.

♦ The multi-scope option method covered in Chapter 6 of this Volume.

ValidRisk does not include the following book methods:

♦ Probabilistic escalation as covered in Volume 1, Chapter 13. For this, spreadsheet tools with MCS add-ons are suggested. However, ValidRisk provides cost and schedule duration probabilistic inputs to an escalation model.

♦ CPM-based analysis as covered in Chapter 4 of this Volume. For this, Safran Risk® is suggested for the CPM elements. ValidRisk provides the parametric element of the P+CPM hybrid approach.

This chapter is intended as a kind of Rosetta Stone to help users understand how the book's methodological content translates into the ValidRisk application. For example, Volume 1, Chapter 11 on the parametric approach uses a simplified Excel® demonstration-of-concept model as the basis for its step-by-step method descriptions.[2]

---

2   The demonstration Excel parametric model is still available to book buyers. A link to it can be found on the publisher's website at www.decisions-books.com. Contact the author for the password at hollmann@validest.com or via LinkedIn or contact the publisher. ValidRisk offers a free, no-obligation trial, which is the preferred approach for getting hands-on insight into the book's methods and tools.

This chapter places the Volume 1, Chapter 11 approach in the context of industrial-duty ValidRisk software. Key content of this chapter not covered in Volume 1, Chapter 11 includes:

♦ Customization of systemic risk rating matrices to match the user's project scope definition process and asset types.

♦ Calibration of the default parametric model algorithm to align its outputs with your company's historical cost growth and schedule slip experience.

These tasks, associated with implementing ValidRisk, align it with your company's phase-gate process, making the ValidRisk parametric model a custom company model rather than a generic industry algorithm.[3, 4]

ValidRisk Implementation

Most users acquire a ValidRisk license after an online, virtual demonstration by the KGC staff, followed by a free trial period. Coordination between the IT staff of KGC and the client is usually necessary, particularly if the software is to be installed on the client's servers. However, procurement and IT business activities are not covered in this chapter. The focus here is on systemic matrix customization and model calibration activities that the client's risk quantification function should undertake, typically in consultation with the KGC partners.

Systemic Rating Matrix Customization

Volume 1, Chapter 11 covers the general systemic risk ratings used in a parametric risk quantification model, focusing on a simplified Excel demonstration model. ValidRisk offers a more extensive

---

3　An obstacle to the acceptance of parametric modeling can be the perception that *"it does not represent our assets, projects, or data"* (i.e., *"we are different"*). While the out-of-the-box model has proven to be a good fit for every industry tested (see Chapter 2 of this Volume), performing calibration will mitigate the *"it is not our data"* challenge. Calibration is recommended for all ValidRisk implementations. Note that owners with a reasonable number of past projects will have the data needed to perform calibration. See Chapter 3 concerning the limitations of data at contractor firms.

4　Supporting customization of systemic risk matrices and model calibration studies are key roles of the author in the ValidRisk alliance with KGC, along with providing training and supporting pilot QRA analysis on a consulting basis.

and customizable set of systemic attribute/risk ratings. These ratings are captured in "matrix tables" that include the systemic attribute or rating item title, followed by the phased levels of definition (e.g., Class 5, 4, or 3) or attribute ratings (e.g., A-E, 0-5, or 0-10), with narrative statements describing the status at each level.

In ValidRisk, every word of the item title and narrative statements can be customized to align with the company's vernacular, project system acronyms, and so forth. The purpose of matrix customization is to make the rating questions as clear and objective as possible, specifying what is expected of that deliverable or how an attribute is to be rated in wording that a project team can readily relate to.

Additionally, a weighting factor can be set for each scope definition item. For a given asset type, the company may feel that one or more deliverables is more or less important (e.g., P&IDs are more important than a spare parts list). Excessive relative weightings are to be avoided, but with many rating items, the average rating of a group of items will usually not change much. The wordings and weightings are not intended to be modified for specific projects.

Table 7.1 shows an example of a ValidRisk matrix item with rating narrative statements and a weight factor that can be edited. For the example item, the parametric tool will ask the user to select from rating levels A to D. The selection rule is that if every criterion in a statement is not met at that time (not tomorrow or as a promise), then the team should select the next lowest rating. The facilitator must enforce this "no-nonsense" rule to counter optimism bias. The customized narrative must therefore be specific about the important criteria while keeping the statement succinct and free of extraneous detail.

Rating: Business Leadership, Ownership, Decisiveness	Weight	5

A. LOW/DEFICIENT: Business-led team leading their own affairs with weak or deficient business sponsor focus, engagement, communication, support, responsiveness and/or decisiveness. Objectives stated but unclear as to alignment with business strategy or in other respects. Immature project system/process.
B. MEDIUM/FAIR: Fair business sponsor focus, engagement, communication, support, responsiveness and/or decisiveness. Objectives documented and generally aligned with business strategy. Moderate project system/process maturity.
C. HIGH/GOOD: Good to Excellent business sponsor focus, engagement, communication, support, responsiveness and/or decisiveness. Clear, documented, signed off objectives well aligned with business strategy. Strong project system/process.
D. N/A

Table 7.1: Example ValidRisk Systemic Rating Matrix Item

If this looks like a process quality assurance tool, that is because it is. Parametric analysis and ValidRisk combine process QA and QRA. If used on every project, the tool will drive company process improvement over time. Because ValidRisk stores each project's ratings in the applicable cloud, it also supports analytical project system analysis later.

Asset Types

When applying ValidRisk, as covered later, the user identifies the "asset type" at the start of a risk analysis. Examples of asset types include process (e.g., plants) and transport (e.g., road and rail). This distinction is important because the planning and design of each asset type require different defining scope deliverables, particularly in engineering. Many deliverables, such as the fundamentals of a good cost estimate or schedule, are universal. However, specific deliverables differ; for instance, process and instrumentation diagrams (P&IDs) are critical for process plant design but irrelevant for roadway design.

AACE International has developed many industry-specific Cost Estimate Classification Recommended Practices (RPs).[5] ValidRisk's default systemic rating matrices are aligned with these industry-specific RPs where applicable. Table 7.2 shows the ValidRisk asset type matrix and RP alignment at the time of writing.

Most companies will have projects for only three to six asset types (e.g., general, process, and pipeline). Therefore, not every matrix needs to be customized. If you have an asset type you want to add, you can modify an existing, unused matrix (e.g., offshore structures) by changing the heading, item titles, and/or narrative statements to better align with your specific asset type (substations, wind farms, etc.). Alternatively, a few items in an existing matrix, such as "process," can be edited with an "or" rating for the few deliverables that vary. For example, "For asset X [state criteria], or for asset Y [state added or different criteria]."

Working with the business units and functional departments to get input and consensus may take several meetings and a few weeks to modify/create matrices as needed. They can always be edited later as teams and analysts gain insights from using the tool.

---

5   See AACE Professional Guidance Document PGD-01, Guide to Cost Estimate Classification Systems, https://library.aacei.org/pgd01/pgd01.shtml.

VALIDRISK ASSET TYPES	AACE CLASSIFICATION RP
Process (can be modified for various types such as oil & gas, chemical, pharms, metallurgical, power plant, etc.)	18R-97: Process Industries 115R-21: Nuclear Power Industries 102R-19: Pharmaceutical and Related Industries
Mine	47R-11: Mining and Mineral Processing Industries
Pipeline	97R-18: Pipeline Transportation Infrastructure Industries
Transmission	96R-18: Power Transmission Line Infrastructure Industries
Transport	98R-18: Road and Rail Transportation Infrastructure Industries
General	56R-08: Building and General Construction Industries
Tunnels	In progress
Hydropower	69R-12: Hydropower Industries
Hazardous	107R-19: Environmental Remediation Industries
Shutdowns	112R-20: Maintenance Turnarounds for the Process Industries
Offshore Structures	87R-14: Petroleum Exploration and Production Industries
Drilling & Completion	
Subsea	

Table 7.2: ValidRisk Asset Types with associated AACE Classification RPs (as of 2024)

In matrix customization, be careful not to deviate from the tool's empirical industry research basis (e.g., Class 3 criteria must not be edited or "softened" to resemble Class 4). However, if systemic matrix customization is done before calibration (next section), any deviation from the industry research basis will be corrected by the calibration (i.e., a calibrated tool will always reflect the company's experience).

Finally, ValidRisk allows unique calibration factors to be set for each asset type. For example, a pipeline company may have different project entities and behaviors for their pipelines versus their facilities (e.g., compressor stations). Another example is power utilities, which usually have separate business units for power generation and power transmission. Each asset-focused entity is likely to have its own project culture and varied external context (governmental, regulatory, social, economic, etc.).

Model Calibration Background

Lognormal Algorithms

ValidRisk's parametric tool is built upon two base algorithm sets that generate lognormal distributions for percentage project cost growth (difference from the base estimate) and percentage execution duration slip (growth and slip are percent differences from the base estimate and duration). Note that it predicts percentages, not absolute costs (i.e., cost outputs are the result of multiplying the percentages by the base cost or duration). The algorithms are based on the research summarized in Volume 1, Chapter 11.

There are separate sub-algorithms for the means and standard deviations (SD) of the lognormal distribution (e.g., the "bias" parameter may only significantly drive the mean distribution, not the SD). As discussed in Volume 1, Chapter 15 and Chapter 2 of this Volume, the uncalibrated models for cost growth and duration slip have proven to be generically applicable to most asset types and projects. However, there may be differences within a company, which is where calibration comes in.

Small Projects are Different

Small project systems almost always have an "over-estimate and under-run (OEUR)" culture, and the base model, based on research of major projects, must be calibrated for them (see Chapter 4 of Volume 1 for discussion of small project cost accuracy). ValidRisk is set up to make the small vs. large distinction and asks the user at the start of a risk analysis whether a project is large or small. Because the ValidRisk parametric model is easy and quick to apply, small project systems with limited overhead budgets and overstretched teams find great value in it, *but only after a calibration study*. Because there are so many small projects, finding current data for the calibration study is rarely a problem for owners. No universal small project calibration factors apply because OEUR cultural biases can vary widely.[6]

---

6   Users have a choice of including small project bias into the algorithm using calibration factors or requiring teams to rate small project estimates as highly conservative project-by-project. However, if the behavior is ubiquitous for an organization, it is generally recommended to address small project bias through calibration. Teams will be reluctant to state that their estimates are so biased.

What is a Small Project?

The main distinction between small and large project systems is that project managers (PMs) and team members on small projects work on multiple projects (often three or more, but sometimes over ten) at the same time. The projects are managed on a portfolio basis where meeting annual portfolio cash flow budget (predictability) is a primary objective. They tend to be sustaining projects. Large projects, often strategic, usually have dedicated PMs and core teams putting all their time into that one project, and the business objective is the least absolute cost and duration (effectiveness) for a given asset output. In cost and duration terms, small projects are usually less than $5 to 20 million and six to eighteen months in execution duration; however, the real distinction is in the objectives and teams. The Pareto principle tends to apply where small projects for an owner make up about 80 percent of the number of projects but only about 20 percent of the total capital expenditures.

Large Projects

Experience from supporting many calibration studies shows that the default model works well for most large projects (at least after considering the statistical significance of any delta found in a study). However, for a given company, business unit, or asset type, there may be unexplained deviations in cost and/or duration mean (e.g., bias) and/or SD (range) behavior. As mentioned, the parametric method supports process QA, and this is no exception. Deviations in behavior flag the need to study the practices used or events occurring to find the cause of the deviation and address it appropriately.

Operations

When setting up ValidRisk for use, the tool steward first defines the "Operations" that own the projects. At multinational firms, this usually reflects some combination of region and business unit (usually product-focused) entities. For example, "Country X, Metal Y Mining." Each company will have a unique structure. In addition to supporting reporting and possibly portfolio analytics (all analyses are captured in the applicable cloud), the calibration factors are applied by Operations as well as by asset type, as discussed previously. Each Operation is likely to have its own project culture and varied external context (governmental, regulatory, social, economic, etc.).

ValidRisk Calibration Capability

The result of calibration is a set of calibration factors (CFs) applied to the mean and SD of the base algorithms. CFs are not proportional; a factor of 2.0 on the mean will not double the mean of the lognormal distribution. CFs are defined by Operation, Asset Type, and Size (small vs. large). This three-way entry allows for a fair degree of CF specificity. For example, a pipeline company could have separate gas and liquids operations that have the same general asset types (pipelines and facilities) but different project system behaviors.[7] A calibration study needs to analyze the cost growth and duration slip experience by operation, asset, and project size group datasets.

CFs	OPERATION: XYZ							
ASSET TYPE	COST				SCHEDULE			
	Mean		Std. Deviation		Mean		Std. Deviation	
	Small	Large	Small	Large	Small	Large	Small	Large
Process	0.8	1.0	1.3	1.0	1.0	1.0	1.2	1.0
Mine	0.8	1.0	1.3	1.0	1.0	1.0	1.2	1.0
Pipeline	0.8	1.0	1.3	1.0	1.0	1.0	1.2	1.0
Transmission	0.8	1.0	1.3	1.0	1.0	1.0	1.2	1.0
Transport	0.8	1.0	1.3	1.0	1.0	1.0	1.2	1.0
General	0.8	1.0	1.3	1.0	1.0	1.0	1.2	1.0
Tunnels	0.8	1.0	1.3	1.0	1.0	1.0	1.2	1.0
Hydropower	0.8	1.0	1.3	1.0	1.0	1.0	1.2	1.0
Hazardous	0.8	1.0	1.3	1.1	1.0	1.0	1.2	1.1
Shutdowns	0.8	1.1	1.3	1.1	1.0	1.0	1.2	1.1
Offshore Structures	0.8	1.0	1.3	1.0	1.0	1.0	1.2	1.0
Drilling & Completion	0.8	1.0	1.3	1.0	1.0	1.0	1.2	1.0
Subsea	0.8	1.0	1.3	1.0	1.0	1.0	1.2	1.0

Table 7.3: ValidRisk Calibration Input Screen for a Selected Operation

---

7   The "Operations" or major business units in large companies never have identical project systems, processes, practices, organizations, or cultures. Most large companies evolve through mergers, acquisitions, reorganizations, and so on. This is dynamic. My rule-of-thumb is that corporate structures, and the Vice Presidents that lead them, have a half-life of 18 months; i.e., within 18 months, half of the organizations will go through a major change. Calibration factors need to be updated.

After the calibration study, the resulting CFs are entered in ValidRisk. This is done by Operation. Table 7.3 shows how ValidRisk CFs are entered in a table for illustration purposes.

Model Calibration Steps

Calibration Overview

Calibration involves:

♦ Calculating actual, normalized project cost growth and duration slip metrics (actual/base estimate)[8] for a dataset,

♦ Applying the base parametric model to get the predicted metric distribution,

♦ Comparing the actual distribution of sample metrics to the predicted distribution, and, if significantly different,

♦ Determining mean and SD calibration factors that result in a close distribution match.

This can be done with varying levels of statistical rigor, such as conducting t-tests to determine whether distribution differences are statistically significant, or using a more practical visual distribution comparison approach.

The first step before calibration is setting up the Operations scheme in ValidRisk and customizing the applicable asset type matrices. This will determine the datasets needed to support the development of calibration factors.

Datasets for Calibration

Creating calibration study datasets with enough reasonably recent projects to yield statistically significant results for a given operation/asset combination is challenging. As a rule of thumb, as discussed in Volume 1, Chapter 10 regarding regression analysis, a minimum sample size of five is desired, but ten or more is much better. Additionally, datasets must be for a given estimate phase (i.e., for nominal Class 5, 4, and 3). For example, a company with five operations and two main asset types in each, and a typical phase-gate system, would need an overall database of 100 projects (5 x 2 x 10) with two or three phased estimates each to cover different possible situations.

---

8   Base Estimates exclude contingency, reserves, and escalation. ValidRisk predicts cost growth and schedule slip from the base (the estimator's view), *not* from the funded amount (the business view).

If the only estimates available are from the sanction gate (usually Class 3 or 2), it will not be possible to ascertain whether the resulting CFs are reasonably balanced across all phases. Also, the projects in a sample should be somewhat independent. For example, a sample of five clone projects done in series by the same team would not be a good sample. Similarly, there should be a variety of complexities. In short, the larger and more varied the sample, the better the calibration.

Identifying Study Projects

Having determined the operation and asset structure, the next step is to identify study projects for use in the calibration. Each operation/asset combination should have five or more observations, optimally for each estimate class. Many companies skip phases for some or all projects (e.g., only Class 5 and 3 gates), shortcut the process (e.g., straight to Class 3), or some phase data is lost, so for a set of projects, there will be different numbers of observations for each class of estimate, with Class 5 usually having the least, and sanction the most. While it is desirable to have recently completed projects executed under the current organization and project system regime (say the last 3-5 years), it may be necessary to include older projects to find enough projects to study. Having a variety of projects (e.g., various complexities) is advantageous.

Be prepared to compromise; very few have a vast amount of data. It is better to determine CFs for a blend of operations or assets than to give up on the task because the datasets are too small for each combination. If calibration is updated annually, the datasets will grow. In the worst case, using ValidRisk without CFs will provide generally reliable results (at least more so than subjective QRA alternative methods).

Data Capture, Normalization, and Metric Calculation

Having identified the projects, the next step is to capture the data. The data required is not highly detailed. Data such as the sanctioned cost and date, actual capital cost, and the completion date can be quickly retrieved from accounting. The rest is usually found in department files from phase-gate reviews, from estimating and scheduling files, and from project close-out reports. Optimally, the company will have a project historical database (Volume 1, Chapter 18).

Tables 7.4 (a) through (d) illustrate the structure of a data collection form (usually using Excel) split into sections for illustration.

Each project will have one row. Notes follow each table describing the data columns and calculations required.

	ESTIMATES (BASE COST AND PLANNED DURATION)						
	CLASS 5			CLASS 4	CLASS 3	CLASS 2	
	Base Cost	Est Basis	Dura-tion	REPEAT COLUMNS AT LEFT FOR EACH CLASS OF ESTIMATE AND SCHEDULE			
	$m	Year	Months				
Project A							

Table 7.4(a): Data collection form: Estimates

Table 7.4(a) notes:

♦ The base cost excludes contingency, reserves and escalation. If only total cost records are available, then make reasonable assumptions as to what contingency, reserves, and escalation may have been included, and deduct them.

♦ The estimate basis date is the year that the base cost represents.

♦ The duration excludes explicit overall contingency buffer duration (not common).

	ACTUALS (COST AND SCHEDULE)						
	COST AND SCHEDULE			ADJUSTMENTS			
	Total Cost	Start Detailed Design	Finish Mech Complete	Major Business Scope Change		Critical Risk Impacts	
	$M	Year	Year	$M	Months	$M	Months
Project A (cont'd)							

Table 7.4(b): Data collection form: Actuals

Table 7.4(b) notes:

♦ The total actual cost is usually recorded in accounting.

♦ The start and end dates are from the start of detailed design through mechanical completion (i.e., the "execution phase" duration).

♦ The parametric model excludes major scope changes and critical (extreme) risk impacts. Search the project close out records and change logs. Rough approximations of the cost and duration of scope changes (+ or -) and risk event impacts (+) is good enough. Teams tend to remember the big ones.

	CALCULATED FIELDS AND METRICS														
	Adjusted Actual Cost & Duration		Mid-point Spend	Normalized Estimates (escalated to mid-point spend) ($M)				Adjusted Actual Cost/Normalized Estimate (metric)				Adjusted Actual Duration/Estimated Duration (metric)			
	$M	Mos	Year	C5	C4	C3	C2	C5	C4	C3	C2	C5	C4	C3	C2
Project A (cont'd)															

Table 7.4(c): Data collection form: Calculated Fields and Metrics

Table 7.4(c) notes:

♦ The adjusted actual cost and duration are the actual values plus or minus the major scope change and critical risk impact amounts as appropriate.

♦ The mid-point of spending year can be approximated as being half of the way between the start and completion years. The base estimate will be normalized to this year.

♦ See Normalization (next section).

♦ The metrics are the cost growth and execution duration slip as a ratio of actual/normalized estimate. These are usually >1.0. For example, a value of 1.20 means the project used or needed 20% contingency.

	APPROXIMATE PARAMETRIC MODEL INPUT RATINGS						
	Asset Type	New Tech.	Process Complexity	Execution Complexity	% Major Equipment	% Fixed $ (FID est only)	Bias
Project A (cont'd)							

Table 7.4(d): Approximate Parametric Model Input Ratings

Table 7.4(d) notes:

♦ If ValidRisk was not used in the past, these ratings, in the format used by ValidRisk, will have to be retrospectively approximated based on analyst and team recollection and interpretation of project reports and records. The average of these values will be used for a given operation/asset group of projects, so the more projects, the better.

♦ Note that the metrics for each Class of estimate are calculated separately, so the key level of definition risk driver is addressed explicitly.

Normalization

The base estimate values represent the recorded "basis" year in Table 7.4(a) and exclude escalation. However, the actual costs will have experienced escalation. To remove the effect of escalation from the actual costs (to get estimate and actuals on an apples-to-apples basis), the estimate costs should be escalated to the mid-point of the spending year. To do this, create a price index table by year using a historical price index representative of capital project costs. Refer to Volume 1, Chapter 13 for a discussion of indices. Using Excel lookup functions, set up a formula in the Table 7.4(c) "Normalized Estimate" cells that multiplies the base estimate by the ratio of the price index at the mid-point of the spending year over the price index at the estimate basis year. The normalized estimate value is then used in the cost actual/normalized estimate metric calculation.

Putting Metrics Data into a Table for Analysis

The calculated metrics data in Table 7.4(c) is next sorted into a form such as Table 7.5, where each estimate is a separate row. The project rows can be grouped by operation and asset group. Table 7.5 uses a function to copy the metrics into estimate class columns on the right to facilitate vertical summation and statistics calculation, which is done by class.

METRICS LISTED BY ESTIMATE				COST (ACT/ESTIMATE)			DURATION (ACT/EST)		
Project	Est Class	Act/Est Cost	Act/Est Duration	C5	C4	C3	C5	C4	C3
Operations X / Asset Group Y									
A	3	1.12	1.08			1.12			1.08
B	4	1.33	1.17		1.33			1.17	
B	3	1.08	0.98			1.08			0.98
C	5	1.76	1.31	1.76			1.31		
C	4	1.24	1.15		1.24			1.15	
C	3	1.18	1.04			1.18			1.04

Table 7.5: Metrics Data in Table Format for Analysis

Data Analysis/Calibration Factor Determination

AACE Recommended Practice RP 42R-08 ("Risk Analysis and Contingency Determination Using Parametric Estimating") describes a calibration approach. The following is a similar and practical and effective approach using traditional actual/estimate metrics (rather than inversed estimate/actual) and employing a visual comparison analysis without the t-test.

Step 1: Determine the Actual Metric Distributions

Using the data analysis worksheet of Table 7.5, and the data corresponding to the operations/asset group of interest, determine the $p10$, $p50$, and $p90$ values of the actual cost and duration metrics for each class of estimate in the Table 7.5 right-hand columns.

Step 2: Determine the Model Prediction Distribution

Run the ValidRisk systemic model (uncalibrated) for a dummy project using the average of the Table 7.4(d) comparison dataset systemic risk ratings as model inputs. For ratings not in the table, assume company-wide average ratings (e.g., Project Controls is 3 on a scale of 0 to 5 for the whole company). When entering the level of scope definition systemic ratings in ValidRisk, do not assume ideal achievement; actual definition almost always lags the optimal. For example, overall project definition ratings are typically 5, 4.4, 3.3, and 3.0 for nominal Class 5, 4, 3, and 2 estimates, respectively (most companies fail to record their Class 5 estimates, if any).

After the representative ratings are entered into ValidRisk, record the predicted $p10$, $p50$, and $p90$ values for cost and duration, which will be in percentages. Convert those to a ratio by adding 1.00 to the decimal percent (e.g., 20% cost growth is a ratio of 1.20).

Step 3: Compare the Actual and Predicted Distributions

Record the actual and predicted metrics in a table such as Table 7.6. The table shown is just for cost; do one for schedule duration as well. In the first go-around, the predicted values will be based on the uncalibrated ValidRisk systemic model (CFs of 1.00).

OPERATION X/AS-SET Y		COST GROWTH: ACTUAL			COST GROWTH: PREDICTED		
		Class 5	Class 4	Class 3	Class 5	Class 4	Class 3
Calibration Factors (CFs)	Mean				1.00	1.00	1.00
	StDev				1.25	1.25	1.25
	p10	0.85	0.87	0.82	0.73	0.79	0.84
	p50	1.16	1.10	0.96	1.14	1.07	0.97
	p90	1.83	1.52	1.18	1.81	1.44	1.14

Table 7.6: Actual vs. Predicted Cost Growth by Estimate Class

Step 4: Plot and Compare Actual vs. Predicted Metrics

Plot the table data on a chart such as Figure 7.1. Compare the actual and predicted lines visually. Through trial and error, adjust the ValidRisk calibration factors (CFs) for the operation/asset group until the predicted values closely align with the actual values without overfitting. Avoid large swings in CFs across estimate classes, as they typically indicate an undisciplined project system. Focus primarily on aligning the $p50$ and $p90$ values, as they are more critical for accurate risk assessment (e.g., in Figure 7.1, the CF that worked for $p50$ and $p90$ at Class 5 was less ideal for $p10$).[9]

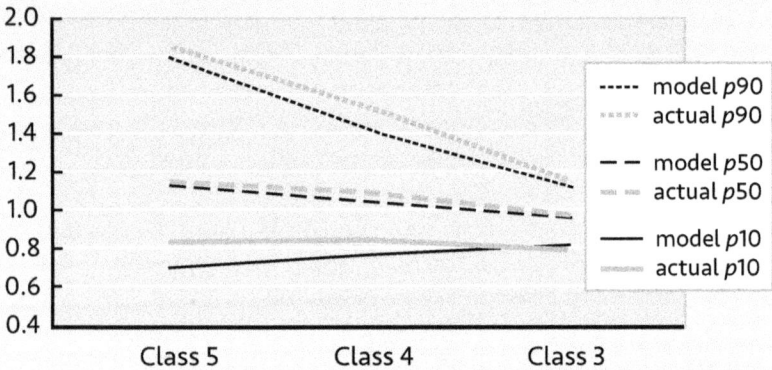

Figure 7.1: Example Comparison of Calibrated Model vs. Actual Cost Growth by Class

Step 5: Refine Calibration Factors

Adjust the CFs iteratively, aiming for consistency across all estimate classes. The end result might look something like Table 7.6 and Figure 7.1, where final mean and SD CFs were 1.00 and 1.25, respectively, for all classes. Favor consistency across classes to maintain reliability. Perfect alignment is rarely achievable, especially with small sample sizes.

Step 6: Review and Analyze

Examine the projects in the dataset for possible causes of any discrepancies. Identify and assess outliers in the actuals, and consider performing comparisons with and without outlier values

---

9   Because capital investment decision making often relies on sensitivity analysis and NPV or similar tornado diagrams, the $p90$ or worst case on capex or start of revenue (project completion) is what separates risky from safer alternatives.

to understand their impact. Consistency across calibration factors is key to reliable prediction.

By following these steps, you can ensure that the ValidRisk model is calibrated accurately, providing reliable risk predictions for your projects.

Track Trends and Utilize Insights

As discussed, ValidRisk serves as a quality assurance tool supporting ongoing project process enhancement through its consistency and data storage capabilities. Regular calibration studies, updated annually (or biennially based on project volume), help identify challenges in project cost growth and schedule slip predictability. These metrics should be viewed as crucial performance indicators. Are the $p50$ metrics showing improvement or deterioration? How are the $p10$ and $p90$ ranges evolving? Concurrently analyzing metric results and trends over time, while considering potential causes suggested by ValidRisk ratings, is essential.

ValidRisk Application

Once the operational framework is established, systemic risk rating matrices are customized, and models are calibrated using the company's historical data, risk analysts can commence project risk quantification analyses with ValidRisk. This chapter serves as a guide to demonstrate the practical application of the parametric and expected value methods from Volume 1 within the ValidRisk environment. It does not provide a detailed, step-by-step user manual, as interface screenshots are likely to evolve over time.

Parametric Analysis of Systemic Uncertainty

A significant enhancement in ValidRisk compared to Volume 1, Chapter 11 examples lies in its expanded and specific systemic rating items. As discussed, narrative statements in ValidRisk are tailored to minimize subjective interpretations of rating intent and criteria.

Volume 1, Chapter 11 extensively covers "Applying the Parametric Models," which applies seamlessly to ValidRisk. In ValidRisk workshops, input elicitation involves projecting each rating question onto screens or sharing them in virtual sessions. Table 7.7 illustrates a typical rating question presentation sourced from the relevant ValidRisk asset matrix (as per Table 7.1). During workshops, the analyst selects an initial rating from a list, typically reflecting project system expectations at that phase. The team then deliberates on whether all criteria are met. If not, a lower (or higher) rating is chosen and discussed, with the analyst documenting the reason for the selection in a note field.

To ensure objectivity, some companies employ voting software that allows knowledgeable team members to confidentially assign ratings. If consensus is lacking, further discussion or rating adjustments may be necessary until agreement is reached.

Q1: Business Leadership, Ownership, Decisiveness
Selections: B. MEDIUM/FAIR: Fair business sponsor focus, engagement, communication, support, ...
Selected Answer: B. MEDIUM/FAIR: Fair business sponsor focus, engagement, communication, support, responsiveness and/or decisiveness. Objectives documented and generally aligned with business strategy. Moderate project system/process maturity.
Note: The business unit engagement is fair or typical for our projects. However, not being strategic, the project does not get top priority business focus and the project phase-gate discipline is sometimes side-stepped. Therefore, a High rating is not justified.

Table 7.7: Representation of the ValidRisk Systemic Risk Rating Input Screen.

After completing all rating questions, the parametric analysis of systemic risk is conducted without the need for simulation. Valid-Risk generates graphical and tabular predictions of cost and duration distributions and provides a summary of the applied systemic ratings. These reports can be exported to Excel for integration into user-designed risk analysis reports and stored in the relevant cloud for archival and potential system analytics.

For projects classified as Class 10 or 5, the analysis typically concludes at this stage. For Class 4 and better, the team proceeds to an Expected Value analysis of project-specific risks and uncertainties, often in a subsequent workshop.

Expected Value Analysis of Critical Project-Specific Risks and Uncertainties

The method described in Volume 1, Chapter 12 closely mirrors ValidRisk's approach, both aligning well with AACE Recommended Practice 65R-11 (*"Integrated Cost and Schedule Risk Analysis and Contingency Determination Using Expected Value"*). The primary aspect not extensively covered in these references is the determination of burn rates, which are multiplied by delay duration to estimate the time-dependent cost impact of a risk. Table 7.8 illustrates a representation of the burn rate table within ValidRisk, situated after entering specific risks and their probabilities of occurrence, and before detailing the impacts of these risks.

Contract/Time Dependent Cost Element	Start	End	Months	Time Dependent Costs	Cost/ Month
Owner/PM/CM, etc.					
Service Contracts					
Civil Contract					
Mechanical Contract					
Electrical Contract					

Table 7.8: Representation of the ValidRisk Burn Rate Summary Screen.

When the user adds a burn rate element or contract (similar to the contracts in Table 7.8), a dialogue box will prompt entry of the element title, start and end dates, and time-dependent costs. ValidRisk calculates the duration in months and cost per month (burn rate), which are then included in Table 7.7. The first two lines of the table are default headings intended for general owner and construction management contractor indirect costs incurred during delays to the critical path.

The time-dependent cost entered should be a rough order-of-magnitude (ROM) estimate specific to the contract, primarily reflecting labor and related indirects such as crane rental costs. Assuming some labor can be repurposed during extended delays, adjustments may be applied (e.g., multiply by a factor like 0.7 for labor costs). The contract's start and end dates should exclude initial and final ramp-up/down durations, instead focusing on the duration when most of the contractor's workforce is mobilized. Estimators, schedulers, and risk analysts can collaboratively develop this table prior to workshops.

When entering a risk's impacts into ValidRisk (refer to Table 12.2 in Volume 1, Chapter 12), select the cost elements from Table 7.7 that are affected by the specific delay risk. For instance, delays due to unexpected soil conditions might impact only the Civil contract, in addition to general items affected by critical path delays.

Tipping Point for Potential Non-linear Behavior

ValidRisk closely follows the method outlined in Volume 1, Chapter 14 for assessing tipping points. Table 14.1 illustrates a representative qualitative output displaying tipping point warnings at the bottom of the Cost Report in ValidRisk. For users seeking a comprehensive quantitative P+EV analysis including hypothesized non-linear cost impacts (e.g., potential blowouts), the "Parameters" tab enables activation of the "Bimodal" switch.

Program Project Cost Consolidation

Program-level cost risk analysis, detailed in Chapter 5 of this Volume, involves consolidating project cost distributions (see Table 5.1). ValidRisk simplifies this step by eliminating the need to transfer p-tables from individual projects to another tool. After conducting risk analyses for each constituent project, users access the "Consolidator" from ValidRisk's Risk Quantification tab. This facilitates aggregation of project risk evaluations by selecting them from a list and specifying correlation coefficients via the Correlations tab. Subsequently, clicking "run simulation" executes a Monte Carlo simulation, presenting the consolidated cost distribution that can be exported to Excel for reporting.

Multi-Scope Option Analysis

Chapter 6 outlines a method for probabilistic cost distribution analysis when projects involve multiple viable scope options (see Figure 6.2). ValidRisk streamlines this process by integrating the analyses of optional projects directly within the tool. Following risk analyses of each optional project, users access "Multi-Option" from ValidRisk's Risk Quantification tab. For Class 10 or 5 estimates, typically only systemic analyses are conducted. Users then add project risk evaluations and assign probabilities for selection, ensuring the sum equals 100%. Clicking "run simulation" initiates a Monte Carlo simulation, presenting a combined cost distribution weighted by probability. Figure 7.2 illustrates a typical "lumpy" wide-shape histogram depicting the varied costs of project options, which can be exported to Excel for reporting purposes.

Analytics

As of the current version, ValidRisk lacks built-in analytics capabilities to comprehensively analyze the complete database of stored risk assessments in the cloud. However, users can export the cloud database for analysis using tools like Microsoft Power BI. Below are some sample analytics that can be conducted; the potential analyses are extensive:

◆ Evaluation of project systemic risk ratings by rating, operation, asset type, and/or year to identify trends over time. Is there improvement in project definition?

Probability Density Chart

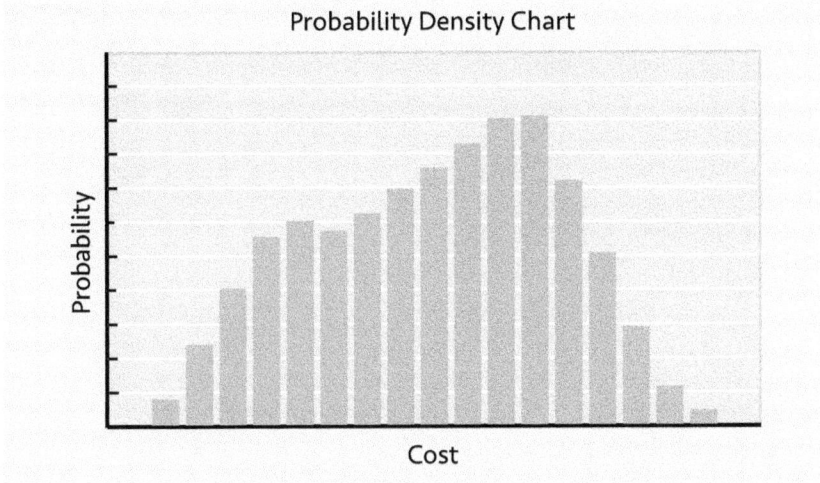

Figure 7.2; Typical ValidRisk Multi-Option Analysis Output Histogram.

♦ Analysis of $p50$ cost and schedule outcomes as percentages by operation, asset type, and/or year to detect trends over time. Are there variations in $p50$ or $p90$ values?

♦ Examination of critical risks identified across the portfolio to serve as a benchmark for future risk identification. Which types of risks are most prevalent, and are there shifts in risk types over time?

As previously mentioned, ValidRisk facilitates ongoing improvement in project processes. At the very least, it ensures consistency in quantitative risk analysis practices across organizational and project portfolios.

Questions

1. What is the purpose of customizing the ValidRisk systemic risk ratings matrices?

2. What is the purpose of calibrating the ValidRisk parametric algorithms?

3. Beyond those outlined in this chapter, can you propose any analytical studies that might leverage exported ValidRisk data to enhance understanding and improve corporate risk management and quantification practices?

Volume 2 Perspective

As the sole commercial software of its kind, understanding the utilization and application of ValidRisk is very important to effectively implement the methods detailed in this book.

Calibration studies are particularly valuable: in many cases, clients have not thoroughly examined their experiences with cost growth and schedule slip, leading to enlightening if not surprising discoveries.

"With data collection, 'the sooner, the better' is always the best answer."
– Marissa Mayer

8

Getting Ready for Machine Learning (Advanced Data Analytics)

Premises

I include this chapter with some trepidation, as I am not an expert in machine learning (ML) or data science. However, I bring over 25 years of experience in predictive analytics, including development of project historical databases and the construction of risk quantification models using inferential statistics (e.g., multiple linear regression; see Volume 1, Chapter 10). Through research, reviewing ML startup products, and discussions with experts in the field, I have gained sufficient understanding to discuss ML-based Quantitative Risk Analysis (QRA). This chapter will explore the challenges and opportunities of ML-based QRA, and how it may compare to the methods presented in this book.

Until recent years, parametric modeling based on regression analysis was the primary empirically-based QRA method in practice. Now, ML-based models are emerging. This chapter aims to provide a non-technical overview of some aspects of ML, the challenges and current state of ML in project risk quantification, and strategies for companies to expedite and leverage ML in their project QRA practices.

The chapter reviews some of the ML-based QRA products available on the market. The inclusion criteria require the method to be empirically based (ML using planned and actual data meets this by default) and to answer a fundamental question for decision makers: *"For a given project with known or potential risk drivers, what are the probabilistic distributions of cost and schedule outcomes?"* Being empirically based and risk driven are criteria for a method to be an AACE Recommended Practice for QRA, such as the methods discussed in this book. Other criteria include integrating cost and schedule analysis, considering trade-offs, and addressing QRA at any decision point in the project life cycle.[1]

Here is a brief overview of my findings from reviewing ML products: no current ML-based schedule QRA product meets all the risk-driven or other criteria, except being empirically-based. The only cost QRA product identified addresses systemic risks but does not integrate cost and schedule risk analysis in a risk-driven way. While all of the products are valuable for validating the outcomes of existing QRA methods (though only at the sanction gate or later), they are not yet suitable as replacements for the methods discussed in this book.

It is Not AI Yet

This chapter focuses on machine learning (ML), not the broader field of artificial intelligence (AI). AI implies that the software is approaching human-like thinking or behavior. Some suggest that AI should feel like magic, with the most common form being "generative AI," which creates things such as artwork or, in our context, an estimate or schedule. While ML falls under the AI umbrella, it is more basic analytically: ML is about identifying relationships in data and continuously learning. Although an ML-based QRA app may involve AI in its development (e.g., natural language processing of an activity or estimate item title), ML (e.g., deep learning

---

1   See AACE RP 40R-08, "Contingency Estimating – General Principles" (this RP is poorly named; it is actually about project cost and schedule QRA in general).

using layers of neural networks) is currently central to developing QRA products.

Competitive Positioning

This chapter is narrowly focused on ML-based predictive analytics for project cost and schedule quantitative risk analysis as a competitor to or potential replacement for the current empirical state-of-the-art combination of parametric modeling of systemic risks with expected value or CPM for project-specific risks.[2] Although I am biased towards the methods presented in this book, I believe that QRA practice disruption *will* occur (if it hasn't already by the time you read this). I encourage ML development, and the purpose here is to constructively support its advancement.

Supporting Project Life Cycle Decisions

To further frame the topic, a key premise of this book is that a robust QRA method, whether ML-based or otherwise, must meet decision makers' needs at all project decision points and gates. In the early phases (Class 5 or 4), QRA is used by owners to quantify the risks of project scope alternatives in various scenarios. It is about selecting the right project. At the final investment decision (FID) or tender gate (Class 3 or 2), QRA focuses on funding and commercial start of revenue decisions by the owner, or bid/no bid and pricing decisions by contractors. QRA also ensures that the "initial state" for managing the Execution phase (detailed engineering through commissioning) addresses potential risks. At this point, it is more about executing the project correctly.[3] Finally, during execution and construction, QRA focuses on forecasting potential final cost and schedule outcomes considering the real-time "current state" and guiding mid-execution corrective action decisions.

For Class 5 or 4, QRA modeling, ML-based or otherwise, depends on inputs reflecting the state of the project and external system as it is or is anticipated to be, as well as physical attributes.[4] At FID (Class 3 or 2), these inputs reflect the initial state for Execu-

---

2   Disclosure: I am a partner in the ValidRisk product covered in Chapter 7 of this Volume.

3   Outcomes of systems are highly sensitive to initial conditions. This is a fundamental concept in chaos theory and relates to why complexity is a major risk driver to explicitly address.

4   The empirical method of Reference Class Forecasting (RCF) is focused almost exclusively on physical attributes as will be discussed later. It is not risk driven and therefore falls short of being a QRA method.

tion. Prior to FID, modeling inputs include little actual performance information other than some preparatory project work. During Execution, near real-time inputs about procurement, fabrication, and construction performance, and externalities to date become paramount for making change management (corrective action) and control decisions.

The distinction between pre-FID and post-FID is significant, as commercial ML products currently offer little QRA value to pre-FID owner decisions that hinge upon inputs regarding the actual state of the project system (project scope and planning definition). These inputs are difficult to capture and process. ML products are primarily focused on FID and post-FID forecasting (and mostly just on schedule). At FID and later, there is minimal opportunity to significantly improve upon the original plan; if the project selected (usually de facto sanctioned well before FID) is a dud, it will remain a dud regardless of actions taken at FID or during Execution. ML-based QRA models must evolve to address early project decisions and consider all risks to fully compete with or replace the QRA methods presented in this book.

ML Background

Parametric Modeling Versus ML

Parametric model development relies on inferential statistical analyses, starting with a hypothesized model of potential risks that might drive cost growth and schedule delays. Only variables hypothesized as relevant based on experience are pursued and structured in a study sample dataset for multiple linear regression (MLR). This is the foundation of the "Rand" models discussed in Volume 1, Chapter 11. The process is slow and relatively costly, often taking years to capture the desired data and develop and update a model. Due to the effort involved, discovering risk drivers beyond the analyst's initial hypotheses is unlikely. Only a few organizations, such as Independent Project Analysis, Inc (IPA), have the resources to spend decades testing new hypothesized inputs and evolving their models (for example, the ValidRisk® model benefited from ongoing published research and includes variables not in the initial Rand models).

ML, on the other hand, can utilize a broad array of data – an entire project historical database as discussed in Volume 1, Chapter 18 – to shape a model by discovering patterns using various techniques such as deep learning. ML learns from the data with varying degrees of analyst supervision. Theoretically, the broader the scope and higher the quality of the database used to "train" the model, the more predictive it will be. A broad database is more likely to discover risk drivers that were not originally hypothesized.

ML: Supervision and Data Structure

ML modeling can be supervised or unsupervised. Supervised ML is similar to traditional MLR, with a "teacher" presenting example inputs (e.g., risk drivers) and outputs (e.g., cost growth or schedule slip), allowing ML to identify input-output relationships from a somewhat narrow database (a traditional, structured project historical database).

Unsupervised ML, however, allows ML to find relationships in broader-input databases, including data from across an ERP system, procurement systems, and more. The more structured and higher quality the data is, the easier the ML analysis effort will be. Structured data is usually quantitative and captured in traditional relational databases. Unstructured data is often qualitative, such as text in narrative reports, and may require techniques such as natural language processing (NLP) to make sense of it. Using unstructured data makes ML more challenging but opens up more learning opportunities.

Main Challenges to ML for QRA

The opportunities for ML analytics to surpass parametric analysis are clear: discovering more relationships between risk drivers and cost growth and schedule delays at all decision points of the project system, doing so more efficiently and closer to real-time, and continuing to learn. However, significant challenges exist. Many companies lack clear objectives for their analytics strategy, especially for QRA. A 2020 IPA survey found that "just 25 percent of owner companies surveyed had clearly defined digitalization objectives linked directly to business goals."[5] Once companies have a vision and strategy, and it trickles down to the project QRA function, the detailed work remains. To encourage owners, contractors, and ML data analysts and startups to focus on improving QRA, the challenges are summarized below.

---

5   IPA, Inc. "Digitalization: New OIIE Capital Project Working Group Launches," December 7, 2020 (https://www.ipaglobal.com/news/article/).

Lack of Structured Data: ML's Achilles Heel

Chapter 2 of this volume concluded with a critique of the engineering and construction industry's project historical data management practices. For most companies, there is little quality, structured cost and schedule data readily available for analysis. For example, when I led a cost engineering benchmarking consortium at IPA, we found that very few major owner clients could fill out a simple cost form with information like the total volume of concrete installed or the number of construction hours spent. I spent many weeks "pre-processing" their low-quality data. Additionally, a few years prior, I discovered my major contractor employer's database consisted of paper close-out records in dusty file boxes (it has likely improved since then). When IPA started collecting initial and final master schedule files for study, we found that their average quality was poor.[6]

Another challenge is collecting reliable phased estimate and schedule data. Phase-gate systems are often ill-defined and/or not rigorously followed, particularly in the infrastructure sector. Analysts can be somewhat confident that plans at the FID or tender gate will be reasonably consistent in nature between projects, but the level of definition before that gate is often poorly documented. This is problematic because the level of definition is a major systemic risk driver. ML-based methods must somehow measure the actual level of definition.[7]

Recognizing these gaps, AACE International developed its Recommended Practice 114R-20, "Project Historical Database Development," aligned with Volume 1, Chapter 18. However, getting management to invest in its data has been challenging. Owners have become largely dependent on their engineering contractors for cost engineering knowledge, and contractors, who come and go from project to project, have different incentives than owners. As discussed in Chapter 3, contractors themselves may lack information about the total capital cost of projects and certain cost elements, such as the ever-increasing owner's costs. Engineering firms that perform many of the construction cost estimates and schedules for

---

6   Griffith, Andrew, "Schedule Practices and Project Success," Cost Engineering Journal, September 2006.

7   There is a practice I call "Class Creep" whereby teams call their definition Class 3 because that is what is expected, but on examination is usually closer to Class 4. The ValidRisk® product helps mitigate that practice.

owners also may have limited firsthand data about construction, as they receive it secondhand from subcontractors.

Creating a database, as outlined in the RP and Volume 1, Chapter 18, requires data cleaning and normalization. Firms need to understand what "good" data is, which requires knowledge of statistics and data analytics. These skill sets may exist in a company but are hard to find among cost engineering staffs (i.e., cost, schedule, risk, project control).[8] Owner companies with an AI strategy usually prioritize business and non-QRA activities, focusing their limited analytics resources on them. For contractors, project cost and schedule are more central to their interests and seem to drive early ML product development, even though their "overhead" budget (tight margins) is typically limited. The good news is that AI/ML interest has raised executive-level interest in data. Additionally, younger staff members, likely exposed to data analytics at the university level, are eager to apply it in their jobs.

The need for data has led to the relatively new terms "data wrangling" or "data munging." These describe the tasks of cleaning, converting, mapping, and storing data so that it is useful for ML. The job descriptions of estimators, schedulers, project control engineers, and risk analysts will increasingly include elements of data wrangling.

Lack of Data from Unstructured Sources: ML's Other Achilles Heel

Empirically-based QRA, as covered in this book, focuses on identifying relationships between attributes and practices of capital project systems (and their interactions with external systems) and project cost growth and schedule slip outcomes. Project systems consist of people, organizations, processes, and practices, and their attributes include factors like complexity, communication methods, decision-making processes, team experience levels, and supply chain dynamics.

Central to project systems are phase-gate scope development processes that span the project lifecycle, from the business identifying an opportunity (Class 5) through alternative selection (Class 4), sanction (Class 3 or 2), and execution to initial asset operation. Research suggests that a project's success or failure can largely

---

8   In a podcast, several AI/ML-based QRA developers agreed it was easier to train someone with a data science background about projects than to train project people about data science.

be determined by the state of, and decision quality in, the project system early on.[9] Once a single scope option is selected at Class 4, commitment bias leads to few projects being canceled or changing course regardless of the business case. Waiting until FID to do QRA is too late for owners to significantly improve return on investment outcomes (the die is cast).[10] If the only data available pertains to physical attributes (scope or asset type, products, size, location, etc.) and cost and schedule at the sanction gate, many systemic risk drivers related to practices over the lifecycle will be missed.

This data gap is evident in the empirically-based practice called Reference Class Forecasting (RCF), which is a form of benchmarking rather than a QRA practice. It is not risk-driven and typically considers differences in outcomes for projects with different physical attributes, often superficially. For instance, examining metrics by "asset type" says little about physical or execution complexity. RCF, as currently applied, lacks practice information except for noting the phase at which the base cost and duration were recorded. Using ML on a practice-less database to generate RCF "uplifts" does little to improve outcomes unless the goal is simply to increase estimates rather than enhance performance. At least RCF results raise a red flag, indicating the team should conduct a QRA.

Information about most project system attributes and practices is primarily located in unstructured data sources, particularly text. This information resides in written reports or deliverables such as business cases, strategy analyses, studies, status reports, and so on. IPA tackled this challenge by having its owner benchmarking client project teams and IPA-trained analysts rate (quantify) the qualities of selected practices and deliverables, mainly through interviews and document examination. This process takes time and money, and I know of no other organization doing this in a sustained way across multiple companies and industries. However, one-off research stud-

---

9   Barshop, Paul,. *Capital Projects*, John Wiley & Sons, Hoboken NJ, 2016. Chapter 1 shares an anecdote of a project where the project failure traces back to failure of executives to reconcile conflicts in objectives early on.

10   During Execution, all that good risk management can do is preserve the value built into the scope and plans (be on budget and on schedule). It can reduce erosion of value *but cannot add to it*. For contractors, any erosion means reduced margin (their life blood).

ies using AI to analyze unstructured project data look promising.[11] For now, the parametric models owned by IPA (proprietary) and those in this book and ValidRisk (which shares roots with IPA via Hackney and Rand, as mentioned in Volume 1, Chapter 3) are the only tools primarily systemic risk-driven and based on research.

For ML to replicate what IPA has done using unstructured data, it will first require access to multiple, often siloed IT systems (SharePoint, ERP, etc.), possibly in multiple languages, including some business-sensitive documents. Getting this access within one company is a challenge; across multiple companies, it may be impossible depending on the depth required.[12] Next, ML will need to perform data pre-processing, such as tokenization, to convert textual data into a numerical representation that can be processed by ML algorithms. This is beyond my knowledge and experience, but I know it won't be easy.

So, what unstructured practice information will ML need to access to find relationships between project inputs and cost growth and schedule slip outputs? What does IPA examine? A project cost and schedule risk management ontology would help guide where to look; however, I could not find a good reference for an ontology in the QRA domain. One could be structured in reference to the AACE International Total Cost Management (TCM) Framework, which is an annotated process map of Cost Engineering, including risk management.

The AACE Cost Estimate Classification RPs[13] are a good starting point for identifying potential inputs. The list shown in Table 8.1 is not all-inclusive but is a sample of key project strategy, planning, and study documents or equivalents that every project should have at least a preliminary draft of in their records at the time of the make-or-break Class 4 (select) decision gate. If these deliverables

---

11 Franzen, Samuel, C. Quang, L. Schweizer, A. Budzier, J. Gold, M. Vellez, S. Ramirez, and E. Raimondo: "Advanced Content Analysis: Can AI Accelerate Theory-Driven Complex Program Evaluation," Independent Evaluation Group. Washington, DC: World Bank. 2022.

12 In that respect, publicly funded infrastructure stands the greatest chance of cross-agency data access. That sector has historically lagged the private sector in implementing phase-gate and supporting empirical research, but having greater ability to force data pooling for AI/ML, may allow them to leap forward in QRA.

13 See AACE Professional Guidance Document PGD-01 "Guide to Cost Estimate Classification Systems," at www.aacei.org.

have not been done, that failure is a measurable systemic risk input. In short, there is a lot of unstructured input data that ML will need to tackle to start quantifying the state of the full project system.

Business Case documentation with Decision Analysis reports	Regulatory and Permitting plan
Technology selection studies	Project Control plan (including cost, schedule, risk)
Contracting/sourcing strategy	Basis of Estimates and Schedules
Organization charts	Estimates and Schedules
Logistics plan	HSE plans
Quality Management plan	Stakeholder Management plan
Integrated Project plan	Geotechnical studies
Project Execution plan	Environmental studies
Start up and Commissioning plan	Constructability (and other Value Improving Practice) Studies

Table 8.1: Unstructured Input Data List

For understanding what happened during Execution, there are further unstructured sources that can be processed and analyzed as shown in Table 8.2.

Tender documents	Risk Registers
Procurement records	HSE Reports
Project Status reports (weekly, monthly, etc.)	Project Closeout Reports/Postmortem studies
Final cost reports and schedules	Claims and Dispute Resolution Documents
Change/Trend Logs	

Table 8.2: Unstructured Input Data List, Execution Phase

A key risk-driver (or perhaps risk mitigation) input is the human side, particularly leadership, which is difficult to measure. A good reference on the topic is the "Leading Complex Projects" book by Merrow and Nandurdikar of IPA.[14] Another risk mitigation input is the alignment of contracting strategy with project objectives. Everyone knows these are critical, but research on them is challenging. Again, Merrow offers a text entitled, *Contract Strategies*

---

14 Edward W. Merrow and Neeraj Nandurdikar, *Leading Complex Projects: A Data-Driven Approach to Mastering the Human Side of Project Management*, Wiley, 2018.

for Major Projects.[15] ML developers would need to take advantage of the decades of empirical learning from IPA and its many major industrial clients.

Add to this list external sources such as news articles and social media postings about the project (important for understanding community issues and stakeholder risks), plus addition of unstructured data from sources such as images, video, and IoT (Internet of Things) devices, and the daunting ML challenge, and potential, becomes apparent.

At this time, I am not aware of any firm or institution (other than IPA) developing ML-based QRA models as commercial products (as opposed to special studies) using unstructured data sourced from most of these key deliverables.[16] Some ML firm literature suggests that there is little to be learned from such inputs, or, put another way, they suggest there is little value in spending time and resources on other QRA methods that address these risk inputs. Such suggestions are specious.

Examples of ML in Project QRA Practice (as of 2024)

Despite these challenges, there are several QRA-related ML-based products of note that illustrate both the opportunity and remaining challenges regarding ML. Some products may have been missed (my apologies), and developments will likely be more advanced than discussed here by the time readers see this; everyone must do their own research.

Two main types of ML-based QRA products have been identified:

♦ Quantitative Schedule Risk Analysis (QSRA): These products are based on CPM models at or near Class 3 or 2 or during execution.

♦ (Quantitative) Cost and Schedule Risk Analysis (CSRA): These products focus on high-level cost at Class 3 or 2 or

---

15 Edward W. Merrow, *Contract Strategies for Major Projects: Mastering the Most Difficult Element of Project Management*, Wiley, 2022.

16 It is not that the ML product developers cannot do it. Most of these firms do bespoke modeling on a consulting basis and they reference their use of some of these types of inputs for specific, but more limited client needs. For example: using unstructured data from risk registers and change logs to help with risk identification, or assessing bidding factors that result in successful and profitable tenders.

during execution, emphasizing contractor finances, including revenue and margins.

No products were found that offer integrated cost and schedule QRA (e.g., address cost/schedule trading).[17] Four QSRA products and one CSRA product were identified. All four QSRA products share a similar general nature, indicating a crowded market space. Although some QSRA product literature mentions cost analysis incidentally, I discounted any CSRA capabilities these products may have, except for Octant AI. Focusing on the QSRA products' general nature is sufficient to draw conclusions about the current state of ML-based QRA methods compared to non-ML QRA methods and to identify opportunities for advancement.

Being on the list does not imply equality in terms of database quality, ML techniques used, the expertise of data science teams, or the quality and reliability of the outputs. Potential users must examine these quality aspects in detail. The products are listed in Table 8.3 below:

Type	Company and URL	QR Code
QSRA	Foresight (www.foresight.works)	
QSRA	Nodes & Links (www.nodeslinks.com)	
QSRA	nPlan; Insights (www.nplan.io)	
QSRA	Oracle Construction Intelligence Cloud Advisor (www.oracle.com/construction-engineering/construction-intelligence-cloud)	
CSRA	Octant AI (www.octantai.io)	

Table 8.3: QSRA and CSRA Products

Note that IPA, Inc. is not included on this list despite having well-established data-driven models that address all QRA criteria (all

---

17   The single CSRA vendor reported that they also offer a product that combines cost and schedule analysis. However, no general marketing literature was available at the time of publication.

risks, all phases, integrated cost and schedule, etc.). IPA uses its models in its benchmarking and consulting practice, but the tools are not marketed alone.

ML-Based Schedule QRA Products

There are four products focused on QSRA, likely because obtaining extensive historical CPM schedule information (usually in Primavera P6 or Microsoft Project format) is relatively easy. Companies often have hundreds or thousands of schedules in their archives, and CPM software data is highly structured based on well-defined CPM scheduling rules (although activity names and scopes may not be well structured or easy to interpret). More importantly, at FID, investors, owners, and contractors all aim to complete their projects on time, creating a relatively good market. Additionally, as already discussed, there is increasing awareness that subjective CPM with MCS-based QRA results are neither realistic nor reliable.

All QSRA-focused products require a baseline, fairly detailed, integrated, critical path network schedule, which is usually available only as the project approaches the Class 3/FID gate. Consequently, ML products focus on executing the selected project scope correctly rather than selecting the right project scope. Some "AI-enhanced" offerings claim to help pick the "best option," but they generally refer to the best "planning and scheduling option," not project scope options.[18]

The various products offer a range of CPM schedule analysis and reporting capabilities with reported AI enhancements. The key point is that they all use ML algorithms to forecast schedule durations based on historical data of schedule performance, focusing on activity duration distribution.

Each product is said to have developed its base models from a large, but often vaguely defined, database of project CPM schedules (both planned and as-built). Data confidentiality is paramount for firms working with these products. Some products emphasize the need to train the base model on the client's data. For example, nPlan suggests providing over 1,000 past client CPM schedules for training.

---

18 Using AI/ML to identify schedule options is similar to what the traditional value improving practice of constructability does. Its purpose is optimization, not QRA per se. The quantitative risk of an optimized schedule still needs to be assessed. One AI-supported product is called ALICE (www.alicetechnologies.com) which refers to what it does as "construction optioneering."

The specific ML techniques used are often unclear in the product literature. However, nPlan, for instance, reports using "deep learning." All products appear to use contextual elements of activities and milestones as inputs, such as activity name and duration, as well as non-contextual elements like whether an activity is on the critical path and its nature in the network.

The products are focused on large projects, typically valued at $50 to $100 million or more. As discussed in Volume 1, small project system behavior is unique and often less disciplined. The focus on large projects is likely due to the high degree of seemingly random behavior in small ones. Additionally, the majority of capital spending, and thus the interest and market for QRA, is in large projects.

QSRA products start by loading the prospective CPM schedule into the system (or selecting one already in the system for CPM software vendors). When a new project schedule is loaded without any actual data from that project, the models rely on their base and compare the previously noted contextual elements to those of the current schedule to forecast the schedule outcome. Most products do this by activity, milestone, and overall. As the project progresses and schedule updates are uploaded, the models use ML to learn from and train themselves on this real-time project-specific data.

Ultimately, the products usually produce a schedule forecast S-curve, allowing users to see the probability that the schedule will be completed on the planned date. All products report providing risk management insights (e.g., identifying risks from the schedule model for mitigation focus). It is then up to the project team to study and decide how to manage the schedule and risks to more likely meet the planned date.

ML Opportunities for Better QSRA

None of the current ML-based QSRA products consider the state of the project system as an input. The only systemic risk drivers they take into account are the attributes of the schedule itself and perhaps some physical attributes of the project and its context. While the empirical basis of these products adds significant value, they fall short of providing substantial insights from ML regarding why historical or current performance is as it is – schedule qualities are far from the only drivers of performance. In this respect, these models resemble Reference Class Forecasting (RCF) for duration but applied at a finite activity level with stronger statistical power. The responsibility for assessing delay causation remains with the team, although the products do allow users to delve into activities and milestones to identify areas for management focus. After a QSRA analysis, generative AI tools (e.g., ALICE) can be useful for exploring alternative scheduling approaches.

Moreover, these products do not utilize ML to assess project-specific risk impacts, such as event risks. Schedule duration encompasses both uncertainty (systemic risks) and discrete risk events, which can significantly affect a specific project. In the Rand research (Volume 1, Chapter 11) underlying the parametric method, critical risk events were excluded from the modeled cost and duration data to ensure that general uncertainty and event risk impacts are assessed separately. Without this distinction, the understanding of ML-derived forecasts is limited. There is a significant analytical challenge in learning from unstructured project system documents and historical risk data in risk registers, logs, and status reports.

Ultimately, the current ML-based QSRA products improve on purely subjective "ranging" schedule risk analysis by injecting reality into the duration forecast at the FID gate or later stages. However, their primary value at present lies in serving as validation or assurance tools to benchmark QSRA results obtained from more integrated, risk-driven, all-phase, empirically-valid methods described in this book. Table 8.4 summarizes the enhancements needed for these products to be considered as the go-to QSRA tool.[19]

Capability Needed	QSRA Product Challenge	Octant AI Challenge
Address schedule duration at any phase, with or without a CPM network.	Capture/assess the level of scope and planning definition at each phase.	Capture/assess the level of scope and planning definition at each phase.
Address the causes of outcomes (not just schedule attributes and broad contextual inputs)	Capture/assess systemic risk inputs (including above) as well as critical project-specific risks	Capture/assess critical project-specific risks
Address integrated cost/schedule risk analysis; tradeoff behavior	Essentially merging the efforts of the above examining correlation of cost/schedule and possible drivers (how to measure trading behavior). Perhaps step away from CPM as the base model for this.	

Table 8.4: Improvements in ML-based QRA Needed

---

19 The ML products often compare themselves to QRA using purely subjective "ranging" QRA methods which, as this book points out, are not reliable. None of the products demonstrated awareness that there are empirically-valid methods in use and a commercial product (ValidRisk) has been available for several years.

ML-based Cost Risk Analysis

Octant AI is the only ML-based product that unambiguously models project cost outcomes. The version evaluated, called "Edge," is primarily tailored for contractors, focusing on forecasting project and portfolio revenue, cost, and margin. This focus likely reflects the available data for modeling and the target market. While it is unclear what base data was used to create the initial Octant ML model, the product produces forecasts over time, indicating that the original data must have been similarly time-phased. The product supports portfolio cash flow analysis, which aligns with the methods described in Chapter 5.

The model uses some contextual information, such as project location and size, as inputs. Users are expected to provide their own "calibration" data (at least 22 projects) to train the ML model on their company's experience. Users input their gross project estimates at FID (including revenue, cost, and margin), actuals, dates, and some contextual information. The trained ML model then provides probabilistic monthly forecasts based on past project financial performance.

In May 2024, a feature was added to Edge allowing users to modify systemic risk parameter ratings using "sliders." This functionality makes it somewhat similar to the parametric model described in Volume 1, Chapter 11. An ML technique was used to address the small initial ratings input dataset, but it is expected to evolve as more data is captured.

Octant AI also reported having an owner's product that examines cost and schedule jointly, though without "sliders" for schedule. No literature on the joint cost/schedule product was available for review. Unlike other QSRA products, the Octant AI product does not use CPM schedule networks as a model, instead relying on overall duration as input.

ML Opportunities for Cost Risk Analysis

Octant AI has taken a significant step towards a more risk-driven approach by incorporating systemic risk inputs and considering both cost and schedule. However, it does not use ML to assess project-specific risk impacts, such as event risks. Additionally, current products only evaluate risks from the FID (Class 3 or 2) estimate, offering little to the owner risk analyst at Class 5 or 4. Nevertheless, like the QSRA products, Octant AI improves on purely subjective cost risk analysis by introducing greater realism into the forecast at the FID gate or later stages.

Table 8.4 outlines the improvements needed for these products to become the go-to QRA tools.

Leveraging ML in Project QRA Practice

At present, ML-based products for cost and schedule QRA (none offer integrated cost and schedule risk analysis) primarily serve a similar purpose as Reference Class Forecasting (RCF) – providing an empirically-based benchmark forecast of cost and schedule outcomes. However, the ML-based methods are more statistically sound than typical RCF practices and are calibrated to learn from the user's own project experience. Given the bias and ineffectiveness of subjective QRA methods in predicting cost growth and schedule slip, including these products in the QRA toolbox is sensible. For major projects, using these tools to validate integrated, hybrid parametric + expected value or CPM-based QRA analyses is worthwhile.

For those in the industrial sector, benchmarking project systems and major projects with IPA, Inc. offers many benefits of robust, established, ML-based models without direct access. The infrastructure sector urgently needs such an organization. A hopeful development can be seen in the Infrastructure and Projects Authority (coincidentally also IPA) of the UK, which published a framework in 2024 for using AI to improve public project delivery.[20]

The narrow QRA focus of this chapter – addressing the question *"For this given project, with these known or potential risk drivers, what are the probabilistic distributions of cost and schedule outcomes"* – is very limited. It leaves many risk management AI/ML tools unexamined. For instance, if QRA outcomes are unacceptable, tools that help improve the plan by generating options (e.g., ALICE) are needed. For every step and task in the risk management process, a similar study of available tools is essential.

For those considering developing in-house tools, these products provide a valuable reference point. Additionally, most of these firms offer bespoke consulting services to help clients develop their own models or customize off-the-shelf models. Numerous AI/ML modeling consultants are ready to assist, but firms that have gone through the rigors of full product development have an edge.

---

20 "Data Analytics and AI in Government Project Delivery," 20 March 2024, www.gov.uk.

The chapter's epigram, "With data collection, 'the sooner, the better' is always the best answer," underscores the importance of capturing and managing data for leveraging AI/ML in any project. This is the foundation for empirically-valid QRA.

ML products will continue to improve, so it makes sense to start now. Many firms offer AI/ML expertise and can assist clients with implementing customized solutions. The ML challenges for QRA, such as using unstructured data, stem not from a lack of ability and know-how at these firms but from limitations in time and resources. Increasing numbers of owners and contractors are investing in their own ML models, leveraging the available expertise.

My AI/ML Wish List

AI/ML is evolving at an amazing pace. I thought it would be fun (maybe even useful?) to describe the project risk quantification-related capabilities and tools I would like to see soon. These stretch goals relate to achieving Level 5 (Adaptive) in the "QRA Maturity Model" discussed in Chapter 10, section 10-8.1 in this Volume.

The first "data sourcing" topics tie to Volume 1, Chapter 18 on "Closing the Loop." The rest relate more to the use of data (i.e., methods) chapters of the book. I hope future readers (and the author of Project Risk Quantification AI-edition) get a chuckle from how far off-base or short-sighted these are.

Data Sourcing: External

♦ Data Trusts: Firms operating in a growing number of regions and industries, with data from hundreds or thousands of peer firms and hundreds of thousands of projects of all types and phases, provide data wrangling services and access to bespoke datasets following strict data confidentiality protocols.

Data Sourcing: Internal

♦ Wrangling: Tools to capture and make useful one's unstructured (e.g., reports, logs, contracts, schedules, drawings, video) and structured (e.g., cost forms, accounting records) data into quality forms for developing AI/ML algorithms. This includes cleaning, normalization, transformation, etc.

♦ Real-Time Data: Leverage tools to obtain real-time tracking, progress, productivity, and conditions data from work sites to be used in tools below.

Machine Learning

♦ Systemic Risks: Assess wrangled unstructured and structured data to identify and rate project system (enterprise) attributes, features, practices, and behaviors, including indicators of culture, bias, competency, and so on (i.e., systemic risk drivers), encompassing all phases of the project life cycle, and stakeholders internal and external (e.g., political and social factors) interacting with the system. Build algorithms assessing the project system using real-time project system data.

♦ Specific Risks: Complement to Systemic Risks, to assess wrangled unstructured and structured (including real-time) data to identify specific project uncertainties and risks that drive KPIs, and build or teach algorithms that identify and estimate the likelihood and consequence of specific risks for a project being assessed.

♦ Supplier Risks: Assess wrangled unstructured and structured data regarding suppliers and market factors, and build or teach algorithms to assess procurement and contracting strategies, support negotiations, and assess supplier risks.

Higher Level AI Tools

♦ Cost, Schedule, and Other Decision Analysis Input Predictions: Build AI algorithms that leverage wrangled Systemic, Specific, and Supplier Risk tools and other inputs to build predictive models that forecast project, program, and portfolio cost, schedule, revenue, opex, operability, as well as other KPI outcomes. These will act through agents that are assessing things as they go.

♦ General Decision Analysis: Leverage prediction algorithms above in building broader AI decision support algorithms that evaluate strategies, including risk treatments, considering alternate scenarios. Use optimization algorithms to identify the best strategy to meet various objectives, whether strategic (e.g., investment/bid) or tactical (e.g., changes/corrective actions).

♦ Contract Strategy/Decisions: Assess wrangled unstructured and structured data regarding bidding/proposals, client and market factors, and build AI algorithms to assess bidding/proposal and pricing strategies using scenarios to maximize margins and revenue considering internal and potential partner resources and capabilities.

♦ Capital Investment Strategy/Decisions: Leverage various tools above and other inputs to build AI algorithms that use capital investment/portfolio scenarios to identify project system improvements needed to achieve capital objectives while being responsive to internal and external risks.

Communicating Risk Quantification Outcomes

This section, which shares the same heading as Volume 1, Chapter 16, discusses how AI/ML can enhance our reporting of QRA outcomes today. Communication leverages the power of generative large language models (LLM), which have already achieved advanced capabilities. Most technical professionals are not great writers and communicators; for many, researching and writing reports is as painful as pulling teeth. To address this, companies like Nodes & Links and nPlan offer generative AI reporting and AI agents to assist in this department.

Whether or not one uses those QRA products, generative LLMs can be used to assist in report writing once they have access to the relevant data. For example, an LLM product was used to edit this book volume. It did not create any new content but cleaned up the writing and was also great at creating succinct summaries from the book text.

Conclusions

Regarding the purpose of this chapter, I do not see these products as replacements for the methods outlined in this book for QRA purposes at this time. None of the ML-based commercial products are risk driven; they do not provide much substantive information about why the forecast is what it is and hence do not directly support significant project practice improvement. They do not yet explicitly consider the impact of critical project-specific risks. They also do not yet support project evaluations at Class 5 or 4. Given the importance of the Class 4 Select gate to owners (do the right project), the ML-based products are best suited for construction contractors (do the project right). Furthermore, they do not yet support integrated cost and schedule risk analysis and cost/schedule trading behavior. However, they do provide empirically-based analysis that can validate the results from any other QRA method; for large projects, this is a valuable addition to any QRA toolbox.

I am very much in favor of using AI/ML. We need these products to improve and eventually supersede the capabilities of the methods in this book. We need improved empirical methods, statistical validity, discovery of new risk drivers, and near real-time learning. I am confident that with sufficient investment and increased data availability, AI/ML firms and agencies will address the QRA gaps pointed out here and likely will have come a long way by the time you read this.

Questions

1. What AI/ML developments would you like to see to support your role on projects?

2. What is the difference between structured and unstructured data?

3. What are some sources of unstructured data that might be useful in ML-based models for QRA?

4. What are some commonalities and differences between the Parametric method and ML-based QRA methods?

5. What are the gaps (as of 2024) between what ML-based commercial products offer and what is needed for robust QRA capability in a project system?

6. What are some opportunities that ML-based QRA may offer to your projects?

7. What might your firm do to prepare for ML-based QRA?

Volume 2 Perspective

When Volume 1 was being written in 2015, OpenAI was just being founded. OpenAI's GPT-1 came out in 2018, followed by GPT-2, GPT-3, and GPT-4. The "big bang" for public AI awareness was the launch of ChatGPT in 2022, which immediately went viral. For QRA, AI/ML startups Nodes & Links and nPlan were founded several years after the Volume 1 rollout, with formal commercial products coming out only in recent years. Here in 2024, practical, commercial AI/ML applications for QRA are still new. Many are probably still feeling some shock and awe regarding AI/ML, and perhaps fear and trepidation, but everyone who is not on the cusp of retirement is or should be asking what this means for their career. Disruption is upon us.

As this chapter points out, in 2024, the AI/ML applications in our domain space are still some ways away from delivering what is needed for robust QRA. However, with the amount of money and intelligence being invested in it, AI/ML products will likely become the main QRA methods by the end of the decade. The main impediment will be gaining access to industry data (and even data within one's own company). For the next few years, database management and learning more about data science should be focus areas for QRA practitioners to help feed the machine now in its infancy. In any case, I trust the data and QRA research and practice fundamentals contained in this book will remain valuable.

"Example is the school of mankind, and they will learn at no other."
— Edmund Burke

9
Risk Analysis Case Histories (Examples)

Readers of Volume 1 requested examples demonstrating application of the book's QRA methods in typical project scenarios (various project phases, perspectives of owners versus contractors, etc.). Examples are provided in this chapter, and are presented in case history format.

Table 9.1 summarizes the cases. Collectively, they utilize the methods discussed in Chapters 11 through 14 of Volume 1, as well as Chapters 3 through 6 of this Volume.

EXAMPLE	QRA METHOD	REF. CHAPTERS	CONTEXT
A	Parametric + Decision Tree	Vol 1, Chap 11 Vol 2, Chap 6	Owner, Class 5 Scoping, Mining
B	Parametric + Expected Value + Escalation; Multi-Phase w/Contractor input	Vol 1, Chaps 11, 12, 13 Vol 2, Chap 3	Owner+Contractor, Class 4, 3, and 2/1, Pipeline
C	P+EV plus Tipping Point and Management Reserves	Vol 1, Chaps 11, 12, 13, 14	Owner, Class 2/1 Execution, Hydropower mega
Chapter 11, Volume 2	Parametric + CPM-based Schedule Risk Analysis	Vol 1, Chap 11 Vol 2, Chap 4	Owner, Class 3, FID, Rail

Table 9.1 Case Histories (Examples)

Each case emphasizes using parametric modeling for systemic risks, highlighting the importance of both identifying and quantifying systemic risks in every analysis. Additionally, all examples employ a combination of methods or models, illustrating hybrid approaches, as no single method effectively quantifies all types of risks.

Although the example projects could have utilized ValidRisk® software (as discussed in Chapter 7), the analyses were conducted before its release. ValidRisk, which includes built-in Monte Carlo simulation (MCS), can be applied to the Parametric, Expected Value, Decision Tree, and Tipping Point methods. For the example using the Escalation method, Excel® with the Lumivero @Risk® MCS add-on was employed, while the Critical Path Method (CPM) example used Safran Risk® with its integrated MCS.

Each case begins with a brief context statement indicating who conducted the analysis, when it was done, its purpose, and the asset or industry type involved. While these examples are set within specific asset/industry contexts, the methods themselves are broadly applicable to engineering and construction projects across various industries. These examples represent actual analyses; however, the details have been altered to maintain confidentiality.

Case History A: Mining Project

♦ Methods: Parametric with Decision Tree
♦ Context: Owner, Class 5 Scoping, Multi-Option, Mining Project

The Situation

This example describes a Class 5 cost and execution duration quantitative risk analysis (QRA) to support a scoping study for a preliminary economic analysis (PEA) of a potentially viable mineral resource. A PEA studies the potential net present value (NPV) and internal rate of return (IRR) of an investment, considering both revenue (metals prices) and costs, including:

♦ Pre-production capital costs (initial capex),
♦ Life-of-mine sustaining capital costs (sustaining capex),
♦ Operating costs (opex), and
♦ Other inputs for the production volumes over the mine life.

The decision analysis (DA) and NPV modeling, which are typically led by the business unit planning personnel, are not covered here (see Chapter 5 of Volume 1 and Chapter 6 of this Volume). Instead, this example focuses on the cost and schedule QRA that is incorporated into the DA. The QRA was carried out by a project risk analyst reporting to a Project Manager, who coordinated with the business unit.

Mining Risk Background

Although there are industry regulatory standards for minerals Scoping Studies, requirements for risk analysis (whether for DA or QRA) are often vague.[1] Guidelines refer to expected cost ranges and emphasize the importance of evaluating risks even at the Scoping stage, as well as the need to study alternative project scopes. However, most published Scoping Study results in the mining industry remain deterministic, reflecting a single option without presenting NPV or other metrics as probabilistic distributions. The argument for a simplistic deterministic approach is that only a small financial commitment is required to move the project to the next phase (pre-feasibility or Class 4), with minimal financial risk at the Scoping stage. However, this approach overlooks the risk of commitment bias, where the initial cost estimate gains undue influence, distorting judgment in later phases.

One example of low industry expectations regarding risk analysis in mining is highlighted in a source that describes the following standard: "Risk assessment is generally given an overview during the Scoping phase, analyzed for fatal flaws during pre-feasibility, and risk workshops with advanced software are conducted during the feasibility study (FS) phase to explore project risks. This primarily affects the contingency percentage, which is 25%, 15%, and 10% for Scoping, PFS, and FS, respectively."[2] In other words, no QRA (only a general risk overview) is typically expected until the final investment decision (FID), at which point unrealistic accuracy expectations often emerge. Traditionally, capital expenditure estimate accuracy in mining Scoping Studies, focusing on a single preferred scope, is arbitrarily assumed to range between +/-25% and +/-50%.

---

1   Common regulatory frameworks include the Australasian Code for Reporting of Exploration Results, Mineral Resources and Ore Reserves ("the JORC Code") and the Canadian National Instrument 43-101 Standards of Disclosure for Mineral Projects ("NI 43-101").

2   Ali Y. Al-Bakri, et.al, "Evaluation studies of the new mining projects," Open Geosciences Journal [De Gruyter Open Access March 23, 2023].

While mining Scoping Studies may not be probabilistic, they often consider profitability sensitivity (NPV) to variations in financial model inputs as a reflection of risk. Figure 9.1 provides an example.[3] Note that the capital cost variance on the *x*-axis extends only to +20%, far below the cost overruns commonly seen in Class 5/ Scoping estimates within the mining industry (also note that sales price is the major profitability driver, a typical finding).[4] I have observed similar narrow sensitivity bands in numerous Class 5 phase analyses across multiple industries. These results reflect a Class 3 mindset regarding risk, where decision makers and investors are shielded from fully understanding the risks involved.

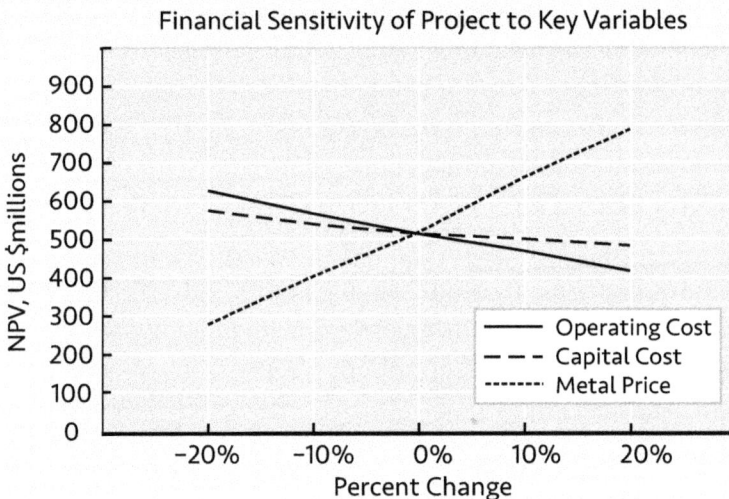

Figure 9.1: Example Financial Sensitivity of a Project Investment (with Narrow Range)

Project Risk Strategy

Unlike many in the industry, the example company chose to conduct a probabilistic NPV analysis during the Scoping phase, alongside a realistic sensitivity analysis. This approach required the use of three-point distribution inputs (*p*10/*p*50/*p*90) for both the capital expenditure (capex) and revenue start-date inputs in the NPV model.

---

3   New World Resources Limited, "Scoping Study Results – Antler Copper Project, USA," ASX Release, 11 July 2022.

4   The Scoping study capital cost estimate included a 22% cost contingency with no mention of its basis. Given that mining companies often assume contingency reflects a notional *p*80 value, 22% at *p*80 implies that the company felt the worst case for capital cost was not much more than that.

Instead of relying on predetermined ranges or subjective inputs from subject matter experts (SMEs), the company used parametric modeling to assess both cost and schedule. Moreover, the project scope presented several potential mineral processing alternatives that varied not only in terms of base cost and schedule but also in terms of technology and complexity – key systemic risk factors that parametric modeling can effectively differentiate.

The Project

The capital project encompasses greenfield underground mine development, processing facilities, material handling, and infrastructure. However, the scope of these various components remains uncertain, including the selection of specific mining methods and the mineral processing technology to be used. These choices will have some impact on infrastructure costs. Although a preferred scope option has been identified, two alternative options are also under consideration.

Table 9.2 outlines the fundamental differences among the scope options, which represent a range of development and asset strategies. These options can be thought of as ranging from a "bargain" to a "deluxe" approach, with all options producing similar metal concentrate output and quality. The primary distinction between them is that the more "deluxe" options offer greater savings in future sustaining capital and operating costs.

Table 9.3 provides the Class 5 base cost estimates for each option. These estimates were developed using historical cost data and various factored estimating methods.

Options	Key Scope Attributes
1	Low complexity; older technology
2	Mixed strategy with increased use of advanced technology
3	Higher complexity; state-of-the-art technology

Table 9.2: Key Scope Attributes of the Options

Capital Cost ($M)	Option 1	Option 2	Option 3
Major Equipment	120	100	150
Mine Development	200	180	250
Process Plant	190	240	280
Infrastructure	70	100	120
Total	$580	$620	$800

Table 9.3: Class 5 Base Cost Estimates for Project Scope Options

Applying the Parametric Model

The cost risk of the three options was assessed using the parametric method outlined in Chapter 11 of Volume 1. The company utilized industrial-grade ValidRisk® software, as discussed in Chapter 7. However, for simplicity and to avoid the inclusion of software screenshots in this chapter, the demonstration-of-concept model described in Chapter 11 of Volume 1 was used for illustration (similar to the case example in Table 11.16).[5]

Table 9.4 presents the systemic risk parameter ratings assigned to the three options. These ratings were determined by the risk analyst in collaboration with business and technical personnel involved in the scoping evaluation. It is important to note that several variables remain consistent across all options – for example, the company's project control capability does not vary.

RISK DRIVER	PARAMETERS		
	Option 1	Option 2	Option 3
Scope Definition (Class)	5		
New Technology	0%	2%	15%
Process Severity	3		
Complexity	2	3	5
Team Development	Fair		
Project Control	Fair		
Estimate Basis	Fair		
Equipment	21%	16%	19%
Fixed Price	None		
Bias	Typical		
SYSTEMIC COST CONTINGENCY % (% TO BE ADDED TO BASE ESTIMATE)			
*p*10	-14	-16	-17
*p*50	26	28	31
*p*70	45	50	56
*p*90	79	86	97

Table 9.4: Chapter 11-Volume1, Parametric Model Inputs and Outputs by Option

---

5   An Excel version of that model is available to purchasers of this book.

At the bottom of the table are the resulting $p10$, $p50$, $p70$, and $p90$ contingency values generated by the model. These percentages are applied to the base estimates (shown in Table 9.3) to calculate the proposed total project cost.

Table 9.5 presents the total projected cost for the three options after applying contingencies at various confidence levels to the base estimates. It also displays the accuracy range around the $p50$ confidence level. Note the difference between the percentages around the $p50$ value and those around the base estimate in Table 9.4. This highlights the importance of being explicit about the reference point when discussing accuracy ranges.

CAPITAL COST ($M)	OPTION 1	OPTION 2	OPTION 3
Base Estimate	$580	$620	$800
$p10$	$500	$520	$660
$p50$	$730	$790	$1,050
$p70$	$840	$930	$1,248
$p90$	$1,040	$1,150	$1,580
Accuracy around $p50$ (80% confidence interval)	+42/-32%	+46/-34%	+50/-37%

Table 9.5: Option Costs Including Contingency and Accuracy

Option 3: The Highest Cost and Most Uncertain Option

Option 3 is the highest-cost option and it carries the greatest uncertainty. This demonstrates how the parametric model helps distinguish the capital cost risk profiles of different alternatives, rather than applying a uniform contingency or +/– range to all options.

At this stage, many companies would typically select one option to use in business case NPV modeling, for disclosures, and for inclusion in long-range capital budgets. The option chosen is often a preferred one for various reasons, such as its ability to easily pass economic evaluation (potentially the lower-cost Option 2). Early selection of a scope option often reflects optimism bias, but is that necessarily a problem?

The key question is: Is the purpose of a scoping study to determine whether any single scope option is viable? Or, should the focus be on assessing whether the overall proposal, considering the range of reasonably likely scope options, is worthy of investment?

The answer depends on the objective. If the goal is to "pitch" or sell an investment, selecting a favorable option might suffice.

However, if the aim is to compare among potential investments being considered, it is critical to evaluate the full risk picture.

For a company with an ongoing phase-gate system, it is essential to report a capital cost figure that is less likely to increase at the next gate – research on estimate accuracy shows that cost increases are common. In this case, the project team decided to evaluate all options to determine an appropriate Scoping capital cost budget and range for NPV analysis and reporting.

Applying the Decision Tree Method

Chapter 6 of this volume discusses the use of a decision tree to quantify the distribution of Class 5 estimates that involve multiple scope options. Simple decision tree modeling is available in Valid-Risk® software (as covered in Chapter 7). However, for this worked example, an Excel model is used (see Figure 9.2), allowing readers with basic Monte Carlo simulation (MCS) software to create their own model and experiment with it.

	A	B	C	D	E	F	G	H
1			Scenario or Alternative		1	2	3	
2		Occurrence or Selection Chance			%	%	%	(add to 100%)
3					A		A:=RiskDiscrete({1,2,3},E2:G2)	
4			Scenario or Alternative					
5			L	$ or months				
6		1	ML	$ or months	B	B:=IF(E$3=1,RiskTrigen(D5,D6,D7,10,90),0)		
7			H	$ or months				
8								
9			L	$ or months				
10		2	ML	$ or months	C	C:=IF(E$3=2,RiskTrigen(D9,D10,D11,10,90),0)		
11			H	$ or months				
12								
13			L	$ or months				
14		3	ML	$ or months	D	D:=IF(E$3=3,RiskTrigen(D13,D14,D15,10,90),0)		
15			H	$ or months				
16								
17					E	E:=RiskOutput("total")+E6+Ee10+E14		

Figure 9.2: Example Decision Tree with MCS Model
(using Lumivero @Risk for Excel)

The $p10/p50/p90$ cost values for the three options from Table 9.4 were entered into the Low/Most Likely/High (L/ML/H) cells of the model shown in Figure 9.2. The team estimated selection probabilities of 30%, 40%, and 30% for the three options, with Option 2 considered the most likely scenario. Since the L and H values correspond to the $p10$ and $p90$ values, the RiskTrigen function was applied.

After running the Monte Carlo simulation (MCS), the results are displayed in the final column of Table 9.6. For comparison, the input costs for the favored Option 2 are also shown. Additionally, a $p95$ row has been included to reflect the possible worst-case scenario for NPV sensitivity analysis.[6] Note that the $p95$ value is significantly influenced by the high cost of Option 3, as the resulting distribution exhibited a long tail.

CAPITAL COST ($M)	OPTION 2	TREE MCS
$p10$	$520	$530
$p50$	$790	$850
$p70$	$930	$1020
$p90$	$1,150	$1,290
$p95$		$1,460
Accuracy around p50 (80% confidence interval)	+46/-34%	+52/-40%

Table 9.6: Decision Tree and Option 2 Cost Outcomes Including Contingency and Accuracy

Inputs to Decision Analysis and Reported Values

In addition to the cost analysis, the project team used the parametric schedule model from Chapter 11 of Volume 1 to forecast the potential range around the base project schedule duration for the three options. The decision tree method was applied to these durations in the same manner as it was for costs. The project duration, in turn, determines the timing of revenue start in the NPV model.

After completing the analysis, the team used the decision tree outcomes for both cost and schedule in the NPV analysis and the business case for capital expenditures (capex). The $p95$ values were used in scenario analysis to account for worst-case scenarios. According to company policy, the $p70$ value was selected for fund-

---

6   The example parametric model in Chapter 11 was not set up to provide the $p95$ value. The output $p95$ is obtained from the decision tree MCS.

ing purposes, so the $p70$ cost outcome from the decision tree was recorded as the budget for long-range planning (referred to as "the number").

The $p70$ of the decision tree outcome, $1,020 million, is 10% higher than the $p70$ of the favored Option 2, which was $930 million. This more conservative value helps reduce the likelihood of unexpected cost increases when the results of the next Pre-Feasibility/Class 4 phase, based on a single option, become available.

Case History B: Gas Pipeline

♦ Methods: Phased Parametric + Expected Value (P+EV) + Escalation
♦ Context: Owner and Contractor, Multi-Phase, Gas Pipeline Transportation

The Situation

This example demonstrates the phased application of the hybrid P+EV QRA method, including probabilistic escalation. Case History A focused on using the parametric method for a Class 5 estimate. Here, we explore how the method evolves as project plans and scope definition progresses from Class 4 (alternative option selection) to Class 3 (FID), and finally to Class 2 (mid-execution, start of construction). This project employed a construction-manager-at-risk (CMAR) contracting strategy, highlighting how owners and contractors might interact in QRA.

Project Background

The example project involved a regulated gas utility replacing and re-routing several kilometers of large-diameter urban gas transportation pipeline. Pipeline transportation serves as a "midstream" asset, positioned between upstream (exploration and production) and downstream (processing) segments in the oil and gas (O&G) industry. The O&G industry has been at the forefront of developing and applying phase-gate project processes, and it drove much of the research on cost growth and schedule delays covered in Volume 1. The first published paper on the hybrid P+EV method was by a major pipeline company.[7] This example reflects that industry legacy.

As with most utilities, the example project was subject to oversight by a regional public utility commission, which regulates utility

---

7   C. Figueiredo and B. Kitson, "Defining Risk and Contingency for Pipeline Projects," 2009 AACE International Transactions. (The project in this example was not done by this company.)

rates and services. Most commissions require utilities to submit project plans for approval, including cost estimates and schedules. In this case, the commission mandated that estimates align with AACE Estimate Classification guidelines (e.g., Recommended Practice RP 97R-18 for pipelines) and that probabilistic QRA be used to assess contingency (e.g., report *p*-values). However, the commission did not specify which QRA methods to use. The gas utility's phase-gate process was aligned with AACE classification standards.[8]

The commission's requirement for project plan approval before full funding and cost recovery meant that project work was suspended for several months between submitting Class 3 permit applications and beginning execution (detailed engineering, procurement, and construction). The commission could impose approval conditions or even reject the plan – risks that had to be included in the QRA, along with economic and market changes during the delay. Therefore, it was essential to update the QRA after receiving commission approval but before project execution.

Although the utility's rates were regulated, there was limited potential to recover cost overruns. As a result, the utility prioritized cost-effective investments, with a project process that included risk management and best-practice risk quantification.[9]

The pipeline being replaced ran through several kilometers of urban area, where potential interferences with residences, businesses, and existing infrastructure posed significant risks of delays and additional costs. The project also faced challenges in crossing roads, utilities, and environmentally sensitive areas. With several major pipeline projects underway in the region, the construction labor and bidding markets were highly competitive.

The project was driven by schedule constraints. It interfaced with another infrastructure project, which created a completion deadline with penalties for late completion. The planned schedule spanned approximately three years from Class 4 through the in-service date, including the required permitting delay.

Project Risk Quantification Strategy

The QRA was conducted by a project risk analyst in collaboration with the project team and Project Manager. The methods had

---

8   However, as is not uncommon, the use of QRA at Class 5 at this utility was inconsistent and no formal QRA was applied prior to Class 4.

9   Some of utility projects are at risk to the owner, making it important that the overall project system is effective for all projects.

been applied in previous company projects. The utility followed a phase-gate process, with QRA methods aligned with AACE recommended practices and the approaches outlined in this book. This was largely a textbook case, using the P+EV method to:

- Analyze multiple route options during Class 4,

- Support sanctioning at Class 3 by analyzing risk transfer in coordination with the CMAR contractor, and

- Perform a Class 2/1 QRA update at the start of construction.

Probabilistic escalation analysis was conducted at Class 4 but was not repeated due to the relatively short time remaining to the midpoint of construction.

The following sections walk through the QRA process by phase.

QRA – Class 4: Option Selection

During Class 4 design development, the project team explored multiple route options. The initial route, referred to as Alt 1 (with two sub-options), was defined and analyzed first. Several months later, two additional routes, Alts 2 and 3, were developed and analyzed, with the original route definition and analysis refined. By the end of the phase, which lasted approximately six months, the business had three fully analyzed route options to choose from. Unlike many teams that make alternative selections without fully considering the risks, this process was thorough and incorporated significant community input into the "optioneering" process.

For each alternative, semi-detailed Class 4 estimates and schedules were developed. The project team, working alongside an in-house risk lead, conducted qualitative risk analysis workshops (first for Alt 1, and later for Alts 2 and 3) and created a risk register to track and plan for risk treatments that could be integrated into the selected option as necessary.

Quantitative risk analyses (QRAs) to evaluate the risk profiles of the alternatives were facilitated by a consultant. The process began by gathering the base estimates, schedules, and associated documentation. The project manager and analyst then discussed the project's primary objectives and determined that the project was schedule-driven. This focus helped in assessing specific risk responses (contingent actions to be taken if risks materialized).

Systemic risk workshops were held (one for Alt 1 and another for Alts 2 and 3 combined) with key project team members. Each workshop lasted several hours. Using the parametric method, the systemic risk quantification was completed immediately after the workshops. The systemic risk profiles were similar across all alternatives since the same project process and team were involved, though one alternative presented more technical complexity.

Next, project-specific risks were assessed. Before conducting expected value (EV) analyses, the risk registers were screened to identify critical uncertainties and risks (those with high potential cost or schedule impacts that could significantly affect the project's success).

Project-specific risk workshops followed, with participants from the systemic workshops joined by additional discipline experts and specialists. At this stage, no construction contractor was involved. The group reviewed each risk, refining descriptions and identifying new risks. Given the schedule-driven nature of the project, the team also proposed "fast" risk responses where appropriate. The probability of occurrence and the low, most likely, and high cost and schedule impacts were elicited, with several risks classified as high impact/low probability (HILP).

The elicited inputs were entered into the EV tool, which is integrated with the parametric tool, forming a hybrid P+EV tool. HILP risk 3-point cost impacts were entered separately without regard to probability, as these would be considered for specific management reserves rather than contingency. Working with the estimator and scheduler, the project's base estimates and schedules were used to calculate burn rates for potential delays. These steps follow the guidelines in Volume 1, Chapters 11 and 12.

Once the P+EV QRAs were completed, the cost and schedule distribution outputs (*p*-tables) were imported into the consultant's probabilistic escalation model. The project costs and start/end dates were entered by cost account, differentiating between types of costs (e.g., steel, concrete, labor). With the exception of a few minor expended accounts, no costs were fixed at this stage. The model was updated with current price indices from an economics consultant, and a Monte Carlo Simulation (MCS) was run to generate a probabilistic escalation estimate, aligned with the method in Volume 1, Chapter 13.

In the end, although the systemic risk and escalation profiles were similar across the alternatives, project-specific risks (particularly HILPs) set the alternatives apart. For instance, one alternative faced the risk of potential horizontal directional drilling

(HDD) failure, while another posed significant risks due to potential construction disruptions in densely populated urban areas.

Based on these analyses, the utility owner selected a single alternative for further definition. Front-end engineering and design for the chosen route began quickly, with the understanding that the contractor would likely continue on through construction under an open book CMAR contract strategy.

QRA – Class 3: Permit Application Submission and CMAR Risk Allocation

Approximately six months after the Class 4 gate, the CMAR contractor completed a Class 3 estimate and schedule, which also served as their open-book preliminary fixed base price proposal for the construction work, excluding contingency. Their deliverables included a contractor risk register. The owner then conducted an updated qualitative risk analysis workshop, incorporating input from the contractor. Once the critical risks were identified and agreed upon, discussions were held to determine which party would be responsible for each.

Following the workshop, the contractor conducted their own QRA to determine the appropriate contingency value for their fixed price proposal, considering the risks they would be responsible for.

The owner then performed an updated P+EV analysis, running two scenarios: one assuming no risks were transferred to the contractor, and the other assuming all agreed-upon risks were transferred. The difference between the two allowed the owner to validate the contractor's contingency proposal. For this project, contingency was set at the $p50$ confidence level.

The owner's QRA also included an analysis of HILP (high-impact, low-probability) management reserve risks, which generally remained the owner's responsibility. The primary HILP risks at this point involved potential interference with underground utilities and community interactions. As the project was schedule-driven, the use of expeditious but costly risk responses was considered acceptable. There was also uncertainty regarding the final CMAR bid price (to be confirmed after the utility commission's review) and the low-probability risk that the owner might need to take an "off-ramp" from the CMAR strategy if the contractor's final price proved excessive. Given the schedule-driven nature of the project, an off-ramp would introduce delays, making such a decision difficult. A specific management reserve was set aside to address any mix of these HILP risks.

No separate escalation risk analysis was conducted at this stage, as the mid-point of spending was only about a year away, assuming timely commission approval. The owner then submitted their application to the utility commission, with most work on hold pending approval.

QRA – Class 2/1: Start of Construction

Following the commission's swift approval, the CMAR contractor finalized engineering and submitted an updated fixed-price proposal. The risks related to permit delays and the potential "CMAR off-ramp" were closed. Given that five months had passed since the previous QRA and the commission approval request, it was deemed necessary to update the QRA. Instead of holding new workshops, updated inputs were gathered from team members as appropriate, reflecting the risks that had evolved through ongoing risk management.

Notably, the perception of HILP risks had shifted. The "interference" risk, which was previously reserved as a specific management risk, was reclassified as a nominal critical contingency risk. However, concerns regarding potential HDD (horizontal directional drilling) failure had grown. As a result, a specific management reserve was set aside to address either HDD failure or the worst-case scenario from potential interferences. No further escalation analysis was conducted, as most costs were now fixed and the project in-service date was less than a year away.

Conclusions

The project was completed within the cost and schedule range forecasted during the Class 4 analysis, including the specific management reserve and escalation. It was delivered more or less on budget (which included specific management reserves) and met the scheduled in-service date set during the Class 3 QRA analysis.

This example demonstrates how risks and their analyses evolve from phase to phase, emphasizing the need for multiple analyses at Class 4 to support alternative selection. At each stage, the same P+EV method was employed, and the sequence of phases is illustrated in the Figure 9.3.

Additionally, the example highlights how contractors and owners can collaborate on risk analysis when appropriate, and under-

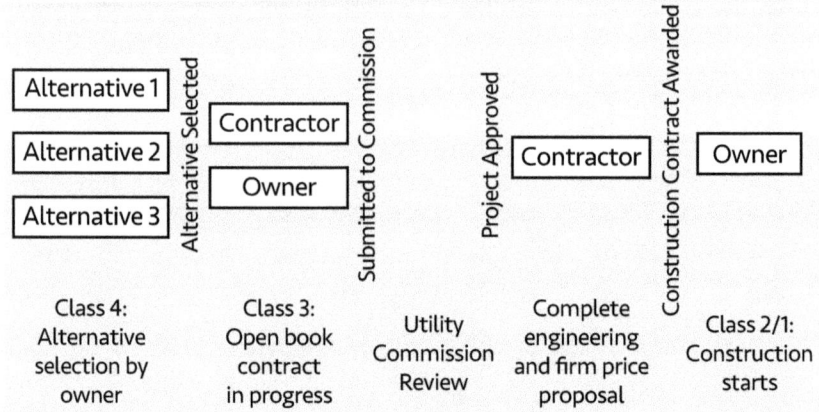

Figure 9.3: Project Phase Sequence

scores the importance of allocating specific management reserves for HILP risks. While this example does not include figures or tables, as it follows a textbook application of the P+EV methods outlined in Volume 1, Chapters 11 to 13, it is important to note that the project was completed shortly before the release of the cloud-based ValidRisk.com software that was discussed in Chapter 7. The tools used were spreadsheet versions that preceded the introduction of ValidRisk.com.

Case History C: Hydroelectric Power

◆ Methods: Parametric + Expected Value (P+EV) + Tipping Point + Reserves

◆ Context: Owner, Remote Megaproject, Execution Phase

The Situation

This example is derived from a case study paper presented by its author and co-author at the AACE International Conference and Expo in 2024.[10] A purpose of the paper was to introduce the hybrid parametric + expected value (P+EV) method to the audience. Further, it sought to demonstrate how complexity and stressors can lead to systemic fragility and non-linearity in risk impacts (relatively common for megaprojects) and to illustrate how the tipping point method (Volume 1, Chapter 14) can help to flag and quantify that

---

10 J. Hollmann and Raminder S. Bali, "Case Study: Use of the Hybrid Parametric and Expected Value QRA Method on the Keeyask Hydropower Megaproject," AACE International Transactions, Morgantown, WV, 2024.

potential impact. Finally, it pointed out the importance of funding specific management reserves to address HILP risks. The example project experienced non-linear impact behaviors, but the final outcome came within the predicted cost and schedule ranges. This is not a story of flawless prediction, but is a practical lesson-learned guide on applying P+EV on a dynamic project in which the nature of the risk evolves and analyses teeter at the tipping point

Project Background / Context

The Keeyask Hydropower Project (Keeyask) is a 695-megawatt hydroelectric generating station located on the Nelson River in Manitoba, Canada. It was developed as a collaborative effort between Manitoba Hydro (MH) and several First Nations. MH managed the construction and now operates Keeyask, which became fully operational in 2022. The project involved building:

- ♦ Earth-filled dams,
- ♦ Earthen dikes,
- ♦ A powerhouse that contains seven turbine units,
- ♦ A seven-bay spillway, and
- ♦ Supporting infrastructure (an access road, construction camps, contractor work areas, power services for construction, borrow areas, cofferdams, and an ice boom.)

The main camp facility ultimately housed approximately 2,400 private rooms.

Keeyask is situated in northeastern Manitoba, about 10 degrees south of the Arctic Circle. Major equipment was transported via a 180-kilometer gravel road from the nearest city. Most of the construction workforce was flown in from Winnipeg, followed by a lengthy bus ride to the site along the gravel road. Workers generally followed a 21-days-on, seven-days-off work schedule. The region experiences harsh, prolonged winters, with temperatures plummeting as low as −40°C. The river freezes during winter, and in spring, ice dams can form, posing flood risks. Although the typical concrete construction season runs from June through October, concrete work on the project extended through several winters, deviating from the original plan.

The civil works (including the dam, dikes, and spillway) comprised a significant portion of the project cost and were responsible for much of the cost overruns and delays. A General Civil Works Contract (GCC) was awarded to a joint venture of three partners under a target-price, cost-reimbursable contract with incentives. The civil scope involved over 17 million cubic meters of earthworks and 330,000 cubic meters of concrete.

During Keeyask's construction, Alberta was experiencing a capital expenditure boom, primarily driven by investments in oil sands development. This led to widespread shortages of skilled engineering and construction labor across Canada, contributing to significant cost overruns and delays in many projects. The hydropower sector was also experiencing a boom, with three other megaprojects underway in Canada at the time.

Company Project System

Manitoba Hydro (MH) employed a stage gate process that roughly aligned with the AACE estimate classification framework, specifically aligning with AACE Class 4, 3, and 2 estimates. The project organization at MH was lean, with a significant reliance on consultants and contractors, typical of many owner firms. However, key roles such as project managers, estimators, schedulers, and project control leads were filled by MH staff. While the team had relevant experience from a smaller generating station, the overall level of project system maturity and project control capabilities could be described as fair but not excellent.

Project Risk Quantification Strategy/Context

For the early Keeyask Class 4 and 3 estimates, MH used a form of "range estimating."[11] However, MH grew concerned about the subjective nature of this method, its consistency from one analysis to another, and its reliability in forecasting the cost growth that was occurring. As a result, MH decided to adopt the P+EV (Probabilistic + Expected Value) method.[12] After piloting the P+EV method on two previous projects and gaining confidence in it, the team was ready to apply it to Keeyask prior to awarding the General Civil Works Contract (GCC) and starting construction.

MH management committed to the P+EV method and was open to using the tipping point approach, funding specific management reserves where necessary. As a regulated entity, MH's project basis

---

11 The ranging method used was consistent with the original AACE International Recommended Practice 41R-08. That RP method was later dropped by AACE because it was inconsistent with QRA principles.

12 While RP 113R-20 for P+EV and this book were not published at that time, the author and others had reported on the hybrid method in several papers.

and analyses were subject to hearings and independent reviews, reinforcing the use of best practices.

The following attributes summarize the key uncertainties and risks associated with Keeyask, identified before the Quantitative Risk Analysis (QRA):

♦ Capex Market: End of the super-cycle, with megaprojects still wrapping up in Alberta.

♦ Hydro Market: Concurrent development of other hydro-power megaprojects in Canada.

♦ Transmission Market: Two parallel MH transmission megaprojects.

♦ Power Market: Commercial agreement in place to supply export power by 2022.

♦ Social License: Development agreement with affected First Nations communities.

♦ Government Oversight: Subject to the Manitoba Public Utility Board and Ministerial oversight.

♦ Remoteness: Workers were flown in on a 21-days-on, seven-days-off schedule.

♦ Weather: Harsh winters; concrete work typically limited to June through October.

♦ Complexity: The GCC was complicated but considered to be moderately complex as it involved no new technology.

♦ Contract Strategy: Target-price, cost-reimbursable contract (shifting most risk to the owner).

♦ MH Project System: Average owner capabilities; facing resource challenges.

These attributes contributed to the systemic fragility of the Keeyask project. The eventual cost overruns and schedule delays were not primarily caused by specific project risks, as identified in typical risk registers, but rather by *tipping point* behaviors.

Prior to the P+EV QRA, MH also drew insights from comparable projects. Two key benchmarking inputs were a recently completed MH generating station project in 2012 and a 2013 joint industry study on cost growth in Canadian hydropower projects.[13] The study indicated that a $p50$ cost growth (i.e., contingency and

13 J. Hollmann, et.al., "Variability in Accuracy Ranges: A Case Study in the Canadian Hydropower Industry," AACE International Transactions, Morgantown, WV, 2014. Used with permission.

reserves required, excluding escalation) was 24%, with a $p90/p10$ confidence interval around a Class 3 base estimate of +63/-1%. The $p50$ schedule slip was 9%, with a $p90/p10$ confidence interval of +54/-23% for a project of Keeyask's scale. These ranges were much wider than expected by most study participants.

MH policy dictated that escalation be estimated deterministically, rather than probabilistically, as recommended in this book. Escalation was included in the impacts of schedule delays. Fortunately, Keeyask's construction period (2014 to 2021) occurred between the end of the oil sands super-cycle boom and the onset of inflation triggered by COVID19.

The remainder of this example explores the execution phase QRA from the perspective of the risk analysts, covering how uncertainties and risks evolved, how risk responses were planned, and the actions taken. Figure 9.4 outlines the timeline of QRA analyses from the start of construction in 2013 to the first turbine unit's in-service date in 2021.

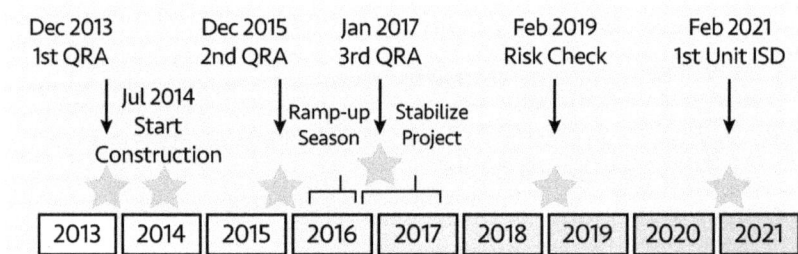

Figure 9.4: Keeyask QRA Timeline

First QRA: Pre-Construction; December 2013

In preparation for regulatory approval and the start of construction in 2014, Manitoba Hydro (MH) updated its nominal Class 3 project estimate and schedule. At this stage, input from the General Civil Works Contract (GCC) was not yet available, but the risk register was updated. The author, along with MH risk staff, led quantitative systemic and project-specific risk workshops, following the approach detailed in Volume 1, Chapters 11 and 12. A draft QRA report was issued two weeks after the workshops (one of the advantages of the P+EV method being its speed). GCC bids were received in December 2013, and the final QRA report was released in March 2014, around the time the GCC contract was awarded. The following summarizes the risk profile at that point.

Systemic Risk

Systemic risks were generally rated as moderate. However, certain areas, including geotechnical definition (there were no borings of the Nelson River bottom), team development, implementation planning, and execution strategy, were rated below Class 3 expectations. MH's project management and systems were still maturing and faced resource challenges. While the physical complexity of the project was relatively low for a megaproject, execution complexity was considered moderate due to the seasonality and remote site challenges.

Critical Project-Specific Risks

Excluding specific reserve risks (discussed in the next section), critical project-specific risks were also rated as moderate. Ten risks were quantified, with the major finding being that, cumulatively, these risks could extend construction by an additional year due to seasonality and constraints related to camp capacity and labor force size.

High Impact/Low Probability (HILP) Risks and Tipping Point

Five potential HILP risks were identified, with a non-trivial probability that one or more could occur, potentially leading to a second year of added construction beyond the contingency risks. With a planned peak workforce exceeding 1,000 and seasonal volatility, along with a somewhat aggressive GCC bid (known by the time the final QRA report was issued), the project was particularly vulnerable to severe impacts on labor productivity, especially for supervisory roles.

The possibility of disorderly, non-linear behavior was addressed through a labor cost reserve analysis. Key concerns in the tipping point analysis included the project size, the aggressive nature of the GCC bid, and challenges with team development and resource availability. While the likelihood of such disorderly behavior was considered low, there was sufficient concern to allocate a specific management reserve for it.

Second QRA: Mid-Construction, Pre-Ramp Up (December 2015)

After the first full construction season in 2015, a mid-project QRA was conducted, including both systemic and project-specific risk workshops. The analysis was based on the remaining cost and schedule of the original control budget, with no major re-forecast. By this time, all major procurements had been bid, and engineering models were nearing completion. Temporary river management structures (cofferdams), which allowed for dewatering and excavation work on the powerhouse and spillway, were complete, and spillway excavation was in progress. Some minor concrete work had also been completed. Overall, the project was on track, and the general perception was that the risk profile had not significantly changed since the first QRA. The team felt confident about the labor force ramp-up for the 2016 GCC season. The following discussion summarizes the updated risk profile recorded at that time.

Systemic Risk

Systemic risks continued to be rated as moderate, with ongoing concerns about team development and staffing. Given the reimbursable contract, where the owner assumes productivity risks, there was still uncertainty about MH's ability to handle project control and change management effectively, especially during and after the critical ramp-up phase in the coming year.

Critical Project-Specific Risks

Specific risks remained moderate and similar to those identified in the first QRA. While two risks were closed (such as the risk of cofferdam overtopping), four new near-critical risks had emerged. The primary critical uncertainty remained labor productivity. As with the first QRA, cumulative schedule risks posed a threat of extending the project by an additional year of construction.

HILP Risks and Tipping Point

As in the first QRA, multiple HILP reserve risk events persisted. An additional HILP risk was identified, maintaining a non-trivial probability that one or more could occur, potentially adding another year of construction beyond the contingency risks. Concerns about labor productivity during the 2016 labor ramp-up remained high. In a forewarning, the QRA report noted that a Canadian hydropower megaproject, which had started about a year earlier than Keeyask, was already experiencing significant difficulties.

Third QRA: Mid-Construction, Post-Ramp Up
(January 2017)

Tipping Point Threat Realized;
Recovery/Stabilization Plan Initiated

During the 2016 construction season, General Civil Contract (GCC) labor productivity fell short of expectations. Despite significant progress in procurement and the completion of engineering work, only 41% of the planned concrete was completed by the GCC. By summer, it became evident that the project faced a potential tipping point. This prompted a call to action, involving the project team, MH, and GCC Executive Sponsors and CEOs. A recovery plan was implemented in September 2016. Additionally, the Manitoba Hydro-Electric Board (MHEB) initiated a review, which concluded in September 2016 that continuing with Keeyask was still the most cost-effective option for meeting future energy demand. The review, which included an independent consulting study, projected substantial delays and cost increases.

As construction continued into the winter of 2016/2017, the recovery plan remained in effect, with improved construction management. MH conducted a thorough evaluation of alternatives for the GCC contract, concluding that amending the existing contract was the best course of action. Other alternatives would introduce significant additional risks and greater impacts on cost and schedule. The QRA, which included tipping point considerations, contributed to this evaluation.

In February 2017, the contract amendment was finalized, and by March, the project was re-baselined with the approval of the Keeyask partnership. The MHEB also approved a new control budget and revised first unit in-service date (ISD) in February 2017.

In terms of the QRA, a project re-forecast was completed in December 2016, serving as the basis for the analysis. Full systemic and project-specific risk workshops were conducted once again. The findings of the third QRA are summarized below.

Systemic Risks

While design deliverables and procurements had advanced, systemic risks remained moderate, with a slight increase from the 2016 QRA. The level of planning definition was considered lower (comparable to a nominal Class 4) due to the contract, cost, and schedule planning baselines being in flux. Execution complexity increased as a result of the recovery plan's actions. Additionally, MH's project system capability was downgraded due to its performance in 2016. This case highlights the importance of conducting systemic risk analysis (parametric) during mid-construction, as project systems can evolve significantly throughout the project lifecycle. It underscores the value of applying full P+EV not only before execution but also during to improve project outcomes.

Critical Project-Specific Risks

Critical project-specific risks remained moderate. However, due to the low productivity assumed in the revised GCC concrete baseline and the increased workforce density, delays from identified critical risks became more costly.

HILP Risks and Tipping Point

As in previous QRAs, multiple reserve risk events persisted, with a non-trivial probability that at least one would occur, resulting in an additional year of construction beyond contingency risk impacts.

With a larger workforce and winter work now part of the plan, the project remained vulnerable to labor productivity challenges. However, no additional management reserve was recommended, given the recovery plans and the revised base estimate's conservative assumptions based on the 2016 concrete productivity levels.

Regarding tipping point analysis, the QRA report stated, *"Once in this distressed mode, control strategies can focus on either 'containment' or 'recovery'. Containment largely accepts the labor and supervision situation and works to ensure predictability with what is at hand. Recovery attempts to restore productivity to something closer to the original plan which adds stress to the project."*

In other words, aggressive actions such as changing contractors risk pushing the project over the tipping point into disorder, from which no typical control strategy can recover. Success requires motivating the team toward achievable goals, as a belief that the project is destined to fail can lead to ever-increasing budgets and timelines, which erode confidence and cause further disruptions. The Keeyask project adopted a stabilization/containment strategy, which was accepted.

Risk Check-Up and Work Transition (February 2019)

The recovery efforts initiated in 2016 proved successful, stabilizing performance through the peak season of 2017 and into

2018. However, the path was not easy. The project owner and GCC worked diligently to meet commitments, seize opportunities, and address risks as they arose. By 2019, as construction shifted from civil and concrete work to mechanical and electrical balance-of-plant tasks, concerns arose about a potential change in the risk profile. In response, a qualitative risk assessment was conducted in January 2019. The energized, focused team concluded that a full QRA update was unnecessary at that time.

Final Results: 2021

The balance-of-plant work progressed smoothly despite the challenges posed by the COVID-19 pandemic during the final stages of the project. The first turbine unit was brought online in February 2021, six months ahead of the date forecasted in 2017.

However, the total project cost increased from $6.5 billion to $8.2 billion (Canadian). The first unit in-service milestone slipped by 15 months to February 2021, but commercial power obligations were still met. When compared to the first QRA risk allowance values set in 2013 (accounting for interest not included in the QRA), the final cost of $8.2 billion fell near the upper range of the 2013 extended P+EV.

Project-Specific Risk Experience

Looking back, more than half of the critical project-specific risks identified in 2013 occurred, including a shortage of skilled labor, low productivity, adverse weather, camp delays, geotechnical conditions, blockades, fire, high water flow, and reservoir filling delays. The team successfully identified these risks, and the P+EV methodology effectively quantified their impacts. While these risks were not exceptional for a major hydropower project, they reinforced the importance of systematic risk assessment.

QRA Lessons Learned

The primary lesson learned is one of success. For the most part, the P+EV method – incorporating HILP risks, tipping point analysis, and specific management reserve funding – handled project uncertainties effectively, except for the tipping point and labor productivity risks. The core issue at Keeyask was systemic fragility, rather than discrete risk events or background uncertainties. In 2013, the potential for a tipping point was underestimated, particularly in terms of the fragility of labor productivity, which proved to be a critical risk.

Another key success was the project's response in 2016. Under strong, pragmatic leadership, Keeyask confronted the tipping point threat head-on and developed a robust risk management strategy. The project avoided the pitfalls of an overly aggressive recovery plan (e.g., unrealistic productivity targets or removing the contractor), opting instead for a contained and manageable stabilization strategy. This approach led to a single, decisive budget increase, unlike other Canadian megaprojects that experienced multiple, incremental cost and schedule overruns over the years.

Tipping Point Learnings

A successful tipping point assessment should produce a qualitative warning of potential disorder or productivity shortfalls, prompting the owner to revise project scope and system attributes to mitigate the drivers (e.g., manage complexity, strengthen teams, treat HILP risks, and reduce aggressiveness). Because the tipping point threat can arise mid-execution, applying the extended P+EV method with tipping point analysis throughout the project lifecycle is crucial. At Keeyask, the 2013 assessment did not meet these expectations. Key lessons for improving tipping point analysis include:

1. Rating Aggressiveness

The aggressive bias in the base cost and schedule was overly generalized, applying a broad "average" perspective to the entire scope. This overlooked the variability and peaks in manpower demand, which surged rapidly to over 1,000 workers within a few months. In hindsight, this aggressive ramp-up should have been flagged in a tipping point assessment. Aggressiveness should be evaluated relative to peak work activity rather than an average across the project timeline.

2. Rating Team Development/Project System Capability

The QRA's assessment of team capability and management systems was also overly broad, failing to consider whether there might be a breaking point under extreme workload peaks. While the MH and GCC management teams performed adequately during 2014/2015's lower activity, they were not equipped for the demands of 2016's peak workload. A refined assessment should consider whether the team has the capacity to handle peak work periods effectively, and if recent, comparable project experience is lacking, the capability should be discounted accordingly.

3. Starting Early with P+EV and Tipping Point Analysis

To manage tipping point drivers effectively, such as systemic fragility, extended P+EV should be applied early – ideally at the nominal Class 4 decision gate when scope and execution strategy are approved. This would allow for proactive management of potential tipping point drivers well before engaging major contractors or finalizing execution plans.

Additional QRA Lessons Learned

While the P+EV with specific management reserves proved effective overall, several practices could have been refined to provide a stronger risk buffer from the outset. These include:

General Management Reserve Funding

Keeyask's contingency was funded at the $p50$ confidence level, without a general "risk tolerance" reserve. Major projects should be funded at a higher confidence level ($p70$ or $p80$) to cover unforeseen risks. It is imprudent to base investment decisions on a $p50$ "coin toss" approach for day-to-day uncertainties, especially for strategic projects of significant economic impact.

Probabilistic Escalation Analysis

MH did not account for probabilistic escalation, only incorporating escalation as a specific risk tied to schedule slippage. Although the project benefitted from a relatively stable, non-inflationary economy during its six-year timeline, no megaproject should be funded without including probabilistic escalation as a major risk. Escalation should be funded at the same confidence level as general reserves (e.g., $p70$ or $p80$).

Conclusions

Overall, the extended P+EV method at Keeyask – along with HILP risk assessment, tipping point analysis, and specific management reserves – was successful, with one exception: the 2013 tipping point assessment did not adequately warn of the labor productivity issues that arose later. Nevertheless, by 2016, the tipping point threat was recognized and addressed with a well-developed stabilization plan. Only one mid-project budget increase was necessary, and subsequent cost and schedule growth were contained.

The overarching lesson is that the Keeyask risk story was one of systemic fragility rather than discrete risk events. Traditional

QRA methods do not directly address fragility; a tipping point or similar non-linearity assessment is essential. To manage such risks effectively, the extended P+EV method should be applied early, providing time to make necessary adjustments to scope, strategy, and project systems before they become critical.

No single QRA method guarantees a project will come in on budget and on schedule. However, by applying a range of methods throughout the project lifecycle, a QRA can realistically capture, quantify, and communicate the risk profile, enabling executive management to make informed decisions. In the end, Keeyask's final cost did fall within the QRA's anticipated range, which, while small consolation, reflects the effectiveness of the analysis.

"'The time has come,' the Walrus said, 'To talk of many things: Of shoes – and ships – and sealing-wax – Of cabbages – and kings – And why the sea is boiling hot – And whether pigs have wings...'"
– From "The Walrus and the Carpenter" by Lewis Carroll

10
Volume 1 Appendix: Updates and Miscellany

Chapters 1 through 9 of this volume introduce significant new stand-alone content since Volume 1 was published. However, several topics that I have learned about, incorporated into my risk analyses or trainings, helped develop tools for, or written papers on since the release of Volume 1, are not extensive enough for full chapter treatment. These are mainly expansions or updates to the topics in Volume 1. They would have been included in a second edition but are appended here to keep Volume 1 unchanged.

For each chapter in Volume 1, in addition to the specific stand-alone content listed in Table 10.1, I provide brief reflections on general industry changes in the topic areas over the ten years since the original Volume 1 content was first drafted.

Table 10.1 lists specific update contents of this chapter that are in addition to the general perspectives. The section numbering aligns with the associated Volume 1 chapter numbers. The updated Risk Quantification Process Map (Figure 7.1 of Volume 1) is highlighted due to its central importance to the book's content.

Number	Vol 1 Chapter	Topic Heading
10-3.1	3	Phase-Gate for Non-Process Commercial / Infrastructure
10-3.2		Cost Overrun by Phase for Transport: Grattan Institute
10-4.1	4	Accuracy Information from RCF Studies
10-6.1	6	Contingency Allocation
10-6.2		High Probability Risks: Where to Fund Them?
10-7.1	7	Risk Matrix/Critical Risks
10-7.2		Updated Risk Quantification Process Map: Figure 7.1
10-7.3		Updated Strengths and Weaknesses of CPM and EV Approaches: Table 7.1
10-8.1	8	QRA Maturity Model and Toolbox: AACE Recommended Practices
10-10.1	10	The J-QPD Distribution; End of the Triangle? (and Focus on the $p90$)
10-12.1	12	Updated EV Method Flowchart, Figure 12.1
10-12.2		Avoid Eventification
10-13.1	13	Lessons Learned: The 2021/22 Covid Escalation Experience
10-14.1	14	Lessons Learned: Tipping Point, Management Reserves and More
10-16.1	16	Risk Communication: Transitioning QRA Methods
10-17.1	17	Cost and Schedule Contingency Drawdown

Table 10.1: Chapter 10 Topics

Chapter 1 Perspectives (Introduction: Why Risks Are Poorly Quantified)

This chapter remains relevant, as the fundamental reasons why risks are poorly quantified have not changed. However, there has been some progress. Awareness of systemic risks has increased, and AACE International continues to publish additional Recommended Practices for quantitative risk analysis (QRA), emphasizing a comprehensive "risk toolbox" to address various risk types and improve organizational QRA maturity. Most notably, rapid advances in machine learning and artificial intelligence have sparked C-level interest in data and analytics. Ten years ago, few executives were inclined to invest in data and analytics as advocated in Volume 1. Nevertheless, projects still face phase-to-phase cost and schedule surprises, frequently overrunning budgets and finishing late due to poor risk quantification. The chapter's "top ten" reasons why risks remain poorly quantified are as relevant as ever.

Chapter 2 Perspectives (Risk: God of the Gate; Creator and Destroyer of Value)

As with Chapter 1, the core principles of this chapter remain valid, as the nature of risk has not fundamentally changed. However, the industry has increasingly focused on sustainability and social license, which act as systemic risk drivers and add project-specific risks. One positive development has been the reduced industry reliance on Reference Class Forecasting. This practice, by largely accepting uncertainty and risk as unavoidable, risked institutionalizing mediocrity, particularly in public transportation projects.

Chapter 3 Perspectives (Phase Gate Capital Project Systems)

Phase gate systems are now widely adopted across industries, including publicly funded infrastructure, although infrastructure projects still often struggle with political challenges to disciplined practices. The application of phase gates in infrastructure is further explored in section 10-3.1. AACE International has continued to develop industry-specific estimate classification Recommended Practices (RPs), now covering most areas in engineering and construction. AACE is also working on a new RP for phase-gate system practices.

The Construction Industry Institute (CII) has also expanded its PDRI tools to include more industry segments, and research linking scope definition levels with cost growth continues, including in infrastructure (section 10-3.2). However, research-backed project risk quantification methods – such as parametric modeling and ML/AI – are still not commonly utilized.

10-3.1 Phase Gates for Non-Process Commercial /Infrastructure

Table 1.1 of this volume (shown again above) includes a "Phase-Gate Rosetta Stone" comparing five different phase naming

AACE	FEL	Process	Mining / Minerals	Non-Process / Commercial
5	1	Conceptual	Scoping	Pre-Design
4	2	Basic Engineering	Pre-Feasibility	Schematic
3	3	Front-End Engineering and Design (FEED)	Feasibility	Design Development / Feasibility
2		No common name: FID / control estimates re-baselined using construction contractor input		Construction Documents or Tender / Bid
1		No name: engineering is near or at 100%; used for changes		

Table 1.1: Typical Phase Name Conventions Compared to AACE Classifications

conventions: Class, FEL, Process, Mining, and Non-Process Commercial. For the commercial/infrastructure industry sectors, the phase names are not standardized. This section adds more detailed name alternatives, descriptions, and comparisons to the process sector for cross-sector clarity. These phases mainly reflect the AIA IPD Guide[1] and an AACE paper by Christopher and Leo Carson, which offers an excellent cost engineering perspective.[2] The phases described are as follows:

♦ Programming/Pre-Design/Conceptualization
♦ Schematic/Criteria Design
♦ Design Development/Detailed Design
♦ Construction/Implementation Documents
♦ Tender/Bid Documents (typical Sanction gate)
♦ Construction
♦ Post-Construction/Closeout

Programming / Pre-Design / Conceptualization

This roughly corresponds to Class 5/FEL 1. The Carsons' treatment is similar to the process "Conceptual" phase; however, the IPD guide includes developing costs by system and understanding the costs of each trade contractor, which goes beyond the process phase content. For buildings, the key scope measure is physical size and

---

1   American Institute of Architects, "Integrated Project Delivery: A Guide," 2007 (rev 1).

2   Carson, Christopher W. and Leo J. Carson, "Implementation of an Integrated Phase-Gate Project Controls Process," AACE International Transactions, 2023.

system (foundations, structure, etc.), compared to capacity and block flow steps for processes.

Schematic / Criteria Design

This roughly corresponds to Class 4/FEL 2. The Carsons' treatment is similar to the process "Basic Engineering" phase; however, the IPD guide addresses tolerances between trades to enable prefabrication, which extends beyond the process phase content. The IPD guide also discusses the selection and initial design of major building systems, compared to process flow diagrams, heat and material balances, and major equipment identification for processes.

Design Development / Detailed Design

This roughly corresponds to Class 3/FEL 3. The Carsons' approach is similar to process FEED, with engineering still being only about 30 percent complete. However, the IPD guide includes carrying the design to the extent of identifying furnishings, which is beyond what FEED provides. The IPD guide speaks of having all key design decisions finalized (if not "fully engineered"), compared to process and instrumentation diagrams, plot plans, and major equipment data sheets for processes. Construction contract strategy is defined.

At this phase, the industry approaches diverge: the process/industrial sectors usually make their final investment decision here (there are no further numbered "FEL" gates), whereas the commercial/infrastructure sectors do not.

Construction / Implementation Documents

This phase is uniquely defined for the commercial/infrastructure sectors. In the process sector, based on cost growth research, construction contract documents (as opposed to the contract "strategy" defined in the prior phase), while important, are not considered critical to bottom-line uncertainty and risk. All detailed engineering and construction activities are performed, typically overlapping, in the uninterrupted "Execution" phase, and no Class 2 or Class 1 estimates are usually prepared by the owner in the process sector.

For the commercial/infrastructure sector, the construction documents phase roughly corresponds to Class 2 in the Carsons' approach, wherein the design is not yet 100% complete. However, the IPD guide indicates that construction means and methods should be finalized and documented, with the construction schedule and cost also finalized and agreed upon, resulting in a "bankable" estimate.

Tender / Bid Documents

This phase roughly corresponds to Class 1, with drawings and specifications ready for construction. According to the IPD guide, commitments are in place for everything required to complete the project, meaning full funds are sanctioned.

Construction

This phase's scope is self-explanatory, taking the project through to substantial completion. In the process industry, detailed engineering and construction usually overlap and are combined in the overarching "Execution" phase.

Post Construction

For all industries, the close-out phase is similar.

Document Handoffs

Regarding contract strategy, the Carsons provided a simple summary of when the design document production is typically handed off to the contractor. This applies to all industry segments, with the key difference being the point at which full funds are sanctioned. The process/industrial segment does not have a formal gate after FEL 3 sanction. Document handoffs include:

- Integrated Project Delivery: Handed off early in Schematic Design (FEL 2)
- Design-Build, EPC, PPP, Multi-Prime: Handed off early in Detailed Design (FEL 3)
- CM at Risk, CM/GC: Handed off at the end of Construction Documents
- Design-Bid-Build: Handed off at the end of Tender/Bid Documents

10-3.2 Cost Overrun by Phase for Transport: Grattan Institute

Volume 1, Chapter 3 includes a section titled "Scope Definition: Driver of Cost Growth and Schedule Slip," which reviews empirical research on the topic by Hackney, Rand, and CII. Research in the publicly funded infrastructure sector has lagged but is beginning to catch up. Increasingly, research is examining the relationship between cost growth, schedule slip, and the level of scope definition. However, it generally has not advanced to addressing other systemic risks.

One example is the use of Reference Class Forecasting (RCF), a form of gross benchmarking, which is starting to consider the level of scope development of an estimate (see 10-4.1).

Another example is shown in Figure 10.1 from the Grattan Institute in Australia, included in their 2016 report "Cost Overruns in Transport Infrastructure" (Terrill), which illustrates the cost growth for different size projects from the pre-commitment (Class 3), commitment (Class 2), to construction phase (Class 1).

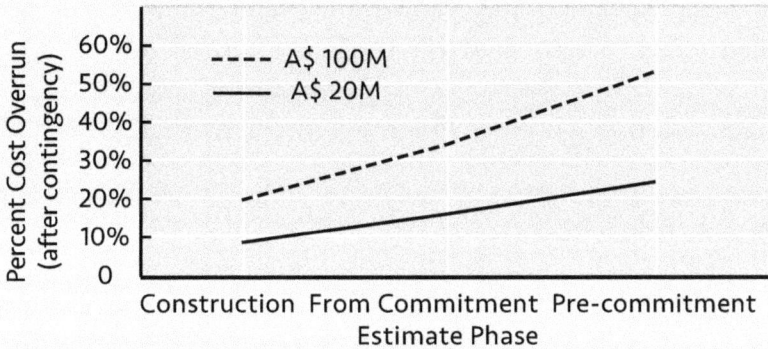

Figure 10.1: Grattan Institute (Aus): Percent Cost Overrun: Transport [2016]

Chapter 4 Perspectives (Accuracy: Confidence and Credibility)

The primary updates relevant to this chapter include heightened attention to the accuracy of publicly funded infrastructure projects, as illustrated in Section 10-4.1. There is also a greater acknowledgment that early estimates must address the uncertainty arising from multiple scope options – an important factor in early-phase accuracy. This topic is now covered in Chapter 6 of Volume 2. Additionally, AACE has published the Recommended Practice 104R-19: *Communicating Expected Estimate Accuracy*, which provides valuable guidance on this topic.

10-4.1 Accuracy Information from RCF Studies

Chapter 4 of Volume 1 reviews "controlled" research studies on accuracy, primarily focusing on the process industries. Although there are published studies on the accuracy of public infrastructure projects, most of these studies are uncontrolled for known risk drivers (such as the level of scope definition at sanction), rendering their conclusions about the causes of overruns and schedule slips suppositional.

Public infrastructure accuracy research has been somewhat handicapped by an academic focus on the planning fallacy: optimism bias as the primary cause of overruns and schedule slips. This industry's use of Reference Class Forecasting (RCF) as a method to avoid overruns (de-biasing) is based on accepting most systemic risks as fate and focusing mainly on predictability at the expense of improving competitiveness. This risk acceptance is partly due to the lack of broad-based benchmarking consortia that share and study project system risks in public infrastructure. Consequently, the industry relies on gross RCF metrics as the best available option.

However, RCF studies are beginning to acknowledge the importance of the level of scope definition, and at least one source now displays accuracy information. For example, Table 10.2, derived from a chart in a 2020 UK Department for Transport guideline on RCF,[3] shows the RCF "uplifts" to bottom-line budgets and schedules recommended for road projects. Note the similarity of the $p90$ cost values to the observed ranges in Figure 4.3 of Volume 1.

UK DEPT FOR TRANSPORT BUSINESS CASE STAGE	APPROXIMATE AACE CLASS	ROAD COST UPLIFT REQUIRED ($P10$ TO $P90$)	
		COST	SCHEDULE
Strategic Outline	Class 5	-35% to +250%	-20% to +120%
Outline Business Case	Class 4	-35% to +90%	-20% to +120%
Full Business Case	Class 3	-20% to +70%	-20% to +100%

Table 10.2: 2020 UK Department for Transport RCF Uplifts for Road Projects

Chapter 5 Perspectives (Investment Decision Making at the Gate)

While owner investment decision-making methods have largely remained the same, this volume introduces substantial new content in Chapter 7 on QRA methods to enhance cost and schedule inputs for NPV/IRR and similar financial models. Additionally, ML/AI is beginning to influence boardroom decisions, though executive-level

---

3   UK Department for Transport, "2020 data update to the 2004 Guidance Document Procedures for Dealing with Optimism Bias in Transport Planning; Updating the evidence behind the optimism bias uplifts for transport appraisals," Appendix A, 2020.

behavioral biases continue to heavily impact capital investment decisions. Chapter 3 of this volume also provides expanded insights into contractors' executive-level bid/no-bid and pricing decisions.

Chapter 6 Perspectives (Budgeting for Risk)

Risk budgeting and project control practices have not evolved significantly, and confusion persists around planning and budgeting for contingency, escalation, management reserves, and schedule buffers. Decision-making bottlenecks, such as slow and indecisive committees with control over contingency funds, continue to be common, as do trust issues between business and project teams and between owners and contractors. Section 10-6.1 further explores these topics. Additionally, management often remains hesitant to allocate adequate funds for necessary management reserves. Section 10-6.2 underscores the critical importance of both general and specific management reserves for strategic initiatives and megaprojects, including escalation provisions.

10-6.1 Contingency Allocation

Chapter 6 of Volume 1 covers "Budgeting for Risk" and describes contingency as a budget account for risk in detail. However, it does not address whether and how contingency might be subdivided or allocated to various parts of a project control budget breakdown. This brief section addresses that topic.

The AACE definition of contingency states it can only be quantified "in aggregate" – it is only quantifiable to the bottom line. However, this raises the question: "the bottom line of what?" Generally, the "what" is the entire project, or a major work breakdown element or sub-project under the authority of a project manager. Each element would have a separate risk quantification analysis; i.e., the contingency is not allocated as such.

However, when major execution contracts are awarded (after tender at Class 2), contract managers may be assigned, and the project may choose to "allocate" or parcel out some or all of the project-level contingency to the contract administrators. This allocation is a form of budgeting for convenience. It shifts authority for contingency use away from the project manager, distancing them from risk control. The act of requesting contingency funds via the change management process is supposed to force near real-time communication with the project manager.

Because we cannot predict which risks will occur (we need to be humble!) and how systemic uncertainties will manifest, budget allocation of contingency will overfund some scope elements and underfund others regardless of the risk quantification method. This sets up potential conflict between work package or contract managers when one needs funds to cover risks that have occurred, but others holding those funds do not want to relinquish them.

As a general rule, try to avoid contingency allocation. Keep contingency management authority with the project manager.

10-6.2 High Probability Risks: Where to Fund Them?

Chapter 12 of Volume 1 discusses "Project-Specific Risks and the Expected Value Method," including a section on "Considering Overwhelming Risks" (high impact/low probability [HILP] risks). Fund these reserves as specific management reserves.

But what about critical[4] post-treatment risks with a high probability of occurring? Volume 1, Chapter 6 suggests funding these project-specific risks via contingency. Volume 1, Chapter 12 calls for applying the expected value (EV) QRA method for these risks (probability times impact with MCS). However, is this the right approach when the probability is very high?

In risk management training classes, I have suggested that if the probability of a specific risk occurring is greater than 50 percent, consider recycling through risk treatment and "including the risk in the base estimate" rather than funding it through contingency via the EV method. However, this statement does not address the real issues. It is more complicated than just saying, "if $p>50\%$, then do X." So, what is really meant by this statement?

The "include it in the base" statement stems from research and benchmarking that show risk occurrences during execution mean change, which can be highly disruptive to project control. Additionally, we know that large projects are fragile. Cost and schedule success depend on good front-end scope and planning definition, and maintaining good discipline during execution (plan the work and work the plan). As a late change, the impact of a critical risk event is often a multiple of the 3-point distribution quantified by the project team using the EV method, particularly for the risk profile defin-

---

4   Recall that the definition of a critical risk is one that, if it occurred, would have a material impact on the project. It individually could threaten the success of the cost and/or schedule success of the project. A critical risk is a serious threat.

ing the "high" point value. This is because a critical risk occurrence may result in lost construction productivity and delays that are not readily apparent, especially if the project system and controls are weak. Therefore, the high impact is not really X, but X+Y, with Y being the penalty for late change and disruption.

Further, tipping point logic suggests that Y may contribute to pushing the project into disorder: impact is X+Y+Z, with Z being the non-linear disorder penalty. As a risk analyst, this worries me. Hence, return to risk treatment and effectively build the risk into the base scope, estimate, and schedule. The reasoning is that as base scope, the relevant work will be done in an orderly, planned way, so the cost of addressing the risk in the base will be less than Y (and much less than Y+Z).

But what exactly should be included in the *base*? This does not necessarily mean just adding the cost impact as a base estimate and/ or schedule duration allowance, although that is an option. It more often means implementing a more aggressive risk treatment that significantly reduces the probability of occurrence. It also means adding the treatment result to the scope of work, not just the estimate and/or schedule.

For example, if the risk of a river overflowing the cofferdam of a hydropower project during seasonal floods, with serious impacts, is greater than 50 percent, an overflow is arguably becoming more of a fact than a risk. Is it better to include some funds in contingency at X% times the potential impact, including potential disruption and disorder at the tail, or to plan and construct a higher cofferdam at a known cost and duration? Changing the design now will reduce the risk probability of occurrence (if the impact is great, the risk may then fall into the potential specific management reserve category for HILPs). The greater-than-50% rule suggests that the team take a harder look at that risk and consider more rigorous treatment.

Another common example is the "migratory bird nest disturbance" risk. Regulations may require that if an active nest is found, the area around it must not be disturbed, which could delay work by weeks or even months. In the past, projects would often "take their chances" and hope, even if the probability was high, that they did not find any active nests (sometimes tucked in the corner of a piece of equipment). However, in recent years, most projects have developed the base plan to avoid clearing or other potentially disturbing work during the nesting season. "Adding it to the base" with a longer planned duration is considered more orderly and economical (and better stewardship of the environment) than the cost of a disruptive delay with potential claims, citations, penalties, and so on. There are many such examples today of potential scope additions to meet regulations, permit conditions, or stakeholder demands.

In summary, avoid mindless risk quantification by applying probability times impact to all post-treatment critical risks directly from a risk register. Consider how an accepted critical risk's occurrence might actually impact the cost and schedule, including the tail risk scenarios. Also, plan the QRA with enough lead time to allow the team to recycle through risk treatment and base plan modification. My experience has taught me to be conservative in QRA; there is little evidence favoring having optimism bias, particularly on large, complex projects.

Chapter 7 Perspectives (Introduction to Risk Quantification Methods)

QRA methods are evolving, as demonstrated in this volume and in new AACE Recommended Practices. AACE has developed a comprehensive QRA toolbox and application guide (Professional Guidance Document PGD-02: Guide to Quantitative Risk Analysis) that readers are encouraged to review. Notably, AACE RP 113R-20 now covers the hybrid parametric + expected value (P+EV) method introduced in Volume 1. Additionally, AACE RP 117R-21, along with Chapter 4 and the worked example in Appendix 1 of this volume, thoroughly explain the hybrid parametric and CPM-based method. Section 10-7.3 below updates Volume 1 Table 7.1, outlining the strengths and weaknesses of the hybrid P+CPM approach. Chapter 5 of this volume explores QRA methods for programs and portfolios, while Chapter 6 introduces a decision-tree method for addressing the uncertainty of alternative scopes and scenarios in Class 10/5 estimates. Chapter 7 presents new commercial software for implementing the P+EV method (ValidRisk®). Finally, Chapter 8 discusses the rapidly advancing ML/AI capabilities and tools available for QRA.

Despite these advancements, industry adoption of modern QRA methods remains slow, with many organizations still clinging to outdated practices. When QRA is applied, it often relies on subjective "ranging" techniques with Monte Carlo Simulation (MCS), a 1980s approach initially developed with MCS spreadsheet add-ons. This method continues to fall short of addressing project estimate uncertainties effectively.

Certain foundational aspects of QRA methodology in Volume 1 Chapter 7 have been updated. Section 10-7.1 below highlights key improvements in risk matrix development and interpretation, while Section 10-7.2 revises the central Chapter 7 QRA methods flowchart to better distinguish between general and specific management reserves. This updated flowchart serves as a major takeaway from the book—a valuable tool that works well as a poster.

10-7.1 Risk Matrix/Critical Risks

Chapter 7 of Volume 1, "Introduction to Risk Quantification Methods," includes a section summarizing the "Expected Value with MCS (for Project-Specific Risks)" and briefly describes the risk or probability-impact matrix used to determine which risks are critical (the Risk Matrix is also defined in the Volume 1 Glossary). Later, in Chapter 12 of Volume 1, "Project Specific Risks and the Expected Value Method," the discussion extends to critical risks and establishing critical capital cost and schedule duration threshold levels, guided by the Risk Matrix. Unfortunately, Volume 1 assumes that readers will have a solid understanding of what a Risk Matrix is and how it should be developed, which is not always the case.

In traditional qualitative risk management, a key tool is the risk matrix, used for prioritizing (ranking) identified risks for treatment.[5] It is prepared before developing the risk register and is usually a 5x5 table with five levels of probability of occurrence on one axis and five levels of impact on the other. An associated document typically describes the criteria for each level. For example, level 5 for impact may be described qualitatively as "extreme," level 4 as "very high," and so on. Best practice involves supplementing these descriptions with quantitative criteria for each objective (cost and duration), such as level 5 for cost being a risk impact greater than +30% or, optimally, an absolute cost impact value. Most 5x5 risk matrix squares are then scored (e.g., 5x5 = 25) and color-coded based on the score (e.g., a score of 20 or above is red or highest priority). These are typical features of the risk matrix.

However, several aspects of risk matrix development and interpretation are often poorly understood:

---

5   The risk matrix is a controversial topic in risk management because some put too much emphasis on it as the main tool in the risk management toolbox. In the methods of this book, the matrix is simply a way of prioritizing risks for treatment. It is *not* the final word for quantification.

♦ The matrix category thresholds must reflect the business objectives, as determined by the business, not the project manager or team.

♦ The cost and schedule impact thresholds must be specific to the project business case, not standard policy (percentages of base cost or duration are discouraged).

♦ The cost and schedule impact thresholds are the focus of risk quantification to determine critical risks (not probability). No high-level risk impact should be coded "green," regardless of probability.

Business Involvement in Matrix Development

A common failing is that the risk matrix numbers (e.g., +30% or $X millions) are either:

♦ defined by canned values that every project uses as policy or simply out of a lack of concern, or

♦ values provided by the project manager or someone they assign.

Both are contrary to the risk management principle that the matrix be defined by the business that sets the business objectives. Only the business (the sponsor) can say what is important to them regarding cost and schedule bottom lines. If the business is not engaged in this exercise, then the "business ownership" systemic risk rating in the parametric model must be rated as deficient.

Impact Thresholds: Use Absolute Values

The risk lead needs to elicit from the business sponsor what each level threshold is. These should be absolute values of money and time, not percentages. Whenever I see percentages, I find that either the matrix has been carbon-copied, or no real thought has been put into the specifics of the project's objectives. If this has not been done prior to risk register development, it will need to be done prior to risk quantification, at least for the highest and next-to-highest impact levels. The highest level of impact is usually set at an amount that, if exceeded, would cause the project to fail to meet its business case objectives. Engaged business sponsors should know very well what absolute cost and duration amounts could bring the project to grief. Most risk management policies require that such risks be treated and preferably eliminated before sanction.

For QRA, Focus on the Impact (Ignore the Probability)

Most matrices use the probability times impact heuristic (e.g., 5x5) for risk scoring. So, a level 5 risk for cost impact, which equates to project failure, may be rated anywhere from 25 (5x5) to 5 (1x5) depending on the probability level rating (scoring math can vary). Most teams will then color the 1x5 box as "green," meaning they can safely ignore the risk for all practical purposes. In effect, they are saying that a high impact/low probability (HILP) risk, which could result in project failure if it occurs, can be ignored. This approach invites teams to pay less attention to such risks, and if they are accepted and occur, falsely blame the failure on unknown unknowns or black swans. In reality, HILP risks often define the project risk profile for major, particularly complex, projects. For risk quantification, consider only the cost and schedule impact when screening for critical risks and ignore the probability. For risk treatment, give the HILPs the priority attention they deserve.

10-7.2 Updated Risk Quantification Process Map (Figure 7.1)

Chapter 7 of Volume 1, "Introduction to Risk Quantification Methods," includes a section on "Overall Risk Quantification Methodology" and Figure 7.1, "Risk Quantification Method Flowchart." This flowchart is considered the methodological heart of the book. However, it needed updating to address topics in Volume 2, such as specific vs. general management reserves and Class 10/5 methods. Additionally, the flowchart has been revised to place Escalation appropriately after Program-level analysis. The revised Figure 7.1 flowchart is shown in Figure 10.2.

Chapter 7 of Volume 1 includes a section on "CPM-Based Model Alternative if Applicable," which refers to the box in Figure 7.1 labeled "Expected Value and/or CPM."

10-7.3 Updated Strengths and Weaknesses of CPM and EV Approaches (Table 7.1)

This section includes Table 7.1, "Strengths and Weaknesses of CPM and EV Approaches," which needed updating to address the now recommended Cost Loaded CPM (Hybrid with Parametric) as covered in Chapter 4. It also references the applicable AACE Recommended Practices. Table 7.1 has been updated as shown in Table 10.2.

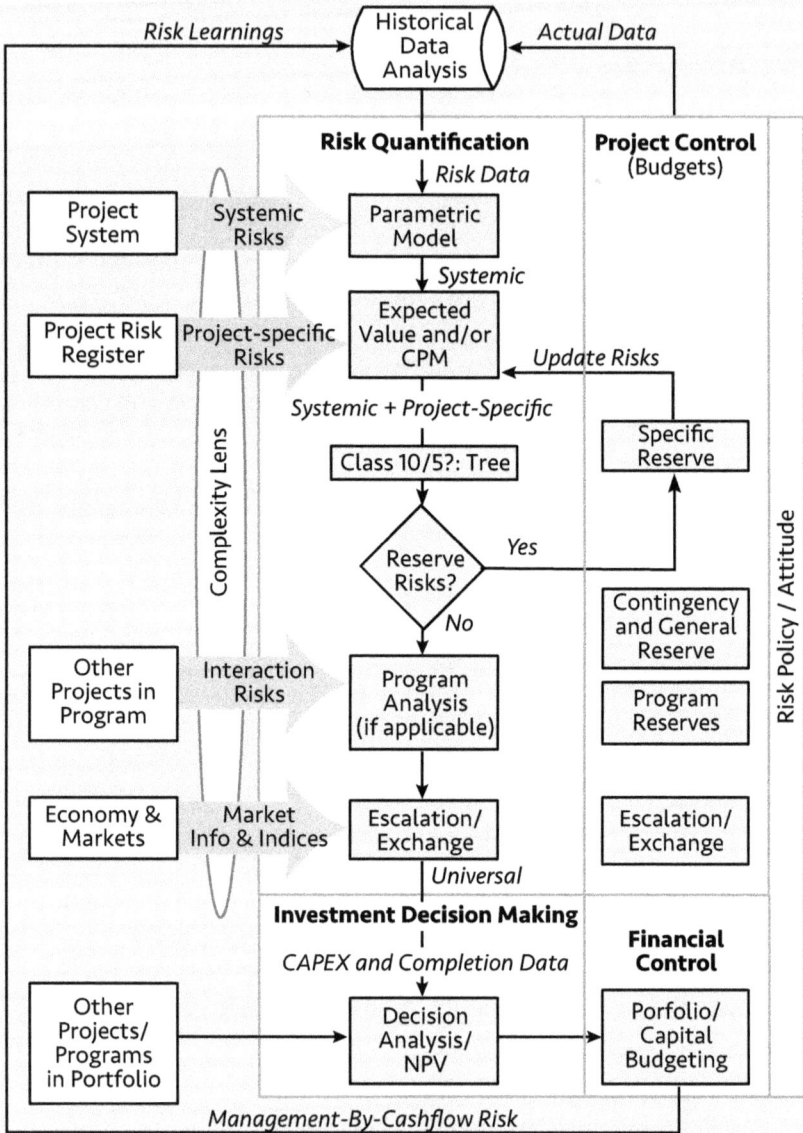

Figure 10.2: Updated Risk Quantification Method Flowchart
(old Figure 7.1)

METHOD	STRENGTHS	WEAKNESSES
COST LOADED CPM (HYBRID WITH PARA-METRIC) RP 117R-21	• Explicit risk-impact linkage • Explicit cost/schedule integration for time dependent costs • Encourages use of quality planning & scheduling methods • Quantify intermediate milestone buffers	• Complex • Requires high quality CPM model, cost-loaded schedule, competent scheduler (consultant) • Not applicable to Class 5 • Static logic assumed and difficult to address cost/schedule trading
PARAMETRIC/ EXPECTED-VALUE RP 113R-20	• Explicit risk-impact linkage • Empirical basis • Applicable to estimates and schedules of any quality • Applicable to all levels of scope definition (phase) • Address risk response • Fairly simple to apply	• Not for intermediate milestone buffers • Schedule risks and cost/schedule integration require more intuitive assessment (more skill and knowledge) • Does not encourage use of quality planning & scheduling practice

Table 10.2: Strengths and Weaknesses of CPM and Expected Value Approaches

Chapter 8 Perspectives (Organizing for Risk Quantification)

Several notable industry developments have enhanced organizational capabilities in project risk quantification. AACE has introduced its QRA Maturity Model, discussed in Section 10-8.1 below, as well as a new risk management certification, the Project Risk Management Professional (PRMP). In terms of competencies, expertise in data science and analytics—particularly in ML/AI, as covered in Chapter 8 of this volume—has now become essential for project organizations aiming to achieve the highest levels of QRA maturity.

10-8.1: QRA Maturity Model and QRA Toolbox: AACE Recommended Practices

Chapter 8 of Volume 1 covers "Organizing for Risk Quantification." The chapter lacked a framework maturity model to guide the development of QRA capability in an organization, which is now available in AACE RP 122R-22, "Quantitative Risk Analysis Maturity Model (QRAMM)."

The chapter also focused (perhaps too exclusively) on the QRA methods recommended by the book (see Figure 10.2 in section

10-7.2). An organization should be familiar with all QRA methods available, which may apply in special situations. AACE now has a product called the "Guide to Quantitative Risk Analysis" in Professional Guidance Document No. 2 (PGD-02). The publicly available PGD is an annotated road map, hyperlinked to all the AACE QRA RPs. It includes an application guide.

These two valuable RPs are summarized as follows:

Quantitative Risk Analysis Maturity Model (QRAMM), AACE RP 122R-22

The AACE QRAMM defines a maturity model for "*assessing the level of capability for quantifying the uncertainty and risks associated with projects, programs, and portfolios within the risk management function of a capital investment or project management organization.*" It follows a 5-level approach common to many industry maturity models. It is intended as a guide for planning, benchmarking, and continually improving an organization's QRA capabilities.

The QRAMM is agnostic as to specific QRA methods; there is no single recommended QRA approach. The QRAMM assumes an organization will need a toolbox of methods consistent with the Guide to Quantitative Risk Analysis, PGD-02, discussed in the next section.

Each QRAMM capability level can be applied with various degrees of rigor. To achieve a high level of maturity, an organization must clearly understand its needs and apply methods in a fit-for-purpose way. The goal is not to be cutting edge if there is no benefit from it. In the QRAMM, the high maturity levels represent having best-of-class practices but also establishing stretch goals, which today represents using advanced analytics incorporating ML/AI (see Chapter 8).

Table 10.3 summarizes the five QRAMM levels with general descriptions of each level, plus my observation of the in-house risk quantification methods usually found in organizations at each level. To see the full QRAMM matrix, refer to the AACE RP. Most organizations are at Level 2 or 3. They generally have only one or two QRA methods (mainly some version of ranging with MCS) and/or they rely on contractors and/or consultants to perform QRA as needed, using whatever tools the third party provides. They also rarely have a useful project historical database, with or without risk information.

LEVEL 1 (REACTIVE)	LEVEL 2 (AD-HOC)	LEVEL 3 (CENTRALIZED)	LEVEL 4 (DYNAMIC)	LEVEL 5 (ADAPTIVE)
No capability exists; intuition-based decision making	Ad hoc / informal processes; infrequent and limited analytical insight	Formal processes; some evidence-based decision making	Formal and dynamic processes; fact-based decision-making	Adaptive and optimized processes; fact-based decision-making
Rules-of-Thumb; no data	Ranging with MCS; little or no data	Partial QRA toolbox; limited data	Full QRA toolbox: this book; robust data	Some ML/AI with excellent data

Table 10.3: AACE QRA Maturity Model with Typical Tools (122R-22)

Only a few companies achieve Level 4 (but I hope this book leads to there being more). I have not worked with any at Level 5 which, by definition, is an aspirational moving target as practices evolve. Leveraging ML/AI in risk quantification is the Level 5 stretch goal as of this writing.

Guide to Quantitative Risk Analysis, AACE PGD-02

As a general principle, organizations should have a "toolbox" of methods. PGD-02 (available free to the public via www.aacei.org) maps a general QRA process and toolbox of methods attuned to the AACE RP library. It summarizes the QRA methods, as well as the inputs to QRA (principles, estimate validation to quantify bias, etc.) and the end uses of QRA output (value management, project control, decision making). It also includes an application guide to align an organization's needs (project size, applicable risks, etc.) with QRA methods that meet those needs.

For the most part, PGD-02 aligns with the methods recommended by this book. However, there are several AACE QRA RPs for "ranging" methods (subjective assessment of inherent uncertainty) that are only appropriate for small, simple projects with few or no critical risks. This book recommends the parametric method, properly calibrated, for use on those small projects.

Chapter 9 Perspectives (Base Cost Estimating and Scheduling)

Base estimating and scheduling practices have remained largely unchanged. While Building Information Modeling (BIM) is increasingly used to generate estimate content, it has not significantly altered the "pump-and-dump" approach described in Volume

1, and spreadsheets continue to be the most common tool for base estimating. Few companies maintain effective project historical databases, and estimators often still bias their estimates without the support of defined cost strategies or robust estimate validation. However, AACE has introduced Recommended Practices for database development (RP 114R-20) and estimate validation (RP 110R-20) to help address these gaps. Additionally, ML/AI applications offer promising opportunities for schedule optimization and validation in the execution phase (see Chapter 7 of this volume), though fully integrated QRA remains a work in progress. Chapter 3 of this volume also expands on contractor estimating strategies.

Chapter 10 Perspectives (Statistics and Models)

The fundamentals of practical statistics and modeling remain mostly unchanged. A minor development is the introduction of a distribution that can simulate the unbounded (long-tail) lognormal distribution with 3-point entry, as described in Section 10-10.1 below. However, ML/AI is increasingly moving empirically based project risk quantification methods from niche practices to mainstream approaches (see Chapter 7 of this volume). While some argue that risk analysts should acquire data science, machine learning, and programming skills in languages like R or Python, the typical role of a risk analyst will more likely involve collaborating with ML/AI specialists to identify, gather, structure, clean, and validate data on risk drivers and outcomes (data wrangling), applying models, and providing insights. A foundational knowledge of statistics, model building, and data quality is becoming essential for risk analyst careers.

10-10.1: The J-QPD Distribution; End of the Triangle? (and Focus on the p90)

Volume 1, Chapter 10, Table 10.1 summarizes the probability distribution functions (PDFs) available to risk analysts. That chapter also includes a section titled "Life is Lognormal." Volume 1, Chapter 11 describes a parametric model based on the lognormal distribution. However, Volume 1, Chapter 12 describes the Expected Value with Monte Carlo simulation (EV) method and recommends using 3-point distributions, namely triangle or PERT, not the lognormal, to quantify risk impacts (binomial is used for probabilities). This section presents a new 3-point PDF that can replicate the lognormal.

In a typical project QRA workshop, 3-points (e.g., low, most likely, high) have proven to be the extent of the cost and schedule risk impact range input that most analysts can expect to obtain from project teams, and triangle and PERT were the only 3-point PDFs available. Neither is an ideal representation of naturally occurring cost growth and schedule slip data. Their main shortcoming is that they are both bounded on the high end. Neither can realistically model tail risk, and as the book has discussed, the high value defines the risk profile, not the most likely, mean, or median.

Risk analysts, attempting to be realistic, often resort to PDF variation (e.g., trigen) and/or attempt to push teams toward the analyst's opinion of acceptable 3-point input. This manipulation can raise stakeholder suspicions about the reliability of MCS, and rightfully so.

The lognormal distribution is a more realistic fit but its use requires the analyst to quantify its mean and standard deviation parameters; that is too much to expect as inputs from a team.[6] What is needed is a lognormally shaped PDF that can be defined with 3-point input.

Fortunately, researchers at the University of Texas at Austin developed a distribution system called the Johnson *quantile-parameterized distribution* (J-QPD) that is able to match the shapes of common distributions, including lognormal and beta, with 3-point input. The author, along with Professor J. Eric Bickel, prepared a paper that reviews the typical QRA PDF use context, describes the J-QPD distribution and its use criteria, and provides practical examples of its application in an MCS-based QRA method. The authors also contacted MCS software vendors to encourage them to include the J-QPD as a distribution choice in their products (hopefully completed by the time you read this).

The J-QPD Distribution

The J-QPD is defined by a low percentile, the median (*p*50), and a high percentile. The low and high percentiles must be symmetric, such as *p*05/*p*95 or *p*10/*p*90. The J-QPD offers several important benefits:

♦ It allows for direct conversion from percentile (or quantile) assessments to a distribution without intermediate calcu-

---

6   If there are critical uncertainty or risk event impact historical data, the data could be used to define the lognormal parameters. Because of the unique nature of project-specific risks, this is unusual.

lations. This is not possible with lognormal, where one had to solve for the mean and standard deviation to match the low and high percentiles. This feature of J-QPDs is why they are called quantile parameterized distributions.

♦ It exactly matches the three input percentile assessments. The lognormal distribution cannot do this because it cannot match three percentiles by adjusting only two parameters (mean and standard deviation).

♦ It exactly matches any coherent set of three percentile assessments, such as $p05$, $p50$, and $p95$. This is not true for the triangular distribution, which cannot match certain valid percentile assessments.

♦ It can closely match common distributions. For example, if one extracts the $p05$, $p50$, and $p95$ from a triangular, PERT, or lognormal distribution and specifies a J-QPD using these values, the resulting J-QPD will be nearly indistinguishable from the original distribution. It can also match PDFs like Beta where the tail is on the low end.

♦ It can represent nearly any degree of skewness and kurtosis (tail thickness). The triangular and PERT distributions are very limited in this regard.

♦ Its cumulative distribution function (CDF) is invertible, making it easily usable in MCS.

Median rather than Mode ($p50$ rather than "Most Likely") and Focus on the $p90$

A challenge in shifting from triangle to J-QPD is getting teams to consider the center value of the 3-points as the $p50$ (median) and not the "most likely" (mode). Due to optimism bias, the "most likely" value provided by a team is often aggressive. Research indicates that for large projects, the "base" estimate typically represents about the $p15$ to $p30$ confidence level; the same applies to major risk impacts. The reference paper shares a heuristic that an analyst can use to "calibrate" team input towards more conservative $p50$ impact estimates.

Another recommendation in the paper is to estimate the high ($p90$) value first when quantifying the 3-point impact inputs. Starting with the center value anchors the team's thinking, causing them to revert to "range-think" rather than assessing the high impact value in absolute terms. For instance, teams often assume a "high" risk impact has a range of about +100%/-50% around the center value, which can be wildly inappropriate for any given risk (hence why QRA methods reliant solely on subjective "ranging" are not recommended). Focusing the QRA workshop discussion on the "worst-case" impact scenario and its possible cost in absolute terms should mitigate ranging bias and encourage more conservative thinking about the center value.

The reference paper includes several charts and tables comparing various PDFs. Table 10.4, for example, reflects a specific "high" risk impact scenario summarized in the paper. It shows percentages of some absolute impact cost. For example, if 100% represents an impact of $1 million, then 245% represents an impact of $2.45 million. The J-QPD exhibits a long upper tail (see the $p95$ row) while maintaining the central tendency of the distribution closer to that of the triangular and PERT distributions that teams are familiar with.

Percentile	Triangular	PERT	Lognormal	J-QPD
5	69%	66%	50%	50%
10	77%	73%	58%	60%
50	113%	106%	100%	110%
90	161%	147%	172%	178%
95	173%	157%	200%	200%
99	188%	173%	267%	245%

Table 10.4: Comparison of Triangular, PERT, Lognormal, and J-QPD Percentiles

The J-QPD may not significantly affect the contingency set at $p50$. However, being unbounded on the high side, it could greatly impact the $p90$ or $p95$, which is crucial for business sensitivity analyses, especially at the Class 4 "select" decision gate. The $p90$ distinguishes the risk profiles of the alternatives being selected from.

The paper provides contact information for those interested in obtaining an application tool for the J-QPD (though hopefully, MCS software vendors will have incorporated it into their products by now).

Chapter 11 Perspectives (Systemic Risks and the Parametric Model)

With over 2,000 copies of Volume 1 sold and the support of AACE Recommended Practices, the concept of systemic risks in QRA is now widely recognized and accepted. Chapter 11 remains state-of-the-art for practical, empirical project risk quantification aligned with phase-gate processes. Integrated, risk-driven ML/AI QRA methods that address systemic risks are still on the horizon. However, a major step toward mainstreaming the parametric method was the 2022 release of the cloud-based ValidRisk® software (see Chapter 7 of this volume). ValidRisk offers a free trial, reducing the need for the simplified Chapter 11 "demonstration" spreadsheet tool, though that model remains available to readers of these books.

Chapter 12 Perspectives (Project-Specific Risks and the Expected Value Method)

Traditional practices that quantify every risk in the risk register while overlooking systemic risk drivers are unfortunately still prevalent. For those adopting the hybrid P+EV method, the core principles in Chapter 12 remain valid, though some details have been expanded. Section 10-12.1 emphasizes the importance of quantifying specific management reserves for high-impact, low-probability (HILP) risks. Section 10-12.2 offers further guidance on distinguishing between risk events and specific uncertainties.

10-12.1 Updated EV Method Flowchart, Figure 12.1

Chapter 12 of Volume 1, titled "Project Specific Risks and the Expected Value Method," includes a section on "Steps in the Expected Value Quantification Method Process" and Figure 12.1, "Expected Value Method Flowchart for Project Specific Risks." This flowchart needed updating to address the distinction between general management reserves (for risk tolerance) and specific management reserves (for HILPs). It also needed to clarify the presence of critical uncertainties and risk events. The revised Figure 12.1 flowchart is shown in Figure 10.3.

10-12.2 Avoid Eventification

Two steps in the Figure 10.3 flowchart involve identifying critical "risks and uncertainties" and then quantifying the probability of occurrence. In many EV risk analyses I review, all risks are quantified as *events*, meaning the probability of occurrence is less than 100%. However, many risks are actually project-specific "condition" uncertainties (with a probability of occurrence equal to 100%), not events. I call this misassessment practice *eventification*.

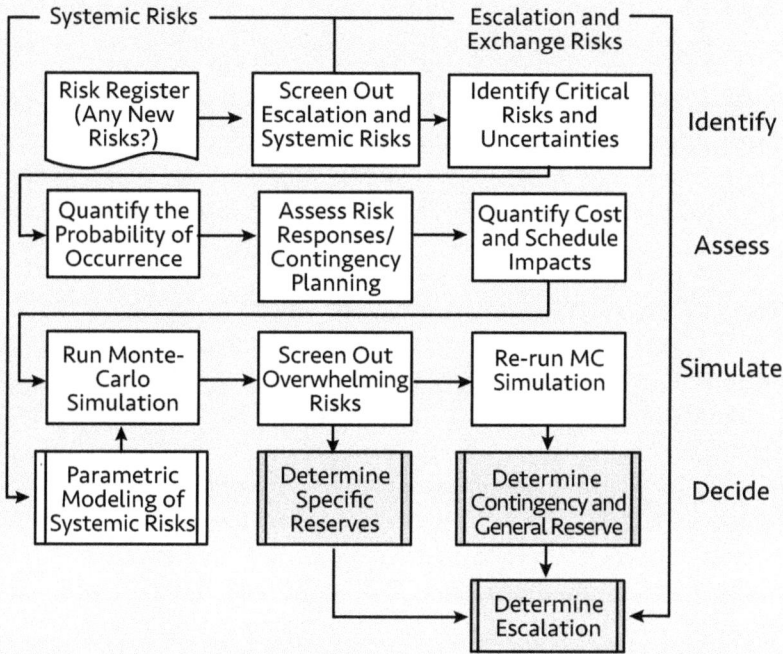

Figure 10.3: Updated Figure 12.1, Expected Value Method Flowchart for Project Specific Risks

Typical "uncertainty" risk register items are general statements such as "poor productivity," "bad weather," "adverse soil conditions," and "late deliveries." These express significant concerns about the general range of variability in quantities, hours, costs, or durations. *Events* are discrete (yes/no) occurrences.

For example, "Category 2 or above hurricane hits site during peak construction" is an event. If the risk register states "bad weather," the team should clarify whether they actually mean a discrete event like a hurricane. If so, they should rename the risk. But if their concern is "the rainy season may be much longer than we planned for," they recognize that weather varies, and they are concerned that the variation may be extreme.

So, how do you quantify "bad weather" in an EV model? First, the probability of occurrence of this risk, as stated, is 100%. In other words, we are 100% certain that the weather will not be exactly as assumed in the Basis of Estimate (BoE) or Schedule. The same is true for general statements such as soil conditions, equipment deliveries, and so on. For example, the BoE may state, "assume 3 lost days of work per month due to severe weather." It could be 0 days or 20 plus days or anything in between, with 3 lost days being the most likely based on historical experience. Another example for the "adverse soil conditions" risk item is that the rock quantity, assumed to be 200 tonnes in the BoE, may be less but could also be several thousand tonnes within reason.

Using a 3-point distribution, the impact of an uncertainty is typically entered with a most likely value of zero (weather or rock occurs as per the plan), a modestly negative low (weather or rock quantity better than plan), and a worst case within reason (e.g., worst observed in the records or in the region).

For example, the weather impact 3-point values, as a cost, may be entered as (-$10,000, $0, +$100,000). However, when teams apply eventification, they commonly input a semi-arbitrary but significant probability of occurrence of, say, 50%, and a 3-point impact logically bounded between $0 (as planned) and +$100,000 (worst case), with some most likely value midway between the low and high based on no particular logic other than perceived balance or symmetry. Note that both event and uncertainty 3-point entries have the same high value and both recognize similarly low values.

As an example of event vs. uncertainty assumptions, let's use the value from the prior paragraph:

◆ Event = 50% probability with ($0, +$50,000, +$100,000) impact versus

◆ Uncertainty = 100% probability with (-$10,000, $0, +$100,000) impact.

MCS simulation with a typical Triangular distribution yields the results in Table 10.5.

CONFIDENCE	TRIANGLE	
	EVENT (*P*=50%)	UNCERTAINTY (*P*=100%)
*p*10	$11,400	$500
*p*50	$25,000	$25,000
*p*90	$40,100	$66,800

Table 10.5: MCS Output for a General Risk Entered as an Event vs. an Uncertainty

The impact modeled as an uncertainty is strongly skewed to the high side, reflecting the tail risk often seen in historical records. If it is an uncertainty, quantify it as such. However, be aware of how that influences the MCS. Some uncertainties (e.g., weather uncertainty)

have a stronger central tendency (and are less likely to be "critical") than others, which may have a steadier march toward costly outcomes (e.g., labor shortage uncertainty).

Chapter 13 Perspectives (Probabilistic Escalation and Currency Exchange)

The fundamentals of Chapter 13 remain unchanged. However, it is concerning that most companies continue to use deterministic methods for estimating escalation and neglect to quantify escalation as a risk – a practice cited as reason #8 in the "Top Ten" list of why risks are poorly quantified (Volume 1, Chapter 1). Section 10-13.1 provides a case example that may help illustrate the importance of probabilistic escalation methods.

10-13.1 Lessons Learned: The 2021/22 Covid Escalation Experience

Chapter 13 of Volume 1 covers "Probabilistic Escalation" analysis. The Covid pandemic and the escalation of 2021/2022 provide a case study demonstrating the method's value. In 2020, prior to the pandemic, an industrial client requested a QRA, including probabilistic escalation, for a very large project. The 2020 analysis reported a $p50$ escalation value of 10% over the course of the project and a $p95$ of 32%.

For various reasons, the project was tabled in 2020. Fast forward to 2023, and the project was restarted, with the estimate updated. During the 2020 to 2023 hiatus, Covid-related escalation (e.g., supply chain risks) significantly impacted the project economy. The project base estimate, with no scope changes, increased by 38% from 2020. This is compared to the 2020 $p95$ forecast value of 32%.

If the client had run an IRR sensitivity study in 2020 as part of the business case using the 2020 probabilistic escalation worst case, the IRR tornado diagram capex bar would have reasonably covered what occurred during the Covid years. While not perfect, it would have been in the ballpark. We have all heard statements like "nobody could have predicted what happened to prices during Covid." This case study suggests that the statement is not true if probabilistic escalation is done using the practices in the book.

Leading up to Covid (and Ukraine), price increases were fairly nominal. The price index distribution, considering the historical record, including the 2003-2012 super cycle, resulted in a long tail on the high side.

However, the Volume 1, Chapter 13 method is not perfect. Another industrial case study project I was involved with was evaluated in late 2021. Covid escalation had already hit hard that year. Unlike in 2020, when most of the price risk was on the upside, it was less clear where prices would go from an elevated 2021 level. Would they continue to increase, level off, or decline? The forecast price distribution at that point, after a year of increase, included both decrease and increase possibilities. The probabilistic analysis prepared in late 2021 forecast a 15 percent increase in the coming years at the $p90$ level; not bad, but that fell a bit short. What we now know is that prices continued climbing sharply through 2022 (e.g., the 38% increase observed in the prior case).

These forecast ranges addressed reality much better than deterministic escalation estimates (usually confusing inflation with escalation), which at the time were falling way short. As discussed in Chapter 3, many construction contractors went bankrupt in 2023. In the case study in section 10-14.1, the owner used deterministic escalation but was fortunate to be pre-2021. Luck should *never* be a strategy.

In 2024, the question most are asking is how much of a price decline is possible (of course, escalation varies by account, region, etc.) and how confident should projects be? These cases highlight the nature of escalation risk during volatile economic periods.

Chapter 14 Perspectives (The Tipping Point: Risk Analysis at the Edge of Chaos)

The fundamentals of Chapter 14 remain relevant. Unfortunately, academia and industry continue to focus on project complexity frameworks and nonlinear cost and schedule behaviors without providing practical solutions for quantifying them. Chapter 14 remains the only practical approach I've encountered for addressing this challenge. Section 10-14.1 includes a case example that may help illustrate the importance and practicality of the Tipping Point method and related practices.

10-14.1 Lessons Learned: Tipping Point, Management Reserves, and More

I have continued practicing QRA using the book's methods on behalf of major client projects since Volume 1 was published. For several projects, I have had the privilege of being involved through to completion. Some projects were canceled or shelved. Some are still in execution. The first lesson (re)learned is captured in this quote from Chapter 1 of Volume 1: *"As a first rule, we must remain humble about our ability to identify risks and forecast their outcome."*

While some projects came in on time and on budget, others did not. However, the projects with overruns came in within the *p*90 values of the QRA. Overruns are never pleasant, but if the business case had confirmed that *p*90 cost and schedule outcomes would meet business objectives (e.g., positive NPV), it is not all bad news.

Consulting experiences are generally confidential, but I can share the learnings from one published case study of an $8 billion Canadian hydropower megaproject completed in 2021.[7] The project was remotely located in an extreme winter environment. To quote the paper, *"It is not a story of prediction perfection, but a practicum on applying P+EV on a project, in which the risk analysis is at the edge of disorder."* The project *"...identified but underappreciated systemic fragility challenges* [that] *led to non-linear behavior; total cost increased from $6.5 to $8.2 billion Canadian dollars and the first unit in-service milestone slipped 15 months from November 2019 to February 2021."*

It should be noted that the project conducted full QRA re-analyses in mid-execution. On megaprojects, QRA is not something done just once; it should be planned for at appropriate milestones. It is also worth noting that the project fully recognized the state of affairs and the risks when it did its mid-stream re-baselining and QRA. The budget increase was once-and-done.[8] In the end, the project outcomes quoted were within the original QRA range. The paper is not repeated here, but the learnings reported are shared below.

Tipping Point and Other Learnings

A Tipping Point (TP) Assessment (Chapter 14, Volume 1) was conducted on this project. TP provides a qualitative warning of potential disorder or deficient productivity so that TP drivers (complexity, aggressiveness, teams, high impact/low probability risks, etc.) can be mitigated. However, the TP assessment for the

---

7   John K. Hollmann and Raminder S. Bali, "Case Study: Use of the Hybrid Parametric and Expected Value QRA Method on the Keeyask Hydropower Megaproject." AACE International Transactions, 2024.

8   A common experience on overrunning megaprojects is to face up to reality slowly resulting in a succession of year-by-year or period-by-period bad news announcements. This tends to support the theory of strategic misrepresentation.

case study project fell short of expectations, leading to several key learnings from the QRA:

1. Rating aggressiveness in TP,

2. Rating team development/project system capability in TP,

3. Starting early with P+EV and Tipping Point,

4. Funding both general and specific management reserves, and

5. Applying probabilistic escalation analysis.

1. Rate Aggressiveness in TP

Aggressiveness and bias of the base cost and schedule were rated too broadly. An "average point-of-view" was applied across the entire project, resulting in a "somewhat aggressive" plan rating. However, the project plan included an extremely rapid ramp-up in manpower in mid-construction, which should have been seen for what it was: extremely aggressive.

2. Rate Team Development/Project System Capability in TP

Similarly, the QRA applied an "average point of view" for team and project system capabilities. While the owner and contractor managed the less demanding pre-ramp-up workload adequately, the project system was not equipped to handle the rapid ramp-up and peak.

A key lesson learned is that unless the owner and contractor teams are coming off a similar project, and ideally from a series of recent projects, expecting a major contractor, particularly a venture partnership, to have strong capabilities and to put them into action quickly and effectively is not a safe assumption. Given the compounded impact of aggressiveness and team capability ratings, the TP analysis should have recommended easing into the ramp-up (e.g., adding a year) while testing and building up capabilities.

3. Start Early with P+EV and Tipping Point

The company was transitioning its QRA practices when the project was being defined. Thus, P+EV and TP were first applied at the same time as the major contract was being awarded and the application for construction approval was being made (between Class 3 and 2). To be effective, extended P+EV should be applied at the Class 4 decision gate when a single scope option and a general execution strategy are approved. Mitigating TP drivers (reducing system fragility) requires challenging and time-consuming efforts such as managing complexity, reducing aggressiveness, strengthening teams, improving capabilities, and so on. Potential TP drivers can then be managed before reaching the Class 3 decision gate and before engaging the major contractor(s), who are optimally brought in early.

4. Fund Both General and Specific Management Reserves

When Volume 1 was being written, the authors believed it was appropriate to fund management reserves either generally (e.g., fund at $p70$ with the difference from $p50$ being a reserve for risk tolerance) or based on specific HILP risks. However, this and other projects have shown this to be inappropriate and unrealistic. The $p70$ is about making prudent investment decisions, i.e., not funding a strategic project with major economic import to the owner on a coin toss ($p50$) concerning day-to-day uncertainty and risks. HILP risks are exceptional, and on a megaproject, the likelihood of one or more occurring is high, if not certain.[9] Both types of management reserve should be funded if HILP risks are present. If the project business case does not hold up when these reserves are included, it is likely not a good project. Management resistance to management reserve funding often indicates unwarranted optimism bias.

5. Probabilistic Escalation

The case study client did not apply probabilistic escalation for policy reasons. However, the project was fortunate to be constructed during an unusual, stable, non-inflationary economy over six years, completing just before the Covid/supply chain major escalation of 2021/2022. Had the project started a few years later (or been slowed down to ease up on the TP risks), the cost overrun would have been greater. No megaproject should proceed without analyzing and funding escalation as a major risk.

Following the project, the company adopted the P+EV method as its core QRA practice. The most important takeaway is the necessity of funding specific management reserves for HILP risks on major projects, along with the more common general reserve for risk tolerance. There is often pushback from management who view specific reserves (and often management reserves of any kind) as overkill; be prepared to strongly support your position. The same is

---

9   In the case-study book *When Mega goes Giga* by Joseph Brewer about the $20 billion Sadura project, Mr. Brewer relates how so called "black swans" "were certain to happen" on large scale projects.

true for probabilistic escalation, which is often resisted by finance departments.

Chapter 15 Perspectives (Estimate Accuracy [and Outliers] for Various Industries and Contractors)

Volume 1 was primarily written from the perspective of owner companies in the industrial and process sectors. Chapter 15 aimed to illustrate how the book's concepts also apply to public infrastructure sectors and contractor companies, although it was somewhat of an afterthought. Drawing on experiences from the past decade, Chapters 2 and 3 of this volume have been added to better demonstrate and explain how the book's methods are universally applicable across all industries, including contractors.

Chapter 16 Perspectives (Communicating Risk Quantification Outcomes)

The fundamentals of Chapter 16 remain relevant. However, experience has shown that even when analysts understand the book and are eager to adopt its methods, convincing organizations to shift from their subjective legacy QRA practices presents a significant challenge. Section 10-16.1 below offers insights into what to expect when proposing or implementing a transition to company-wide QRA practices.

10-16.1 Risk Communication: Transitioning QRA Methods

Chapter 16 of Volume 1 is titled "Communicating Risk Quantification Outcomes." It focuses on how to convey the story told by the QRA analysis of a given project or program. However, it does not cover communication with organizational and project system leaders, as well as external stakeholders, about what to expect when transitioning company-wide QRA practices. The 2022 roll-out of ValidRisk software (Chapter 7 of this Volume) highlighted the need to discuss this challenge. Companies offering empirically-based ML/ AI QRA software will face similar communication challenges.

Most companies, agencies, and investors have been using or seeing the results of subjective ranging with MCS methods for cost and schedule QRA. As discussed in Volume 1, Chapter 4 on "Accuracy: Confidence and Credibility" (see Figure 4.3), the results from these methods are typically unrealistic and tend to replicate the accuracy range expectations that management and other parties have. These expectations are shaped by various industry accuracy range publications that lack a reliable empirical research basis. As pointed out in Chapter 4, the actual high end of ranges is 2x or more the "standard" values.

For organizations changing from subjective ranging methods with MCS to empirically-valid methods, such as the parametric method (Volume 1, Chapter 11) and/or a QRA validation method using ML/AI tools (Chapter 8 of this Volume), the risk leader needs to prepare management and external stakeholders for what might be called QRA sticker shock.

For example, in the mining industry, the prevailing practice has been to fund projects at the $p80$ confidence level of the cost QRA outcome. This practice evolved because subjective ranging QRA cost outcome distributions are consistently too narrow. The $p50$ of such methods tend to result in low contingency values, such as 8-12%, which most in mining correctly perceive as being too low given the high risk of their projects (e.g., usually in remote locations with geotechnical and social license risks). Therefore, they moved along the cost distribution curve to the right until they saw a contingency that seemed reasonable, typically around the $p80$ level. This usually provided a contingency of roughly 20%, which most in management felt was reasonable.

Nobody seemed to question why they were using a QRA method where the value they found to be reasonable for contingency was close to the QRA method's worst case (reflecting a prevalence of "contingency-think" and neglect of the importance of the high or $p90$ value to the risk profile). Those who use the $p90$ cost and schedule values in their business case sensitivity analyses may discover that newly realistic $p90$ values render the project economically unviable.

When an empirically-valid QRA method is introduced, the $p50$ values will look like the old $p80$ at around 20% (i.e., the $p50$ of reality is the $p80$ of subjective QRA). The new $p80$ might now have values of 30% or more. The organization will need to change their funding policy to revert to the $p50$ or mean, where it should have been all along if the QRA had been realistic. The $p90$ may kill the project or force a recycle through alternative evaluations, causing confusion, shaken confidence, or even shock.

Communicating with Internal Organization Management

When changing QRA methods from subjective to empirically-valid, plan for preparatory training backed by research (e.g., this book). The best confidence-building practice is to conduct a "calibration study" as discussed in Chapter 7 of this Volume. If an ML/AI method is involved, it should be "taught" using the company's own data. When management sees their own actual cost growth and schedule slip data compared with the QRA method outputs, most concerns will be addressed. Another good idea is to plan a pilot phase where side-by-side QRA analyses are done using the old and new methods; this will also serve as part of risk analyst training.

Communicating with External Stakeholders

The cost and schedule risk analyses of government-owned or government-funded projects will typically be subject to review by government agencies. The same is true for projects in regulated industries (e.g., utilities where rates are regulated). If not self-funded, projects may have to answer to financiers. Finally, the analyses may be inputs to claims and dispute resolution forensic analyses.

While most analysts will not communicate directly with these external stakeholders, it is important to remember that one's analysis may be reviewed or used by them. Therefore, it is crucial to be as clear as possible in reports, recognizing that these external parties may have a limited grasp of statistical concepts and methods. You must use ethical practices and align with current standards and guidelines, such as those from AACE International where applicable.

With government authorities and regulators, a main challenge is that they may have their own standards or guidelines that are not aligned with the most recent best, empirically-valid practices. Even if they have no formal guidelines, agencies have been seeing a steady stream of too-low submittals based on ranging methods. Some authorities (and in hearings, etc.) may also rely on independent reviewers who may not be using empirically-valid practices.

A common example that flags a communication problem is being asked by a stakeholder, "Why didn't you use the AACE International standard range?" The answer is that AACE has not had standard fixed ranges since 1998, and the accuracy range values they do publish are too narrow relative to research. I have encountered all these external stakeholder situations in one way or another. Good communication tends to become an educational process that calls for credibility built on the knowledge and competence of the communicator.

Chapter 17 Perspectives (Budgeting for Risks and Account Control)

The fundamentals of Chapter 17 remain applicable. However, experience indicates that confusion persists regarding the best practices for managing cost and schedule contingency. Section 10-17.1 below offers more specific guidance on this topic.

10-17.1 Cost and Schedule Contingency Drawdown

Chapter 17 of Volume 1 addresses "Budgeting for Risks and Account Control." It includes a section on "Drawdown," which provides a summary description of the general cost contingency drawdown approach as part of change management. Given the many questions I receive on this topic, the following details how to develop a drawdown plan and discusses schedule contingency drawdown, which was not covered in Chapter 17 (this is not a project control text).

Drawdown Plan

The change management process includes allocating cost and schedule contingency (and escalation for cost) to the accounts and activities impacted by a risk event or condition. The principle is that the current budget and schedule control base must accurately reflect the current scope and plans for work activity. As money and time are shifted from the contingency and escalation accounts to other accounts (i.e., when a change is approved), this transfer (drawdown) from contingency to other control accounts is tracked over time. Variance from the planned drawdown signals a need to reassess the risk situation.

Tracking drawdown starts with developing a baseline contingency expenditure plan, represented as an S-curve chart with contingency value on the y-axis and time on the x-axis. I recommend a contingency expenditure curve proportional to labor and labor-related cost expenditure (including engineering and construction labor and labor indirects). Confidential research on actual drawdown curves supports this approach, as labor and labor-related costs are most subject to cost growth. A similar approach links the plan curve to the planned project progress curve. However, this can overweight early major procurements, resulting in overconfidence as actual drawdown appears less rapid than planned.

Some advocate linking the plan curve to the risk register, which involves quantifying the expected value (EV: probability times impact) of each risk, estimating start and end dates, spreading EV costs accordingly, and summing all risk EV expenditures. However, this approach suffers from "illusion of control" bias, as it fails to address systemic risk, which typically drives most cost growth but does not appear in risk registers. The resulting curve is choppy, reflecting high-impact risks hitting sporadically. This method is not recommended for primary risk quantification.

Schedule Contingency Drawdown

Using explicit schedule contingency is less common than cost contingency. For owners, schedule contingency may be allowed between project completion and the promised delivery date to a client, visible only to the business, not the project team. Schedule contingency is often applied at various points in the schedule network, such as buffers before key milestones. However, if there is an explicit schedule contingency, a time drawdown curve similar to cost can be used, with days on the y-axis instead of cost. The same general procedure tied to project control change management applies.

Chapter 18 Perspectives (Closing the Loop)

The fundamentals of Chapter 18 remain relevant. However, as noted in that chapter, "very few owner and contractor companies capture, analyze, and use project historical data." The good news is that AACE has published Recommended Practice RP 114R-20, *Project Historical Database Development*, which provides comprehensive guidelines to support the development, maintenance, and application of all the QRA methods outlined in these books. Additionally, the rapid advancement of ML/AI has sparked significant interest in data among senior management (see Chapter 7 of this volume).

Volume 2 Perspective Wrap-up

There are 16 update sections in this chapter, touching on almost every chapter in Volume 1. This book project began as a 2nd Edition effort in 2023 but grew unwieldy due to extensive new content, now included as chapters in this Volume 2. Volume 1's content remains solid and relevant. The shift to a Volume 2 effort failed to capture many 2nd Edition draft revisions not substantial enough for standalone chapters, resulting in the need for this miscellany chapter. For many topics, readers may find it useful to refer back to the corresponding Volume 1 chapter; references are noted in each section.

Working on this chapter reminded me that learning is a continuous process, regardless of age. Several new chapters and topics in this chapter evolved from papers I authored or co-authored since 2016. I thank coauthors J. Eric Bickel of the University of Texas at Austin, who developed the J-QPD distribution covered in section 10-10.1, and Raminder S. Bali of Manitoba Hydro, project control lead on the Keeyask project described in section 10-14.1. My thanks also to Publisher/Editor Dave Charlesworth for his patience and perseverance, essentially undertaking this effort twice (switching from a 2nd Edition to a 2nd Volume was his idea).

11

Appendix 1
Example Hybrid Parametric plus CPM-based Method

Background

Chapter 4 of this volume describes a critical path schedule method (CPM) based quantitative risk analysis (QRA) that integrates parametric modeling (Volume 1, Chapter 11) with risk-driven CPM using Monte Carlo simulation (MCS), referred to as P+CPM. The chapter recommends using P+CPM in addition to the hybrid parametric plus expected value (P+EV) method. Employing both methods provides assurance and practicality, especially for major projects.

This example uses the method covered by AACE RP 117R-21, "Integrated Cost and Schedule Risk Analysis and Contingency Determination using a Hybrid Parametric and CPM Method." The P+CPM method from Chapter 4 differs from that RP to reduce complexity (an objective of this book's approach to QRA). RP 117R-21, and this worked example, add the following to the Chapter 4 approach:

◆ Ranging of inherent uncertainty and a heuristic to deduct the "inherent uncertainty" from systemic uncertainty, resulting in "net systemic risks," and

◆ Quantifying nominal weather uncertainty using weather calendars.

As new content, the *net systemic risk concept* is described before working the example.

The RP 117R-21 approach is used by Mr. Colin Cropley, managing director of Risk Integration Management Pty Ltd (RIMPL), who generously prepared the draft worked example and was the primary contributor to the RP.[1] Mr. Cropley and the remainder of this chapter refer to the RP 117R-21 approach as "P+IRA" (Parametric plus CPM-based Integrated [Cost and Schedule] Risk Analysis).

[Editor's Note: Screen shots do not reproduce well in print or eBook formats, so we have replicated the screen shots as closely as possible using Adobe Illustrator and/or InDesign in this chapter.]

Acronyms

The discussion and example include many acronyms; for clarity, they are defined in Table 11.1 below:

ACRONYM	DESCRIPTION		ACRONYM	DESCRIPTION
d	day		RC	Rainfall Calendar
h	hour		RE	Risk Event
NSRF	Net Systemic Risk Factor		RF	Risk Factor
NSCRF	Net Systemic Cost Risk Factor		SR	Safran Risk
NSDRF	Net Systemic Duration Risk Factor		TD	time-dependent
P+EV	Parametric plus Expected Value		TI	time-independent
P+IRA	Parametric plus Integrated Risk Analysis			

Table 11.1: Acronyms and Descriptions

General CPM Tools, Methods, and Preconditions

Software and Risk Factors

The fundamental schedule risk analysis methodology used in the example is the Risk Factor (RF) approach. This fundamental RF (without parametric analysis) approach is covered in AACE RP 57R-09, "Integrated Cost and Schedule Risk Analysis Using Risk Drivers and Monte Carlo Simulation of a CPM Model."

---

1   Contact Mr. Cropley via www.riskinteg.com or info@ riskinteg.com. Mr. Cropley and I have worked together on several major international QRA assignments. Computer files for the worked example later in this appendix can be obtained on the riskinteg.com website.

The CPM-based risk analysis software with MCS used in the example is Safran Risk (SR). The worked example, particularly the Net Systemic Risk content, is highly specific to SR software tabs and functions. It is assumed that users are already familiar with AACE RPs 57R-09 and 117R-21 as well as SR software. Those with other CPM-based QRA software that can integrate cost and schedule risk analysis can use it for modeling inherent risk and mapping risk events to identify and rank pathways of varying schedule and cost uncertainty for risk optimization. For example, the P+IRA method was developed using Oracle's Primavera Risk Analysis (PRA). The Chapter 4 approach, which replaces ranging with systemic outputs as the source for general or background uncertainties, may be an option.

Risk Factors

In risk analysis, *uncertainties* have a 100% probability of occurrence (an attribute or fact of the project), while *events* have less than a 100% probability of occurrence. RFs can be used in risk impact quantification for both uncertainties and events. RFs are multipliers of the base costs or durations in the model, usually expressed as percentages.[2] RFs based on Subject Matter Expert (SME) input are typically described by 3-point probability distributions in the MCS software (e.g., Triangular), but other distributions (e.g., Lognormal) can be used if data supports their definition. A triangular 3-point RF distribution with low, most likely, and high values may be something like 80%, 110%, and 150% (note that a value of 100% does not change the base value).

Uncertainties and Net Systemic Risk

The most common way to quantify duration uncertainties (as opposed to risk events) in CPM-based schedule risk analysis (SRA) is known as "ranging." A group of SMEs with relevant knowledge and experience in a facilitated workshop assesses the project schedule and assigns consensus values for the 3-points of the duration RF distribution. They usually do this for groups of related activities (there may be thousands of activities at the Class 3 level of definition). Empiricism is generally not explicitly included in ranging.

---

2   Some use the term *Risk Factors* as a synonym for uncertainties. That term usage can confuse the concepts of risk type and how the risk type impact is quantified.

A similar ranging process is followed when costs are overlaid on the schedule in CPM-based integrated cost and schedule risk analysis. An additional division of costs is required into time-independent ("fixed") costs and time-dependent ("variable") costs because, to simplify the modeling, only cost uncertainty is assumed to act on fixed costs while only duration uncertainty is assumed to act on variable costs. A more sophisticated approach allows for the rates of time-dependent costs to be subject to uncertainty, as well as the duration of the activities to which they apply.

The P+CPM approach discussed in Chapter 4 eliminates the ranging (which quantifies inherent uncertainty) and nominal weather uncertainty quantification steps, sacrificing the SME expertise and specific local weather modeling, which usually includes probabilistic weather calendars based on historical weather data and may be due to multiple weather factors, depending on the project. Offshore projects or projects in locations with highly seasonal effects cannot omit weather effects independent of the activities, which can slip into and across such effects. Omitting weather in such seasonal projects would prevent schedule and consequent cost impacts from being properly modelled and optimised.[3]

The P+IRA approach preserves this ranging step while also using parametric modeling of systemic risks (see Volume 1, Chapter 11). However, to avoid double counting the overlapping inherent and systemic uncertainties, P+IRA uses a heuristic to deduct the inherent uncertainty from the systemic uncertainty to yield *net systemic risk* – the total uncertainty contribution is then the sum of inherent plus net systemic.

But systemic risk does not always exceed inherent risk. Where the SMEs are experienced, their inherent risk assessments can exceed (and have exceeded!) systemic risk. Usually the systemic risk spread ($p90$–$p10$) exceeds the inherent risk spread. But on numerous occasions the $p50$ (systemic) is less than $p50$ (inherent). In such situations, the Net Systemic Risk Factor should still be added. This ensures that both SME input and empiricism are incorporated. The complexity of the net systemic risk heuristic can be seen in the example for users to judge.

---

3   Mr. Cropley and I disagree on the added value of SME and weather uncertainty inputs. We agree that SME involvement will usually improve team buy-in of the result. Critical weather events (such as hurricanes or wildfires) are quantified as risk events in either method. If you have the time and expertise, full P+IRA (RP 117R-21) should be considered.

The Venn diagram of Figure 11.1 illustrates the overlap of uncertainty types.[4] Inherent uncertainty, quantified through SME inputs using ranging, typically does not include much uncertainty outside the immediate SME experience, even if they often discern useful relative uncertainties of different schedule pathways or cost line items.

For example, the ambiguous impacts of a weak project system or project complexity are difficult for SMEs to grasp. SMEs are also prone to bias, particularly optimism. Systemic risk, quantified using parametric modeling, encompasses all inherent risk plus some of the impact of nominal (i.e., minor or less than critical) risk events (sometimes referred to as *contingent risks*). Net systemic risk then is represented by the full, large light grey circle in Figure 11.1, including the bite into risk events, but minus the darker grey inherent risk circle.

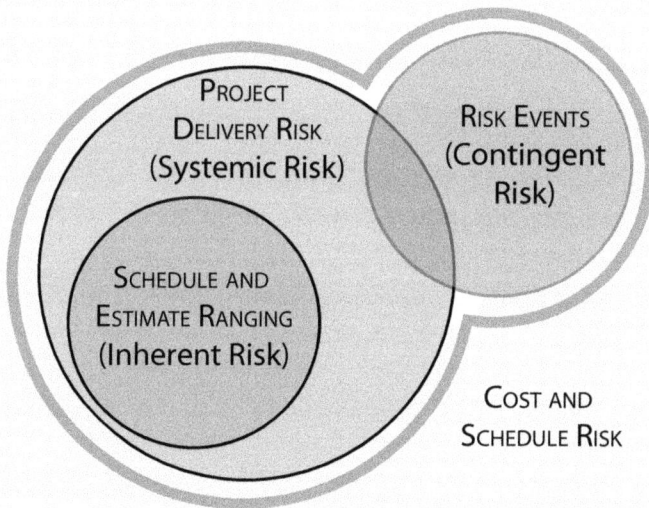

Figure 11.1: Venn Diagram Comparing Risk Types

Schedule Quality and Size

To produce reliable CPM-based risk analysis results, the schedule network's technical quality must be high. This includes having minimal *open ends* (activities without start predecessors or finish successors), except for the project start and finish milestones. There

---

4   Figure 11.1 is from AACE RP 117R-21 and is also used in AACE Professional Guidance Document PGD-02, *Guide to Quantitative Risk Analysis* (with permission).

should also be no mandatory constraints (constraints that override schedule logic) on any activities with predecessor logic. The goal is to have a flexible and responsive schedule that can fully reflect changes in the timing of any parts of the project. A rule of thumb is that a fully linked schedule will typically have a ratio of links to total activities of two or more.

Safran Risk (SR) software can handle schedules with many thousands of activities and still produce Monte Carlo simulations (MCS) with thousands of iterations within minutes. However, the smaller the schedule model, the faster the MCS, and the faster schedule drivers can be evaluated. Generally, it is preferable to use the project level 3 master control schedule rather than creating a separate summary or study schedule. This helps reflect the merge bias effect (resistance of projects to finishing earlier or being accelerated due to logic complexity) and avoids the time and effort involved in creating quality, representative summary or study schedules.

Basic SME-based Methodology

The P+IRA method starts with the common cost-loaded CPM with MCS, using risk factors (RFs). This approach is covered in AACE RP 57R-09. Without going into detail (see the AACE RPs), the approach can be summarized as follows:

- ♦ A suitable base schedule model (e.g., level 3 master schedule) of the project, containing the main inter-dependencies, is overlaid with the project base estimate that is split into time-dependent and time-independent costs.
- ♦ Time-dependent costs are loaded into hammock activities and linked to the start and finish of the groups of activities to which they relate, so that as those groups of activities vary in duration, the time-dependent costs change proportionally.
- ♦ Appropriate cost and schedule impact RFs are identified in workshop sessions or interviews with SMEs and mapped into the model, producing inherent (100% probable) duration and cost uncertainties in groups of tasks and line items, with concomitant correlation effects (due to the interaction of overlapping RFs).
- ♦ In some cases, the RFs are considered to describe project cost or schedule uncertainty related to other schedule or cost RFs. In these cases, correlation is applied between

RFs, using judgment as to the strength or weakness of the correlation.

♦ Critical risk events (<100% probable) from the project risk register are reviewed in a workshop, their probabilities and cost and schedule impacts assessed and mapped into the model where logically applicable, forming risk-tasks.

♦ Probabilistic weather calendars are defined and applied based on time series weather data, usually available from government weather station data, where applicable for construction activities.

Common practice is to stop there and report on the analysis findings and recommend possible risk treatments, contingencies, and management reserves. However, this purely SME-based approach (apart from weather history input) will usually not reflect the full impact of systemic risks as captured in industry (and hopefully company) empirical research, unless the project is a close repeat of similar previous projects working with the same team under the same project system. That is why the P+IRA methodology was developed.

Incorporating Parametric Analysis of Systemic Risks

To add "net systemic risk" to the purely SME-based model above, first quantify the total systemic cost and schedule risks using parametric modeling as described in Volume 1, Chapter 11.

A systemic risk workshop is usually held with senior project and corporate personnel responsible for the project and the project system (many systemic risks are owned by the business, such as assuring strong processes and organizational capabilities). The resultant systemic risk ratings are incorporated into the parametric model to generate the systemic cost and schedule uncertainty distributions. This parametric (P) analysis step is the same for a P+EV, P+CPM, or P+IRA approach. A worked example of applying parametric analysis is included in Chapter 9.

Having obtained the systemic cost and schedule distributions, quantify the net systemic risk. In SR software, this is quantified by using MCS to subtract an inherent risk probability distribution from a systemic risk probability distribution for each of the cost and schedule impacts. These subtractions result in net systemic cost and duration probability distributions. These two distributions are approximated by RF distributions for MCS. Because the parametric model (e.g., ValidRisk®) generates a lognormal distribution, that data can be used to define a lognormal RF distribution; otherwise, the trigen ($p10$, $p90$) distribution is often used (whichever gives the closer approximation to the source net systemic probability distribution). These two RFs – one for costs and the other for durations – are applied to all time-independent cost distributions and all execution phase activity duration distributions, respectively, in the P+IRA model.

Table 11.2 shows the sequence of the combined P+IRA methodology. This can be compared to the P+CPM flow chart in Figure 4.2 of Chapter 4 in this volume. A logic diagram that shows P+IRA flow chart steps in more detail is included in AACE RP 117R-21 (the reference source for Table 11.2).

STEP	DESCRIPTION
1	Receive / critique project schedules, estimates and risk register (including strategy, alignment, and technical quality).
2	Conduct schedule and cost ranging workshops (through assignment of risk factors), systemic risk workshops, and project-specific risk workshops.
3	Incorporate required schedule changes; make sure schedule and estimate are aligned. Review risk register.
4	Configure parametric model for systemic risk from workshop inputs. Determine probability distributions for cost growth and schedule slip.
5	Incorporate schedule risk factors to drive duration uncertainty with automati correlation in the IRA model to form the Base Schedule model.
6	Map labor costs to schedule in structured cost hammocks and materials costs to cost sheet. Include cost risk factors in the IRA model to express the Base Estimate model.
7	Run IRA range analysis, capture distributions for cost and schedule, deduct from parametric distributions using MCS. Build cost and schedule distributions for Net Systemic Risk Factors for P+IRA analysis.
8	Map net systemic risk factors to all activities and fixed costs and map critical project-specific residual risk events to appropriate schedule and cost elements in P+IRA model.
9	Build and incorporate weather model into P+IRA model (as applicable), assigning probabilistic weather calendars to matching weather-exposed activities..
10	Run Integrated Cost and Schedule Risk Analysis of P+IRA model including Net Systemic Risk Factors. Run validation checks and prepare initial reporting.
11	If project team changes model, re-analyze, run Quantitative Exclusion Analysis sensitivities, and prepare final report.

Table 11.2: Flowchart for the P+IRA Method Used in this Example

Worked Example: Rail Extension Project

Example Project Scope

The example is based on a major proposed Rail Line Extension Project to expand and upgrade an urban transport network. The project included the following scope:

♦ An approximately 15 km passenger railway line interconnecting two radial metropolitan rail lines.

♦ Duplication of about 3 km of track along one of the radial passenger lines.

♦ Relocation of about 11 km of rail freight lines.

♦ Developing two new stations and associated infrastructure, including car parking, bus interchanges, cycling facilities, and passenger amenities.

♦ Upgrading of the terminal stations at each end of the interconnecting line.

♦ Upgrading one road bridge and one rail bridge and constructing one footbridge.

♦ Constructing about 12 km of shared cyclist/pedestrian pathway along the railway line route.

An appropriate, integrated Class 3 schedule and estimate were prepared by the team, along with a risk register. These formed the starting point inputs to this P+IRA contingency assessment using Safran Risk (SR) software (along with some ancillary information). These inputs are described in the following sections.

Base Cost Estimate

The base project cost estimate is summarized in Table 11.3. Labor, Plant and Subcontractor costs were all treated as time dependent (TD) costs.[5] Materials are treated as time Independent (TI) costs. Costs were imported into the SR Cost tab by Excel spreadsheet using a structure defined with the SR Grouping functionality. Part of the TD costs is shown in Table 11.4, along with the hammock activities defined to receive the costs (each receiving 100% of the base cost).

Corresponding time independent (TI) costs were imported in the same file, as shown in Table 11.5. By defining 0% allocation to

---

5   This would be typical for a project with a reimbursable cost contract strategy. With other strategies, some of the contractor costs may not be time dependent to the owner.

the hammock activities, the costs were designated as TI and incorporated in the SR cost sheet fixed cost breakdown.

ELEMENT	TOTALS	LABOR	PLANT	MATERIALS	SUBCON-TRACTORS
Construction Costs	$426,913	$108,673	$66,531	$117,688	$134,021
Owner's Costs	$103,615	$49,497	$377	$17,362	$36,379
Base Estimate	$530,528	$158,170	$66,908	$135,050	$170,400

Table 11.3: Summary of Rail Extension Project Base Cost Estimate ($000s)

OUTLINE	ID	DESCRIPTION	BASE	ACTIVITIES
Labor	1.1.00.TD	Owners Project Management Overheads	$48,434,640	[C110000; 100]
Labor	1.1.01.TD	Land acquisition costs		[C111000; 100]
Labor	1.1.02.TD	Advance works costs	$26,317,916	[C112000; 100]
Labor	1.1.03.TD	Traction power costs	$11,499,991	[C113000; 100]
Labor	1.2.00.1.TD	Contractors design costs	$35,700,832	[C120010; 100]

Table 11.4: Part of Time Dependent Costs Imported into SR

OUTLINE	ID	DESCRIPTION	BASE	ACTIVITIES
Materials	1.1.00.TI	Owners Project Management Overheads	$2,018,110	[C110000;0]
Materials	1.1.01.TI	Land acquisition costs	$9,567,276	[C111000;0]
Materials	1.1.02.TI	Advance works costs	$5,777,104	[C112000;0]
Materials	1.1.03.TI	Traction power costs		[C113000;0]
Materials	1.2.00.1.TI	Contractors design costs		[C120010;0]

Table 11.5: Part of Time Independent Costs Imported into SR

Base Schedule

The base execution phase schedule ran from Funding Approval on 24 May 2018 to Practical Completion on 17 March 2023, covering a duration of 1,758 days. This overall duration was based on construction work being estimated and scheduled for a 6-day x 11-hour working week. However, the schedule model activity durations were based on construction being worked to a 5-day x 11-hour working week, effectively incorporating a 20% inclement weather allowance.

A comparison with 60 years of rainfall records indicated that the annual lost time in the area due to wet weather would be about half of this allowance on a $p50$ basis. This assumption was based on Earthworks and Civil work stopping if more than 5 mm of rain fell in a day and all other construction work stopping only if more than 10 mm of rain fell in a day. These assumptions took into account the open, sandy nature of the soil in the project region, suggesting that about 10% schedule contingency was built into the base project duration on top of the required weather allowance. Table 11.6 lists the schedule summary activities.

ACTIVITY DESCRIPTION	START	FINISH	DURATION
Rail Extension Project	24/05/2018	17/03/2023	1758
Land Acquisitions	24/05/2018	21/09/2018	120
Advance Works	25/09/2018	18/09/2019	358
Traction Power	12/02/2019	7/08/2019	176
Contractors Design	9/08/2019	22/10/2020	440
Preliminaries and General Items	1/10/2019	17/03/2023	1263
Civil works Preliminaries	7/11/2019	17/03/2022	585
Track works	7/11/2019	27/05/2022	633
Structures - Preliminaries	1/10/2019	19/08/2020	221
Stations - Preliminaries	1/10/2019	12/02/2021	342
Shutdowns - M Line Tie-ins	17/02/2020	8/03/2020	15
Earthworks, Drainage and Fencing	7/11/2019	17/03/2022	861
Retaining Walls	22/11/2019	2/08/2021	619
Noise Walls	29/04/2020	13/07/2021	440
Rail Webbing	2/06/2022	14/07/2022	29
Ballast Matting	10/02/2021	23/12/2021	316
CE & CR Bridges	7/11/2019	14/05/2020	189
Bridgeworks & Roadworks - RR	8/11/2019	19/07/2021	619
Buildings, Platforms & Carpark- RRS	7/11/2019	5/11/2020	364
C Stn Platform Extension	9/03/2020	4/11/2020	240
T Station	24/07/2020	17/06/2021	328
Bldgs, Platforms & Carpark - NRS	31/01/2020	25/03/2021	419
Freight Rail Relocation	10/02/2021	9/02/2022	364
Freight Rail Signalling - Foundations	29/06/2020	18/08/2020	50
Freight Rail Signalling - Installation	5/11/2021	8/02/2022	60
Rail works	8/01/2020	10/03/2021	427
OHLE	8/01/2020	3/10/2022	993
Communications	10/02/2021	2/06/2022	477
Signalling	2/08/2021	15/06/2022	317
Testing and Commissioning	3/10/2022	15/02/2023	91

Table 11.6: Rail Extension Project Summary Activities

The schedule quality was checked and minor issues corrected. The final schedule characteristics are summarized in Table 11.7. Note the use of 35 hammocks and the 2-to-1 ratio of links to total activities.

PROJECT SUMMARY							
TOTAL SUMMARY		**PROGRESS**		**LINKS**			
No.	Parameter	No.	Paramater	No.	Parameter		
163	Activities	0	Act Starts	94	Start-Start		
35	Hammocks	0	Act Finishes	0	Start-Finish		
0	Summaries	0	Rem Durns	230	Finish-Start		
2	Start Milestones	0	Pct Complts	85	Finish-Finish		
1	Fin Milestones	0	Out of Seqs	Included:			
201	Total Tasks	0	In Progress	88	Btw Hammocks		
		0	Completed	0	Btw Summs		
409	Links			409	Project Links		
2.0	Links : Total Tasks			0	Cross Proj Links		
35	Resources						
CONSTRAINTS				**LOGIC**			
No.	Parameter	No.	Paramater	No.	Parameter		
0	Must Start On	0	As Late As Poss	1	Logic Starts		
0	Must Finish On	0	Suspended	1	Logic Finishes		
1	Start No Earlier	0	Must Start On	0	Free Stdg Activs		
0	Start No Later			No loops			
0	Finish No Earlier						
0	Finish No Later						

Table 11.7: Rail Extension Project Schedule Characteristics

Project Risks

The project risks were provided by the team in an Excel spreadsheet and included 57 risks, categorized as follows:

- ◆ 37 Inherent Uncertainties (Risk Factors): These have a 100% probability of occurrence and include duration and/or cost impact distributions. The team assigned these uncertainties to schedule activities and costs.
- ◆ 20 Critical Risk Events: These have probabilities of less than 100%. They were derived from the project Risk Register, with the inclusion criterion being a cost impact (or equivalent delay impact) that exceeded 0.5% of CAPEX.

All of these uncertainties and risks were imported into the SR Project Risks tab, where the pre- and post-mitigated probabilities of occurrence and impacts could be defined and edited. All impacts were quantified as 3-point distributions, either Trigen (10%, 90%) or Triangle.

Tables 11.8 and 11.9 show selected examples of pre-mitigated uncertainties (Risk Factors) and pre-mitigated Risk Events from the Risk Register Excel Input sheet, respectively.

RISK FACTOR	PROB.	DURATION IMPACT	TI COST IMPACT
NSCRF Net Systemic Cost Risk Factor	100 %		Trigen(88% ; 102% ; 122% ; 10 ; 90)
NSDRF - Net Systemic Durn Risk Factor	100 %	Trigen(98% ; 106% ; 117% ; 10 ; 90)	
RC05 5mm/day Rainfall Risk Calendar	100 %	As defined in prob. weather calendar	
RC10 10mm/day Rainfall Risk Calendar	100 %	As defined in prob. weather calendar	
RF001 Owners Costs uncertainty	100 %		Trigen(90% ; 100% ; 130% ; 5 ; 95)
RF002 Existing Utils (excl oil co pipeline)	100 %	Trigen(90% ; 100% ; 120% ; 5 ; 95)	Trigen(90% ; 100% ; 120% ; 5 ; 95)
RF003 Earthworks Scope uncertainty	100 %	Trigen(90% ; 100% ; 120% ; 5 ; 95)	Trigen(90% ; 100% ; 120% ; 5 ; 95)
RF004 Drainage uncertainty	100 %	Trigen(90% ; 100% ; 150% ; 5 ; 95)	Trigen(90% ; 100% ; 150% ; 5 ; 95)
RF005 Retaining Walls uncertainty	100 %	Trigen(90% ; 100% ; 120% ; 5 ; 95)	Trigen(90% ; 100% ; 120% ; 5 ; 95)
RF006 Noise Mitigation uncertainty	100 %	Trigen(90% ; 100% ; 110% ; 5 ; 95)	Trigen(90% ; 100% ; 110% ; 5 ; 95)
RF007 Bridges uncertainty	100 %	Trigen(90% ; 100% ; 120% ; 5 ; 95)	Trigen(90% ; 100% ; 120% ; 5 ; 95)
RF008 Stations & Platforms uncertainty	100 %	Trigen(90% ; 100% ; 130% ; 5 ; 95)	Trigen(90% ; 100% ; 130% ; 5 ; 95)
RF009 Track uncertainty	100 %	Trigen(95% ; 100% ; 110% ; 5 ; 95)	Trigen(95% ; 100% ; 110% ; 5 ; 95)
RF010 OHLE uncertainty	100 %	Trigen(90% ; 100% ; 120% ; 5 ; 95)	Trigen(90% ; 100% ; 120% ; 5 ; 95)
RF011 Traction Power uncertainty	100 %	Trigen(90% ; 100% ; 130% ; 10 ; 90)	Trigen(90% ; 100% ; 130% ; 5 ; 95)
RF012 Signalling uncertainty	100 %	Trigen(90% ; 100% ; 130% ; 5 ; 95)	Trigen(90% ; 100% ; 130% ; 5 ; 95)

Table 11.8: Selected Example Pre-Mitigated Uncertainties (Risk Factors)

Risk Event	Prob.	Duration Impact	TI Cost Impact
T013-Delay in completion of the PDP for submission	30 %	Trigen(20d ; 40d ; 60d ; 10 ; 90)	
T015-Delay in endorsement of the Business Case	5 %	Trigen(160h ; 480h ; 960h ; 10 ; 90)	
T016-Local community delays and conditions	10 %	Trigen(160h ; 480h ; 960h ; 10 ; 90)	Trigen(200000 ; 500000 ; 1000000 ; 10 ; 90)
T018-Legal approvals or permits	5 %	Trigen(160h ; 480h ; 960h ; 10 ; 90)	
T020-Environmental approvals and more stringent conditions	50 %	Trigen(160h ; 320h ; 480h ; 10 ; 90)	Trigen(5000000 ; 10000000 ; 20000000 ; 10 ; 90)
T021-Heritage and Indigenous approvals	5 %	Trigen(7d ; 14d ; 21d ; 10 ; 90)	Trigen(200000 ; 500000 ; 1000000 ; 10 ; 90)

Table 11.9: Selected Example Pre-Mitigated Risk Events

These tables provide a snapshot of the types of uncertainties and risks considered in the analysis, highlighting their potential impacts on both schedule and cost.

The first two uncertainties (Risk Factors) are Net Systemic Cost and Duration Risk Factors produced using the P+IRA methodology, which will be explained later in this example. The following two are daily Rainfall Calendar (RC) distributions derived from historical weather data. The Risk Factors with RF prefixes were generated based on SME input during schedule and cost uncertainty assessment workshops. These workshops had access to past project performance data, although such data was typically quite limited.

Risk Events

Risk Events are usually based on project Risk Register items but may be late additions identified in the preceding P+EV quantification workshop or in the schedule or cost ranging Risk Factors workshops.. These are project-specific, critical risks (refer to Volume 1, Chapter 12) identified in an Expected Value analysis as part of a P+EV analysis done prior to the P+IRA (see Chapter 9 for a P+EV example).

Risk Factors Mapping

The RFs were used to drive the time-dependent cost and schedule uncertainties in the model through the SR Risk Mapping tab. The cost RFs were applied to the TI cost resources. The TD costs were loaded into the cost hammocks, and the TI ("Materials") costs loaded in the SR Cost tab were the targets of the applicable cost RFs to apply cost uncertainty against the corresponding cost breakdown structure values.

Parametric Modeling of Systemic Risk

To assess systemic cost and schedule uncertainty using the parametric method, this worked example makes use of the parametric tool in ValidRisk® software (see Chapter 7). A worked example of using ValidRisk software for parametric modeling is in Chapter 9. However, any parametric model (e.g., the demonstration model in Volume 1, Chapter 11) could be used to generate the cost and schedule "P-tables" to be shown later. If a full P+EV analysis had been done using ValidRisk, as recommended, the ValidRisk EV analysis would not be used in the CPM analysis; that is done in SR software to help confirm the P+EV results.

Applying a parametric tool requires systemic parameter "ratings" to be input into the parametric model, a simple task. The ratings would be obtained in a top-down assessment workshop, which typically takes about two hours. For more information on ratings using the AACE Classification measure, readers should review the AACE Estimate Classification RPs for the applicable industry.[6] For example, RP 98R-18 defines Classes for road and rail transportation infrastructure projects. In addition to rail, this project included considerable station and structural (e.g., bridges) scope. RP 56R-08, which addresses building and general construction projects, might be a better fit for that scope.

ValidRisk software has rating matrices for most industries that are aligned with AACE Class RPs. If the project work breakdown structure was of a program nature, made up of separate rail and station sub-projects, the systemic risk of each sub-project could have been assessed separately with rating matrices specific to them, The parametric output is then applied to the respective sub-project schedule networks, plus one for the overall program (see Chapter 5). For this project, the rail matrix was applied to the entire project scope for simplicity. Some notes on the choice of parameter ratings for the Rail Extension project are discussed below.

---

6   See AACE Professional Guidance Document PGD-01, "Guide to Cost Estimate Classification Systems."

Systemic Risk Rating Inputs

Scope Definition

♦ General: This category rates the level of definition of various aspects of the project scope. For the example, the scope was assessed to be at AACE Class 4 level of definition rather than the preferred Class 3. It is not unusual to find projects not achieving full desired definition despite being labeled a "Class 3" project. This often lags in the general category, which includes problematic scope elements such as permitting, community involvement, and team development. In particular, as a government-owned project with a Design and Construct (D&C) contractor yet to be engaged, the team development was rated as only Fair.

♦ Planning: For this group of ratings, addressing the level of definition of various aspects of the planning of the rail project, the overall average of the ratings was about a Class 3.

♦ Engineering: This group of ratings addresses the level of definition of engineering deliverables. For the rail project, the average level of definition of these deliverables was also about Class 3 development.

♦ Overall: The level of scope definition averaged about Class 3.3. Note that while AACE Classes are a threshold metric – there is no fractional class – the parametric tool uses it as a continuous variable.

Estimate Basis

The estimate was rated as Good given the quality of the Basis of Estimate documentation and the team's good cost knowledge and experience with this scope in this location.

The base cost estimate was assessed to be Average: neither significantly over nor under-estimated (conservative or aggressive) relative to norms. No explicit validation had been done, so this rating was subjective. The parametric method is highly sensitive to base bias, so validation or benchmarking is highly recommended.

Schedule Basis

The schedule was rated as Fair overall. There was no specific Basis of Schedule; the planning basis was a section incorporated in the Basis of Estimate. Because the work was to be done on an operating rail route, the progressive replacement and relocation of existing lines was complex, and the team's confidence in durations was Fair. Investigation of weather records as part of the QRA suggests the team's allowance was quite conservative, reflecting their uncertainty with conditions.

There were indications of over-estimation of contractor productivity in this complex, brownfield project environment. While somewhat countered by the conservative weather assumption, schedule bias was rated as somewhat aggressive relative to norms.

Project Control:

The project control process, systems, and capabilities were well established, so this was assigned a rating of Good.

Procurement

The percentage of major mechanical and electrical equipment was estimated to comprise around 3% of the base estimate.

As the project was not yet approved and no contracts were in negotiation, the fixed price percentage was entered as 0%.

Technology and Complexity

♦ New Technology: It was difficult to identify the level of new technology applicable to the rail project from the information available. Assuming that controls, communications, and signaling involved some degree of new technology, a level of 1 was chosen on a rating scale of 0 to 5.

♦ Operational Severity: Considering the nature of the project (parallel freight and passenger lines and stations with somewhat heavy traffic), a rating of 2 on a rating scope of 0 to 10 was used.

♦ Project Complexity: The project had a fair degree of physical complexity with parallel freight and passenger lines, switching, multiple stations, interconnection of two main passenger lines, brownfields conditions, and so on. The execution complexity was also somewhat complex with the size of the project, a number of competing stakeholders, and interaction with the community. On average, a complexity rating of 3 was applied on a scale of 0 to 10.

Parametric Model Results

Based on the above inputs, the mean cost and schedule duration contingencies suggested for systemic risk are both about 14%. However, for the P+IRA method, the output needed is the systemic risk cost and duration distributions. These are derived from the P-tables: the predicted cost and durations at various percentages of confidence of underrunning the value. These are used to produce systemic cost and duration probability distributions for input into SR for use in MCS. With a base estimate of $530.5 million (m) and base schedule duration of 1,758 days, the P-tables from the parametric models are shown in Table 11.10.

P-VALUE	COST (M)	DURATION (D)
10%	$496	1,776
20%	$526	1,840
30%	$550	1,890
40%	$572	1,936
50%	$594	1,981
60%	$617	2,031
70%	$643	2,087
80%	$675	2,153
90%	$725	2,248

Table 11.10: Systemic Risk Cost and Duration Distributions

Deciles and ValidRisk Reports

Deciles are shown here for brevity, but ValidRisk reports *p*-values in increments of 5% by default. Interpolation can be used to derive 1% increment values, enabling 100 percentile values (including 0 or 100). Exactly one hundred percentile values are required to create a discrete distribution in SR, from which the base IRA cost distribution can be subtracted using MCS, as explained in the next section.

P+CPM Method Variation

If the P+CPM method variation were to be used per Chapter 4, these systemic risk distributions would be the only ones needed to quantify general cost and schedule uncertainty in the CPM-based model when represented as Risk Factors. In this case, there would be no SME input or quantification of "inherent" risks, nor a net systemic risk heuristic.

Assessment of Net Systemic Risk Factors

As discussed, the P+IRA approach starts with the quantification of inherent uncertainty based on SME input and ranging, then uses parametric modeling to add an increment of systemic uncertainty, bringing empiricism into the analysis. At this point, the inherent and systemic uncertainties are represented by impact probability distributions for cost and duration separately.

The next step is to quantify the two (cost and duration) Net Systemic Risk (NSR) distributions to avoid double-dipping by subtracting the base inherent uncertainty probability distributions from the systemic uncertainty distributions using MCS in the SR software. The cost and duration NSR distributions are characterized in SR as Risk Factors, which are applied to the fixed cost line items and to the schedule activities respectively in the CPM-based model to produce the complete P+IRA model.

Base Schedule and Cost Distributions for Inherent Uncertainty

The base cost and Base Schedule distributions for inherent uncertainty are produced by applying the RFs for cost to the fixed cost line items to which they are mapped in the SR Cost tab, and applying the RFs for duration to the schedule activities in the SR Risk Mapping tab. Using the SR Analyze tab, the following SR Included Risks checkboxes are to be unchecked or excluded (assuming the use of the final model):

- ♦ NSCRF & NSDRF (the Risk Factors to be determined),
- ♦ RC05 & RC10 (probabilistic weather calendar risks), and
- ♦ Risk Events (with probability <100%).

This leaves the base CPM model with inherent uncertainty only to be analyzed using MCS. SR will create base cost and schedule distributions (not shown here: typical outputs for SR and other CPM-based risk software).

Export of IRA Base Cost and Duration Percentiles

To provide the IRA cost and duration distribution inputs for performing MCS subtractions from the corresponding systemic distributions, follow these steps:

1. Display the Cost Icon in the SR Distribution Graph (3 coins icon) tab, highlighting the Total Project Costs.

2. Select the SR <Export> icon from the Distribution Graph ribbon.

3. Click on the bottom Percentiles icon.

This will generate an Excel file with two tabs: Schedule and Cost. Save and open the Excel file. Use the Percentile and Duration columns in the Schedule tab, and the Percentile and Cost columns in the Cost tab. Their use is explained in the next section.

Assessment of Net Systemic Cost and Schedule Risk Factors

To produce Net Systemic Risk Factors (NSRFs), set up a simple separate project in SR. Using MCS, the separate project will subtract:

♦ The Base IRA duration impact distribution from the parametric duration impact distribution.

♦ The Base IRA cost impact distribution from the parametric cost impact distribution.

For convenience, assume all tasks have the same remaining duration as the planned Rail Extension Project execution duration: 1,758 days. This duration is not necessary for cost-related tasks, which are assumed to be 100% time-independent. The NSRF schedule is shown in Table 11.11 (next page).

During a simulation, the hammock task 00030 might show +182 days duration, while task 00040 would be −182 days, but it cannot be negative, so it shows as 0 days. The Net Systemic Cost Distribution (NETCOST), Systemic (80), Base Execution (90), and Net Systemic Duration and Cost Risk Factors are also shown with their simulation values for a particular iteration.

Description of Activities in the NSRF Schedule

The purposes of each activity in the NSRF schedule are detailed in Table 11.12. In the SR Risk Factors tool, uncertain input task durations and cost line items are driven by risk factors. This requires defining and mapping Risk Factors for each uncertain input duration task and cost, as outlined in the last column of Table 11.12.

Note that two hammock tasks (00030 and 00040) are required to capture the full net systemic-inherent duration distribution. During iterations, more often, task 00010 duration exceeds task 00020 duration (making hammock 00030 positive and hammock 00040 = 0, as shown in Table 11.11). Less frequently, task 00020 duration exceeds task 00010 duration (making hammock 00040 positive and hammock 00030 = 0). For most iterations, when their durations would equal zero, the hammocks would be negative, but task durations cannot be negative. How this is circumvented is described in the next section.

Activity ID	Description	Dura-tion (Days)	Risk Mean Cost
Rail Ext Proj	Net Systemic Cost & Schedule Determination	2162	1,122,457
DUR	Net Systemic Duration Determination	2162	
10	RailExtn Systemic Risk Dur Distribution	2162	
20	RailExtn Base Plan Execn Dur Distbn	1980	
30	Hammock Systemic - SRA Base Plan	182	
40	Hammock SRA Base Plan - Systemic	0	
NETSYSDUR	Net Syst Dur Distbn	1794	
DURRF	Net Systemic Duration Risk Factors	1652	
NETSYSDRFN	Net Systemic Risk Dur Risk Factor (LogNormal)	1565	
NETSYSDRFT	Net Systemic Risk Dur Risk Factor (Trigen)	1652	
NETCOST	Net Systemic Cost Distribution	1758	18,499
80	Rail Extn Systemic Risk Cost Distribution	1758	603,065
90	Rail Extn IRA Base Plan Execution Cost Distbn	1758	-584,566
NSCRF	Net Systemic Cost Risk Factors	1758	1,103,958
NETSYSCRFN	Net Systemic Risk Cost Risk Factor (LogNormal)	1758	553,329
NETSYSCRFT	Net Systemic Risk Cost Risk Factor (Trigen)	1758	553,329

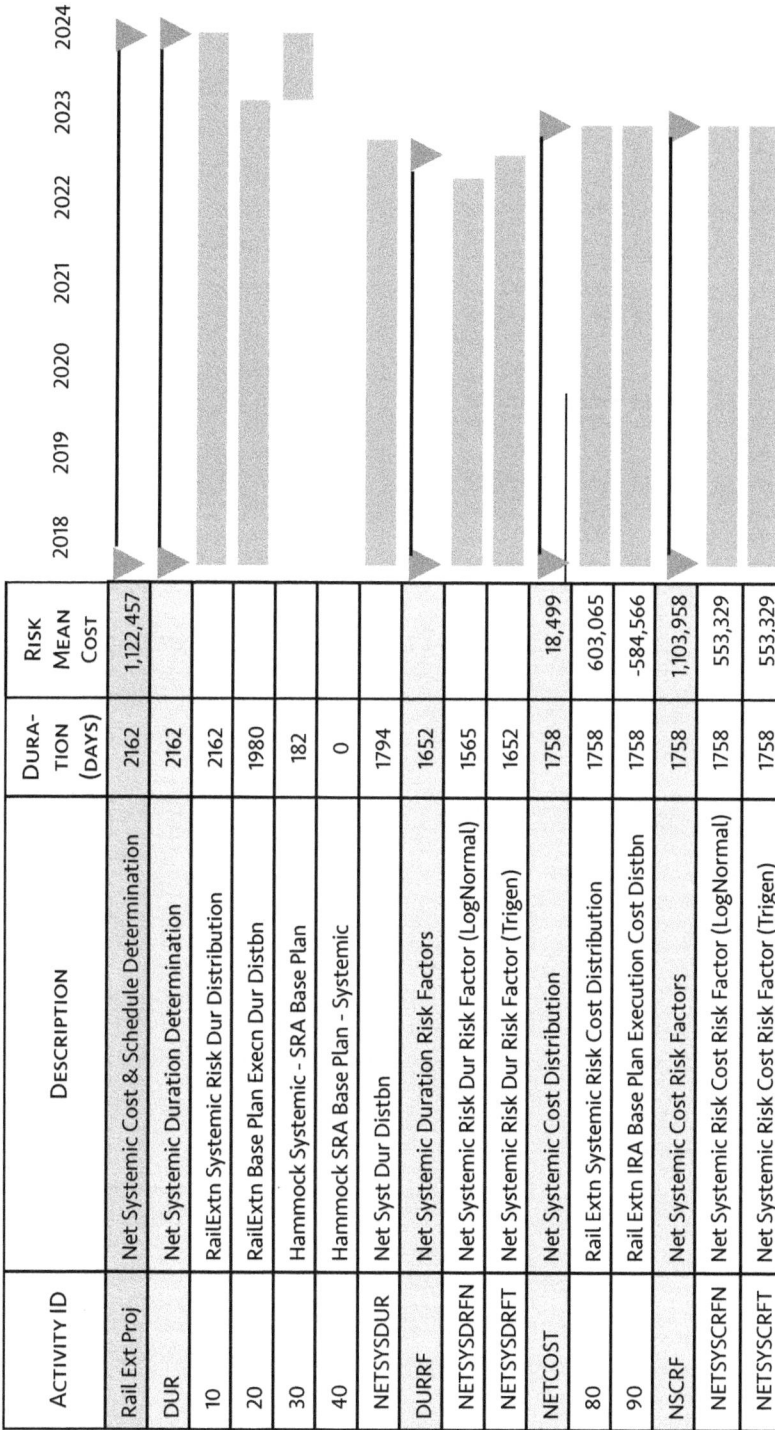

Table 11.11: Rail Extension Net Systemic Risk Factors Schedule

Act. ID	Description	Purpose	Comment, RF
DUR	Net Duration Distribution Determination	Groups duration impact tasks together	Grouping function: distribution - not required
00010	Rail Extn Execution duration (Systemic distribution)	Task to which Systemic duration impact risk distribution is applied	Project Risk Factor Risk–001 is applied (correlated +80% to Risk-002)
00020	Rail Extn Execution duration (IRA Base Plan distribution)	Task to which IRA inherent duration impact risk distribution is applied	Project Risk Factor Risk–002 is applied (correlated +80% to Risk-001)
00030	Hammock Systemic - IRA Base Plan	Collects positive differences from iterations when Systemic duration > IRA duration (otherwise 0)	Distribution to be combined with that from task 00040
00040	Hammock IRA Base Plan – Systemic	Collects positive differences from iterations when IRA duration > Systemic duration (otherwise 0)	Distribution to be combined with that from task 00030
NETSYS-DUR	Net Systemic Duration Distribution (based on correlation +0.8 between Risk-001 & Risk-002)	Task on which net systemic duration distribution produced from combining hammocks 00030 & 00040 (through Risk-006).	Risk Factor Risk-006, produced from the combination of hammocks 00030 & 00040 is applied.
NETSYS-DRFT	Net Systemic Duration Risk Factor (Trigen)	Task duration distribution derived from distribution parameters of NETSYSDUR duration distribution.	Net Systemic Duration RF Risk-007 distribution built from NETSYSDUR output values using Trigen (10,90).
NETSYS-DRFN	Net Systemic Duration Risk Factor (LogNormal)	Task duration distribution derived from distribution parameters of NETSYSDUR duration distribution.	Net Systemic Duration RF Risk-010 distribution built from NETSYSDUR output values using LogNormal.
NET-COST	Net Cost Distribution from MCS (based on correlation -0.8 between Risk-004 & Risk-005)	Groups cost impact tasks together and collects cost impact difference distribution between Systemic Cost Risk and Base Cost Estimate Risk Distributions	Correlation negative because Base & Systemic costs have opposite signs. Net cost risk distribution generated on the summary task by the MCS iterations.
00080	Rail Extn Systemic Risk Cost Distribution	Task to which Systemic cost impact risk distribution is applied	Risk Factor Risk-004 is applied (correlated -80% to Risk-005)
00090	Rail Extn IRA Base Plan Execution Cost Distbn	Task to which IRA inherent cost impact risk distribution is applied as negative costs.	Risk Factor Risk-005 is applied (correlated -80% to Risk-004)
NETSYS-CRFN	Net Systemic Risk Cost Risk Factor (LogNormal)	Cost distribution derived from distribution parameters of NETCOST cost risk distribution.	Net Systemic Cost RF Risk-008 distribution built from NETCOST output values using LogNormal.
NETSYS-CRFT	Net Systemic Risk Cost Risk Factor (Trigen)	Cost distribution derived from distribution parameters of NETCOST cost risk distribution.	Net Systemic Cost RF Risk-009 distribution built from NETCOST output values using Trigen (10,90).

Table 11.12: Duration and Cost-related NSRF Activities and RFs

Each of the four distributions to be input to Risk 001 – Risk 005 are imported into SR as histograms. These histograms are discrete distributions, consisting of discrete values interval by interval, along with their probabilities of occurring in each interval. Once these four distributions are input to SR, MCS analysis can be initiated, and outputs obtained.

Subtraction of Distributions

The analysis requires subtracting the inherent risk base schedule distribution from the systemic risk schedule distribution. For duration, this involves subtracting the Base IRA Inherent duration risk discrete distribution from the Systemic Duration risk discrete distribution (interpolated from percentiles from Table 11.10 duration distribution) using two hammock activities to measure the differences between iteration values.

For cost, the Base IRA Inherent Cost risk discrete distribution is subtracted from the Systemic Cost risk discrete distribution (interpolated using percentiles from Table 11.10 cost distribution). This is achieved by making the Inherent Cost distribution negative and adding it to the Systemic Cost distribution, automatically storing the combined net distribution in the summary grouping task NETCOST.

Risk Correlation

To ensure a like-for-like comparison, a high correlation must be input between the pairs of distributions. This ensures that if a high or low systemic value is chosen, a similarly high or low inherent risk value will be selected for the same MCS iteration. As shown in Table 11.13, for Risk 001 to Risk 002, both distributions are positive, so the correlation coefficient must also be positive.

The Risk 001: Risk 002 pair was assigned a correlation coefficient of +0.8 (though +0.9 could also be chosen for a slightly higher NSDRF). For Risk 005 (IRA Base Cost distribution), the cost distribution is negative, resulting in higher p values (e.g., $p99$) being considered mathematically smaller (more negative) than lower p values (e.g., $p01$). This means that when a large systemic cost value from Risk 004 is selected for an iteration, a large magnitude but mathematically smaller value must be selected from the Base IRA Cost distribution to produce a credible net cost distribution.

The Risk 004 to Risk 005 pair was assigned a correlation of -0.8 (-0.9 could also be used for a slightly higher NSCRF, but -1.0 or 1.0 should be avoided for discrete distributions with limited values to select).

CORRELATIONS						
			RISKS			
			001	002	004	005
			Schedule	Schedule	Cost	Cost
RISKS	001	Schedule		0.80		
	002	Schedule	0.80			
	004	Cost				−0.80
	005	Cost			−0.80	

Table 11.13: Correlation Pairings for MCS Subtractions

MCS Assessment of Net Systemic Cost Risk Factor

Net Systemic Cost Risk Factor determination is straightforward once the Parametric and IRA Base distributions have been loaded into the Net Systemic Risk Project via the two Risk Factors, Risk 004 and Risk 005. Using the SR Analyse tab, a NETCOST Cost distribution can be produced. Based on the statistics from that distribution, Net Systemic Cost Risk Factors can be produced using either:

♦ Lognormal distribution (using Mean / Standard Deviation) of 18.5k / 64.9k, or

♦ Triangular distribution (P10, P50, P90) with values of -64.2k, 10.7k, 116k.

The NSCRF is normalized by adding the deterministic cost and dividing by the deterministic cost, as shown in Table 11.14.

DETERMINISTIC COST = ($000s)		530,500		RISK 008	RISK 009
Distribution:	NETCOST	NETCOST + DetCost	(NETCOST + Det Cost)/	NSYSCRFN	NSYSCRFT
Parameter	($000s)		DetCost (%)	LN	Trigen (10,90)
Mean	18,500	549,000	103.5%	104%	Low
Std Devn	64,900	64,900	12.2%	12%	Likely
					High
p10	-64,200	466,300	87.9%		88%
p50	10,700	541,200	102.0%		102%
p90	116,000	646,500	121.9%		122%

Table 11.14: Lognormal and Trigen NSCRFs from NETCOST Distribution

Either distribution function could be chosen for the NSCRF, depending on which gives results closer to the NETCOST distribution values. SR limitation of requiring whole percentiles can drive the choice for closer results.

MCS Assessment of Net Systemic Duration Risk Factor

Net Systemic Duration Risk Factor assessment is more complicated than that of the Cost Risk Factor because negative durations are not permissible in CPM schedules. It is necessary to use two hammock activities to track the difference in durations between the systemic risk schedule slip activity (00010) and the base schedule inherent risk activity (00020), driven by Risk 001 and Risk 002, respectively. The two hammocks produce two parts of a single distribution defining the net systemic duration uncertainty distribution. However, the two parts must be combined in Excel to handle the respective negative portions, expressed in the hammock duration distributions as zero duration.

Export Percentiles of Both Histograms

SR enables export of duration percentiles from 0% to 100% at 1% intervals to Excel files from each of the two hammock activity distributions. When examined in Excel, it becomes apparent that the large number of zero duration "hits" in each distribution almost entirely represent the negative values displayed as positive in the other hammock distribution.

Combine Histogram Percentiles

It is necessary to manipulate the non-zero data from Hammock 00040 to express it as negative and reverse the order of the numbers so they can be combined with the Hammock 00030 data. This process is first shown in the export file from Hammock 00040 (Table 11.15).

The data highlighted is combined in the export file from Hammock 00030 (Table 11.16).

Upload Combined Percentiles to SR Risk-006

The light grey highlighted columns on the right in Table 11.16 are pasted into SR as was done with costs. These percentiles constitute the Net Systemic Duration Risk discrete distribution.

	A	F	G	H	I
1	Project: Rail Extension Project Net Systemic Risk				
2	Analyzed on: October 15, 2020 7:26:44 PM				
3	Percentiles for 00040 – Hammock IRA Base Plan – Systemic				
4					
5	Percentile	Duration			
84	78		Step 2	Step 3	Step 4
85	79		Convert to negative numbers	Reverse order values	Copy this set to Percentiles for 00030 – Hammock Systemic-IRA Base Plan
86	80				
87	81	0	0	–163	
88	82	2	–2	–103	
89	83	6	–6	–91	
90	84	7	–7	–79	
91	85	11	–11	–70	
92	86	16	–16	–59	
93	87	21	–21	–53	
94	88	24	–24	–49	
95	89	30	–30	–42	
96	90	33	–33	–38	
97	91	38	–38	–33	
98	92	42	–42	–30	
99	93	49	–49	–24	
100	94	53	–53	–21	
101	95	59	–59	–16	
102	96	70	–70	–11	
103	97	79	–79	–7	
104	98	91	–91	–6	
105	99	103	–103	–2	
106	100	163	–163	0	
	Not shown: Trimming off "d" suffix, convert text to values.				

Table 11.15: Positive Tail Hammock 00040
(converted to negative, order reversed)

	A	F	G	H	I
1	Project: Rail Extension Project Net Systemic Risk				
2	Analyzed on: October 15, 2020 7:26:44 PM				
3	Percentiles for 00030 – Hammock IRA Base Plan – Systemic				
4			Step 7	Step 8	
5	Percentile	Duration	Pasted from Table 11.14, Column H	Probability	Value
6	0	0	–163	0	–163
7	1	0	–103	1	–103
8	2	0	–91	1	–91
9	3	0	–79	1	–79
10	4	0	–70	1	–70
11	5	0	–59	1	–59
12	9	0	–53	1	–53
13	7	0	–49	1	–49
14	8	0	–42	1	–42
15	9	0	–38	1	–38
16	10	0	–33	1	–33
17	11	0	–30	1	–30
18	12	0	–24	1	–24
19	13	0	–21	1	–21
20	14	0	–16	1	–16
21	15	0	–11	1	–11
22	16	0	–7	1	–7
23	17	0	–6	1	–6
24	18	0	–2	1	–2
25	19	0	0	1	0
26	20	3		1	3
27	21	4		1	4
28	22	6		1	6
29	23	11		1	11
30	24	16		1	16
31	25	19		1	19
	Not shown: Trimming off "d" suffix, convert text to values				

Table 11.16: Negative Tail of Hammock 00040
(combined with positive part of Hammock 00030)

Run MCS to Generate Inputs for Net Systemic Duration Risk Factors

Another MCS is run on the Rail Extension Net Systemic Risk project to produce a distribution in the task NETSYSDUR from Risk-006. This is the net systemic duration uncertainty around the deterministic Base Schedule duration of 1,758 days.

Production of Net Systemic Duration Risk Factors (NSDRFs)

The NETSYSDUR distribution provides the input metrics to produce Net Systemic Duration Risk Factors, either Lognormal or Trigen (10,90) to produce realistic spread. The Lognormal RF is based on the NETSYSDUR Mean and Standard Deviation, while the Trigen RF is based on the $p10$, $p50$, and $p90$ inputs from NET-SYSDUR. Both are input as Relative functions because SR adds any Absolute distribution to the deterministic value but multiplies the deterministic value by a relative distribution. This reduces the precision of the relative distribution because SR only accepts percentages to the nearest percent.

The metrics of the two duration RFs are compared with the parent NETSYSDUR distribution in Table 11.17. The NSDRF is normalized by dividing by the deterministic duration to produce the Relative NSDRF.

DETERMINISTIC DURATION	(DD, DAYS):	1,758	RISK 010	RISK 007
Distribution:	NETSYSDUR	NETSYSDUR	NSDRFN	NSDRFT
Parameter	(days)	/ DD (%)	LN	Trigen (10,90)
Mean	1,876	106.7%	107%	Low
Std Devn	124	7.1%	7%	Likely
				High
$p10$	1,728	98.3%		98%
$p50$	1,857	105.6%		106%
$p90$	2,064	117.4%		117%

Table 11.17: Lognormal and Trigen NSDRFs from NETSYSDUR Distribution

As with costs, either distribution function could be chosen for NS-DRF, depending on which gives results closer to NETSYSDUR values. Again, the whole percentages limitation of SR may drive which function (Lognormal or Trigen) is closer to NETSYSDUR values.

Assessment of P+IRA Cost and Schedule Contingencies

Add Net Systemic Risk Factors and Map to Tasks and Costs

Once the choices of NSRF distributions have been made, they are added to the SR Project Risks tab as Risk Factors. Assuming Trigen (10,90) distributions are used, the following are added:

◆ NSDRF – Net Systemic Duration Risk Factor: Using Trigen ($p10$; $p50$; $p90$): 98%; 106%; 117%

◆ NSCRF – Net Systemic Cost Risk Factor: Using Trigen ($p10$; $p50$; $p90$): 88%; 102%; 122%

The NSDRF Risk Factor is mapped into the model using the SR Risk Mapping tab. To map the risk factor to all activities in the schedule, click the NSDRF Risk Factor button at the top Project Level in the SR Risk Mapping tab.

For the NSCRF Risk Factor, click the green triangle in the Risks column of the SR Costs tab at the Time Independent Costs level. This will bring up the available risks picklist, allowing the NSCRF Risk Factor to be selected. Confirm this by clicking the OK button, mapping the NSCRF to all material costs in the project.

Run Model With and Without Added Net Systemic Risk Factors (NSRFs)

Once the NSDRF and NSCRF risk factors have been mapped to activities and fixed costs respectively, the P+IRA Risk Factors model is complete and ready for analysis. The effects of the NSRFs are substantial, as seen from the following tabulated cost and schedule comparisons with (P+IRA) and without (IRA). Tables 11.17a and 11.17b are for cost, and Tables 11.17c and 11.17d are for duration.

Note that the addition of NSRFs has significantly widened the spread of the probability distributions, particularly at the pessimistic ($p90$) end. For example, the predicted $p90$ duration slip (increase over base) for P+IRA is about 38% compared to about 27% without NSRFs. The $p90$ defines the risk profile and is crucial for investment decision-making and making commitments (e.g., "when will service start?").

COST WITH NSRFs				
Data ($,000S)	Planned	p10	p50	p90
Funding to Practical Completion	$530,530	$592,504	$659,910	$731,141
Delta from Planned:	-	$61,974	$129,380	$200,611
Planned % Prob / % Delta from Planned:	0%	11.7%	24.4%	37.8%
% Variance around the p50:	-	-10.2%	-	10.8%

Table 11.18a: Cost Results Based on P+IRA Model Results with *NSRFs*

COST WITHOUT NSRFs				
Data ($,000S)	Planned	p10	p50	p90
Funding to Practical Completion	$530,530	$579,790	$620,070	$663,750
Delta from Planned:	-	$49,260	$89,540	$133,220
Planned % Prob / % Delta from Planned:	0%	9.3%	16.9%	25.1%
% Variance around the p50:	-	-6.5%	-	7.0%

Table 11.18b: Cost Results Based on P+IRA Model Results without *NSRFs*

DURATION WITH NSRFs				
Data	Planned	p10	p50	p90
Entire Plan - Execution Phase	17-Mar-23	7-Sep-23	1-May-24	16-Jan-25
Duration from start of Execution Phase (days):	1758	1932	2169	2429
Planned % Prob / % Delta from Planned:	1%	9.9%	23.4%	38.2%
% Variance around the p50:	-	-10.9%	-	12.0%

Table 11.18c: Duration Results Based on P+IRA Model Results with *NSRFs*

DURATION WITHOUT NSRFs				
Data	Planned	p10	p50	p90
Entire Plan - Execution Phase	17-Mar-23	20-Jul-23	15-Dec23	28-Jun-24
Duration from start of Execution Phase (days):	1758	1883	2031	2227
Planned % Prob / % Delta from Planned:	1%	7.1%	15.5%	26.7%
% Variance around the p50:	-	-7.3%	-	9.7%

Table 11.18d: Duration Results Based on P+IRA Model Results without *NSRFs*

Optional Assessment of Drivers Using Quantitative Exclusion Analysis (QEA)

At this point, the P+IRA analysis has provided the team with information to decide on cost and schedule contingency and management reserve funding at the decision gate. However, further analysis can be done using Safran Risk's automated capability to compare cost and schedule uncertainty with and without selected individual cost or duration Risk Factors. This greatly enhances the analyst's ability to identify and quantify the drivers of schedule and cost uncertainty at multiple selected P-levels.

This QEA capability (called Sensitivity Analysis in SR) supports the prioritization of risk treatments for risk management, which is a primary reason for using P+IRA analysis. Therefore, this capability is best practiced well before the decision gate or during execution when improvements are being evaluated.

Glossary

Note: Where an AACE definition is referenced, the source is *Cost Engineering Terminology*, Recommended Practice 10S-90, AACE International®, Morgantown, WV (www.aacei.org).[1] Refer to the latest version of that RP; it is updated regularly as Industry practices evolve. While I tend to favor AACE terminology, unless otherwise indicated, these definitions are my own or the source is cited.

Artificial Intelligence (AI) refers to the capability of devices or software to perform tasks akin to human learning and decision-making. Machine Learning (ML), a subset of AI, focuses on developing algorithms that enable computers to learn from data.

Bias in estimating, scheduling, and quantitative risk analysis refers to systematic errors that lead to over- or under-estimation relative to a stated cost objective. For example, small projects often overestimate base costs, despite aiming for cost-effective investments.

A **Black Swan** is a high-impact risk event not recorded or quantified because it is considered unrealistic or overly pessimistic. When such events occur, they are sometimes mislabeled as Black Swans to excuse the failure to record or quantify them (see also **HILP**).

Bonds: Sureties are financial products bought from a surety that promise to cover part of another party's failure to fulfill an obligation. In risk management, bonds transfer some risk, often required by regulations to cover uncertain decommissioning or closure costs.

Buffer: See **Contingency: Schedule**.

Burn Rate refers to the time-dependent costs (e.g., per day, week, or month) incurred when a project-specific delay risk occurs. The delay's cost impact equals the delay length multiplied by the burn rate.

Calibration: Model per AACE refers to adjusting a parametric model to better predict empirically observed results. **Calibration: Workshop** involves improving the alignment of expert risk probability estimates with actual outcomes.

---

1 Excerpts from RP10S-90 with permission of AACE International, 1265 Suncrest Towne Centre Dr., Morgantown, WV 26505; http://www.aacei. org, Copyright ©2016 by AACE International; all rights reserved.

Classification: Unclassified/Class 10 is a new AACE estimate class for long-range estimates (e.g., over 10 years) where scope changes are likely, such as in life cycle cost analysis or capital budgeting.

Complexity Lens (for Non-Linearity) refers to a QRA step that assesses potential non-linear risk behavior, where outcomes are disproportionate to inputs. Non-linearity becomes more common in complex projects.

Consolidation (with MCS) refers to using Monte Carlo simulations to combine cost distributions from multiple projects into a program-level cost distribution. Dependencies between projects must be accounted for, as only the mean values of distributions are additive.

Contingency Drawdown is the process of tracking cost or duration contingency usage over time compared to a planned estimate, often charted using an S-curve. The book recommends an S-curve proportional to labor-related costs or project progress.

Contingency Management involves monitoring and assessing contingency usage and determining whether remaining contingency is sufficient given the uncertainty and risks of the remaining work.

Contracting Strategy refers to the planned approach for contract types in a project, focusing on how best to allocate risk between parties. The aim is to assign risks to the party most capable of managing them (see Chapter 3 of Volume 2 for contract types).

Cost Loading in CPM-based QRA methods links cost estimates to schedule activities, allowing for the quantification of time-dependent cost impacts of uncertainties and risks.

Data Analytics encompasses strategies and processes for managing and analyzing data to discover patterns and insights that support business and project decisions.

Data Trust/Pooling refers to combining data from various sources into a common repository under a legal and procedural framework that ensures appropriate data stewardship, often seen in benchmarking and industry consortia.

Data Wrangling/Mungling/Shaping involves transforming and organizing data to improve quality and usability, commonly used in ML/AI but also applicable to project database normalization.

Deep Learning, a subset of ML, uses algorithms to process data through multiple layers, with each layer refining information for better predictions.

Early Contractor Involvement (ECI) is a contracting strategy where contractors provide input during the design phase to optimize design, reduce uncertainty, and mitigate risks.

Enabler projects in multi-project programs are necessary for other projects to add value (see also **Kindler**).

Eventification refers to mistakenly assigning probabilities of less than 100% to uncertainties that are not actual events. For example, the uncertainty of how much rock will be found in soil is not an event but an expression of variability.

Fat Tail (also Blowout) describes a distribution where the frequency of very high values is significant, unlike a long tail with a low occurrence of extreme values.

Gigaproject refers to extremely large projects, often over \$10 billion in 2024 dollars, with significant regional economic and social impacts (see also Megaproject).

Go-No Go refers to a contractor's decision on whether to respond to a tender or request for proposal based on evaluating both opportunities and risks.

Hammock Activity in scheduling spans two points in a project schedule, and overarching risk impacts can be assigned to it in risk-driven CPM-based QRA.

HILP Risk refers to risks with a high impact but low probability. Such risks should be considered for funding as specific management reserves (see also Black Swan).

Hybrid QRA methods combine different approaches to address varying uncertainties and risks most effectively.

Kindler projects in multi-project programs add value to other projects (see also **Enabler**).

Large Language Models (LLMs) are a subset of NLP that uses deep learning models to generate and interpret human-like text (see also **NLP** and **Deep Learning**).

Life Cycle Cost Estimating and Analysis (LCCE/LCCA) involves estimating and analyzing costs across the lifecycle of an asset, including capital (CAPEX) and operating (OPEX) costs, often used with net present value (NPV) to compare investment alternatives.

Margin (including **Incentives**) in contracts typically refers to the difference between revenue and costs for executing the work. This profitability measure is often a focus in quantitative risk analysis for bid decisions.

Markup refers to the amount contractors add to the direct costs of executing the contract work to cover overhead and allow for profit (see **Margin**), including provisions for cost risk and uncertainty.

Intermediate Milestones are zero-duration events or decision points within a schedule (excluding the completion milestone). While the overall project duration can be analyzed without schedule-based QRA, analyzing durations to or between intermediate milestones may require such methods.

ML/AI Data Structure: Structured vs. Unstructured. Structured data is typically quantitative and stored in relational databases. Unstructured data, often qualitative, such as narrative reports, may require techniques like natural language processing (NLP) for analysis.

ML/AI Modeling: Supervised vs. Unsupervised. In **Supervised ML**, a teacher provides example inputs (e.g., risk drivers) and outputs (e.g., cost growth), leaving the algorithm to identify relationships. **Unsupervised ML** allows the algorithm to explore relationships in a dataset with little to no guidance.

Natural Language Processing (NLP) encompasses AI/ML techniques enabling machines to understand, interpret, and generate human language. NLP is often used for preprocessing data, while large language models (LLMs) handle more complex cognitive tasks.

Optimism Bias (Planning Fallacy) refers to the tendency of analysts and decision-makers to underestimate project durations and costs relative to historical data. Empirically-based QRA methods help reduce this bias.

Optimization focuses on enhancing project value by maximizing benefits while minimizing costs and resources. It typically targets opportunities, but with sufficient lead time, QRA methods can be applied to evaluate alternatives for optimization.

Optioneering refers to analyzing project plan or scope alternatives to find an optimal solution (see also **Optimization**).

PDF (3-point) refers to probability distribution functions defined by three input points. Widely used in Monte Carlo simulations, these inputs (low, most likely, high) are easy for project teams to provide. Common forms include **Triangular**, **PERT**, or **LognormAlt** (using P(X), P50, and P(100-X)).

Phase Gate: For phase naming conventions across industries, see Table 1.1 in Volume 2, which compares them with AACE class designations.

Principal-Agent Problem arises when a contractor acting as an agent for the owner has different goals. For example, a contractor conducting a QRA for an owner might be incentivized to push project approval if they expect to benefit from the project later.

Program Agility refers to the tendency of risks to emerge or evolve during long, complex programs. As a result, mid-execution risk quantification should be anticipated and planned for.

Program Phasing: Parallel vs. Sequential refers to considerations in QRA method selection, based on whether program projects will be executed in parallel or sequentially. Analyzing the overall duration of parallel projects requires CPM-based schedule risk analysis.

Project Objectives (Predictability vs. Effectiveness): These refer to strategic objectives driving capital project performance. Financial concerns prioritize predictable capital spending (e.g., avoiding overruns and delays, risk-averse), while profitability concerns emphasize cost-effectiveness (e.g., minimizing costs for the same results, risk-tolerant). Few companies effectively balance both.

QRAMM (QRA Maturity Model) refers to AACE International's five-level scale for measuring an organization's QRA capabilities, supporting continuous process improvement.

RCF Uplifts refer to the recommended percentage increase (uplift) applied to project estimates or durations to match the mean of the RCF dataset, ensuring predictability relative to past performance (see **Project Objectives**).

Request for Proposal (RFP) is a form of solicitation for contractors to bid. Unlike Tender, an RFP allows more flexibility, including the option to revise or withdraw a proposal. A successful tender bid, however, usually requires entering a contract.

Reserves (Specific Management Reserves) are funds set aside for specific risks or uncertainties not covered by contingency funding (see also **HILP Risks** and **Black Swan**). These reserves are distinct from general management reserves meant to address overall risk tolerance.

Risk Allocation refers to deciding which party in a contract will carry which risks and uncertainties. The goal is to allocate risks to the party best equipped to manage them.

Risk Factors in QRA methods refer to percentage multipliers for duration or cost, used to calculate variations due to risk or uncertainty. These are typically entered as a 3-point distribution (e.g., 95%, 100%, 125%).

Risk Mapping in CPM-based QRA refers to applying risk factor distributions to the schedule's activities and costs (or groups of activities).

Risk Matrix (Parametric Model) is a table of pre-determined systemic risk inputs in a parametric model, such as key scope definition deliverables, with respective ratings (e.g., 0-5) and model weighting criteria.

Risks: Inherent Uncertainty vs. Contingent: These terms differentiate between general uncertainty (Inherent) and risks tied to specific events or conditions (Contingent). Inherent risks are a subset of systemic risks, which also include minor contingent risks.

Schedule: Master refers to an owner's composite schedule, typically maintained at a summary level, that includes all project or program activities. CPM-based QRA methods usually rely on a master or study schedule for modeling.

Schedule: Study refers to a simplified schedule created specifically for CPM-based QRA on projects with large, complex schedules.

Strategic vs. Sustaining Projects: Strategic projects create new assets to support business plans (e.g., adding production, entering new markets), while sustaining projects maintain or enhance existing assets.

Tender is a form of solicitation for contractors to bid. Unlike an RFP, a tender follows strict rules where the successful bidder must enter a contract.

Time-Driven Cost refers to cost risks caused by schedule delays (e.g., labor or equipment rental costs), as opposed to non-time-driven costs (e.g., physical repair costs due to a risk event).

Tokenization refers to breaking text into smaller units (tokens) for natural language processing (NLP).

ValidRisk® is commercial cloud-based QRA software that combines parametric modeling of systemic risks with Monte Carlo simulations to assess specific project risks and uncertainties.

Weakest Link refers to overall program risk quantification in parametric modeling, where a parameter rating reflects the sub-project with the highest systemic risk (e.g., least defined, most complex). This reflects the idea that weak performance in one project can negatively impact others.

Winner's Curse refers to a situation where a contractor wins a bid due to its low price, but the price reflects underestimation of costs, leading to little or no profit or even a loss. This is often caused by underestimating risk and uncertainty in the bidding process.

Index

Note: This index does *not* include Volume 1. Readers and researchers on the topic of quantitative risk analysis are advised to review Volume 1 as well.

(Schedule/scheduling, continued)
  optimization/optimized/optioneer-
    ing, 73-74, 80, 174, *See also* Quan-
    titative Exclusion Analysis
  quality/assurance (QA), 64, 65, 70,
    74, 86, 233
  re-baselining, 219, *See also* risk
    response
  risk analysis, *See* Schedule Risk
    Analysis
  slip, See schedule slip/slippage
  study schedule, 86, 234, 266
schedule-driven, *See* Objectives
Schedule Risk Analysis (SRA)
  cost-loading, mapping, 57, 64, 72,
    234, *See also* time dependent/
    independent
  hybrid with parametric (P+CPM), 4,
    50, 60, 63-76 (flowchart, 69), 80,
    82, 120, 202
  hybrid with parametric (P+CPM) for
    program, 86-87
  hybrid with parametric (P+IRA)
    worked example, 229-259, *See
    also* Cropley
  ranging with MCS (no hybrid), 46,
    66
  risk driven with MCS (no hybrid), 57,
    66, 68
    risk factors, 66, 68-69, 266, *See
    also* risk mapping (schedule)
  risk mapping, events/factors, 73-74,
    266
  strengths and weaknesses (CPM vs
    P+EV)(updated table), 207
  time-driven/non-time driven (inte-
    grate with cost), 72-73, 263
schedule slip/slippage, 2, 9, 21. *See
  also* contingency, contract disputes,
  delay, overrun/underrun
    accuracy/studies of metrics, 23-28
    data quality of metrics, 22-23
    model of, 22, 28, *See also* Quantita-
    tive Risk Analysis
Schematic/Criteria Design (phase),
  194-195, *See also* Rosetta Stone
Schroeder, Brett R., 13
Schweizer, L, 149
Scope
  alternatives/options/variation, *See*
    Multi-Option

business, 102
change, 57, 84, 90, 103, 111 *See also*
  change management
contract 102, See Contract-scope
  structures
definition/level of definition, *See*
  Classification
Scoping Study (mining phase/Class 5),
  166 *See also* Rosetta Stone
Seib, Gerald, 31
Select decision gate (Class 4), *See* de
  facto sanction, decision-alternative,
  Phase-gate
self-correcting model, *See* parametric
sensitivity analysis, 30, 54, 103, 105,
  107, 166, *See also* Multi-Option
    tornado diagram, 106
    worst case, 30, 35
severity of process/service (risk driver), *See also* complexity, parametric,
  technology
    measure/level of, 16, 18
Sharepoint, 149
Shephard, Alan, 39
Shrestha, Pramen 24
Siem, K., 32, 48
Siemens, 48
Skinner, David C., 106
small modular reactor (SMR), 34
social license/community, 2, 6, 27, 98,
  124, 151, 181, 193
Southern Company, 33
Sovacool, Benjamin, 13, 18
stage-gate, *See* phase-gate
stakeholders, 27-28, 34-35, 84, 107, 151,
  202, 224
  indigenous/First Nation, 179
startup, 23, *See also* commissioning
statistics, *See also* accuracy, probability distribution functions
    descriptive, 11
    inferential, 11, 46, 54
      multiple linear regression (MLR),
      parametric model basis, 144
Steers, S, 60
strategic misrepresentation (lying), 19,
  30, 90, 219, *See also* optimism bias
    exploitation; "if politicians grasp
    the profession's failure," 21
strategic versus sustaining projects,
  See Portfolio

Other Books from Probabilistic Publishing

Here is a list of our other books, all of which can be ordered from https://www.decisions-books.com.

TITLE	AUTHOR
Project Risk Quantification, Vol. 1 (A Practitioner's Guide to Realistic Cost and Schedule Risk Management)	John Hollmann
Presents a practical, realistic, and integrated approach to project cost and schedule risk quantification. Written for managers, engineers, and risk analysis practitioners.	
Introduction to Decision Analysis, 3rd Edition (A Practitioner's Guide to Improving Decision Quality)	David Skinner
Comprehensive decision analysis (DA) handbook for DA consultants, DA practitioners, and graduate-level MBA and engineering students.	
Introduction to Bayesian Inference and Decision, 2nd Edition	Robert Winkler
Foundational mathematical treatment of Bayesian statistical theory and practice.	
Why Can't You Just Give Me The Number?, 2nd Edition (An Executive's Guide to Using Probabilistic Thinking to Manage Risk and to Make Better Decisions)	Patrick Leach
Leach presents a compelling, insightful, practical and understandable case for using probabilistic analysis as part of everyday business decision-making.	
Game Theory for Business (A Primer in Strategic Gaming)	Paul Papayoanou
Presents a straigtforward, practical for understanding and applying game theory.	
Problem, Risk, and Opportunity Enterprise Management (How to use language, data, information, and analytics that easily align with the ways we think.)	Brian Hagen
Dr. Hagen has tailored a decision making process to correspond with the way that our brains actually function. This comprehensive book shares his methodology and the basis for it, including powerful insights that are not found elsewhere..	
The Business of Negotition (An executive's guide to getting what you want)	Craig MKnight
This book presents the clearest and most comprehensive guide to negotiations that is available today..	
Creating a Culture of Profitability (A Revolutionary Model for Managing Culture)	Rob and Aviva Kleinbaum
The Kleinbaums used Lawrence Harrison's 30-year study of successful cultures as the foundation for a powerful, practical, and logical framework for analyzing and improving business culture.	
Your Mother Should Know, (From Liverpool to Los Angeles)	Angie McCartney
Beyond Zoar Valley (The Extraordinary Life of Carrie Busekist)	Edna Busekist
Generations, (Growing Up on a Farm during the Great Depression)	H. Charlesworth

www.ingramcontent.com/pod-product-compliance
Lightning Source LLC
Chambersburg PA
CBHW052109030426
42335CB00025B/2904